PENGUIN COOKE[...]

SOPHIE'S TABLE

Sophie Grigson was born in 1959, the daughter of Jane and
Geoffrey Grigson, cookery writer and poet. She has contributed
to many magazines and writes a daily column for the London
Evening Standard. Her first book, *Food For Friends*, was published
in 1987, and she is also the author of *Sophie Grigson's Ingredients
Book* (1991). She lives in north London.

SOPHIE GRIGSON

SOPHIE'S TABLE

PENGUIN BOOKS

PENGUIN BOOKS

Published by the Penguin Group
Penguin Books Ltd, 27 Wrights Lane, London W8 5TZ, England
Penguin Books USA Inc., 375 Hudson Street, New York, New York 10014, USA
Penguin Books Australia Ltd, Ringwood, Victoria, Australia
Penguin Books Canada Ltd, 10 Alcorn Avenue, Toronto, Ontario, Canada M4V 3B2
Penguin Books (NZ) Ltd, 182-190 Wairau Road, Auckland 10, New Zealand

Penguin Books Ltd, Registered Offices: Harmondsworth, Middlesex, England

First published by Michael Joseph 1990
Published in Penguin Books 1992
1 3 5 7 9 10 8 6 4 2

For Jane Grigson and Jess Koppel,
my best friends

CONTENTS

Acknowledgements

In November of 1986 a phone call came straight out of the blue. It was Fay Maschler, restaurant reviewer and for the past year cookery columnist for the London *Evening Standard*. Would I take over the daily recipe section? I took the plunge, and have been writing for the paper ever since. I owe Fay and the staff at the paper a great debt. Thanks to them I became, virtually overnight, a full-time food writer. Without them this book would not exist.

Michael Bateman, former Deputy Editor of the *Sunday Express* Magazine has given me constant support and encouragement since the day he asked me to write my first article. My mother has always been there to share my excitement at new discoveries, making helpful but unobtrusive suggestions when I moan that I cannot possibly ever think of another recipe again.

Three marvellous assistants have patiently unravelled scribbled notes and tested recipes for me: Charlotte Lyon, Puff Fairclough and Deirdre Shillaker. Gail of Synchronicity took on the mind-numbingly dull task of sifting through my computer files to locate particular recipes.

Finally, I'd like to thank the many friends who have cheerfully eaten their way through both my culinary successes and my disasters, tactfully steering me away from serious mistakes, in particular Jess Koppel, Seamus Cassidy and Dominic Owens.

INTRODUCTION

There is no theme to this collection of recipes. The majority first appeared in my daily column in the London *Evening Standard*, but not all. Some are quick to run up, others demand a degree of time and patience. Many use ordinary, every day ingredients, others incorporate more unusual ones. There are classics peppering their way through foreign dishes and my own ideas. There are recipes for one or two people, and others to feed a whole crowd.

This is the way I cook. I bear no particular allegiance to one style of food or another. I love the full, heady flavours of the Mediterranean, but I relish the spiciness of Eastern food and the perfumes of the Middle East. Then again, there are times when I long for something homely and satisfying. Usually I am cooking for myself and perhaps one or two close friends, but I also enjoy preparing a large meal to share with a full table of people.

So the only link between all the recipes that follow is that I like them, and think they are worth passing on. Dip in and use the ones that appeal to you and suit the way you cook. Scattered throughout the text are hints on choosing the best ingredients and simple ideas for using them.

I do not see my recipes as absolute. Quite the opposite. Cooking and eating should be enjoyable experiences, fun and exciting, whether you've only got five minutes to throw together a sandwich or can indulge in the luxury of spending a whole day preparing a special meal. Recipes are guidelines, indications of how to get the best out of raw foodstuffs. I often suggest alternatives to the

1

ingredients given. Adapt the recipes to your liking. If, for instance, you don't share my passion for olive oil, use a lighter, bland oil. If fresh coriander isn't your cup of tea, or isn't available, use basil or marjoram instead.

There are, of course, a few rules that it would be foolish to ignore. Always stick with one set of measurements, imperial or metric (both are given here). Remember that spoon measurements mean rounded spoonfuls, unless otherwise stated. Always season lightly at first; you can add more later, but you cannot take away. Taste dishes as they cook; you are the arbiter and the only one who knows what tastes good to you.

Don't expect timings to be exact – the size of your pans will be different from mine, and your oven settings are unlikely to be identical to mine. Check occasionally to see how things are doing as they cook, and adjust timings and temperatures accordingly. At the back of the book is a chapter with notes and comments on some of the ingredients and basic techniques used. Ingredients and methods marked with an asterisk* are explained in this section.

I hope that you will derive as much pleasure from using this book as I have from cooking and eating the recipes in it.

Sophie Grigson
Spring 1990

Soups

Pumpkin and Ginger Soup

As a child in autumnal France, I would while away car journeys by counting golden objects. By the end of October, or early November, the game became impossible – the whole countryside was a glorious, riotous blaze of yellows and oranges. Maize, poplar trees and pumpkins, everywhere. And what pumpkins! Huge, bulbous things, squatting smugly amongst their foliage. As the nights grew colder, they began to disappear from the fields and reappear on the table, in the guise of puddings or pies, or warm, comforting soups.

In London, shops and markets suddenly flood with pumpkins around the end of October, in time for Halloween and bonfire night. They are sold, primarily, for the making of lanterns, not for eating, but it is a shame to waste the flesh. Greengrocers serving areas with large ethnic communities continue to sell pumpkin throughout the winter months.

Try to buy a whole pumpkin for this recipe, so that the soup can be served in the pumpkin shell. You will need a pumpkin that weighs a good 2½ kg (5 lb) or more, to get the required amount of useable flesh. If you see them, use little individual pumpkins instead, weighing around ¾ kg (1½ lb) each.

Slice a thick lid from the top of the pumpkin. With your hand, pull the mass of fibres and seeds from the centre and discard. Using a sharp-edged spoon, or a small knife, carefully cut the flesh from the pumpkin, leaving just enough to give a firm shell. Use the cut flesh to make soup, and brush the insides of the pumpkin shell with melted butter. Dust with salt and pepper and bake, placing in a large oven-proof bowl to give extra support, at 180C/350F/Gas 4 for 1–1½ hours. Fill with soup, and as you serve scrape a little of the softened flesh into each bowl.

If you don't have your own transport, or a pumpkin-selling shop round the corner, then go for a slice cut from a larger pumpkin – you should only need ¾–1 kg (1½–2 lb) then. Just scrape away the seeds and fibres, and discard the skin.

SERVES 4

1 onion, sliced
1 cm (½ in) piece of fresh ginger, finely chopped
30 g (1 oz) butter
500 g (1 lb) prepared pumpkin (see above)
300 ml (½ pt) milk
1 tablespoon sugar
½ teaspoon ground nutmeg
salt and pepper
6 rashers bacon
4 tablespoons sour cream
fresh chives, chopped

Cook the onion and ginger in the butter over a low heat until soft. Add the chopped pumpkin and stir to coat in butter. Pour in the milk and add the sugar, nutmeg, salt and pepper. Simmer until the pumpkin is tender. Liquidise and adjust the seasoning.

Meanwhile, grill or fry the bacon until crisp. Crumble. Reheat the soup if necessary, and serve with the cream swirled in, scattered with bacon and chives.

Avgolemono Soup

Make Avgolemono soup for supper the day after you've cooked a roast chicken. Save all the small pieces of leftover cooked chicken (you don't need exactly 125 g (4 oz), that's just a rough guide), and turn the bones into stock (page 269).

Good stock is essential. A chicken stock cube just won't do. There aren't enough other ingredients even to begin to mask the false chemical taste of a stock cube.

Once you've got the stock, Avgolemono is quick and easy to rustle up and its clear lemony freshness makes it a thoroughly welcome soup, whatever the time of year. But be sure that the stock has cooled a little and is no longer boiling, before you beat in the eggs. Overheat and the eggs will curdle.

To vary the recipe, add a quartered fennel bulb, or a branch of fennel herb (or dill) to the stock. Taste the stock and, if you think the aniseedy flavour is not strong enough, cook small cubes of fennel with the rice in the soup.

SERVES 4

1 litre (2 pt) chicken stock
45 g (1½ oz) long-grain rice
125 g (4 oz) cooked chicken
salt and pepper
2 large eggs
juice of 1 lemon

Bring the chicken stock to the boil. Add the rice and simmer for 10 minutes. Add the cooked chicken, torn or cut into small pieces. Cook for a further 5 minutes or until the rice is cooked. Season, and turn down the heat as low as possible.

Separate the eggs. Whisk the whites until stiff. Fold in the yolks and then the lemon juice. Take the soup off the heat. Little by little, beat a mugful of the hot, but not boiling, soup into the egg mixture.

Once it is all mixed in, pour the mixture back into the soup which should by now have cooled a little. Stir and taste. There should be quite a strong waft of lemon, so add extra if necessary. Serve quickly, with warm crusty bread.

Caldo Verde

Virtually every restaurant and café in Portugal has *Caldo Verde* on the menu. In smaller cafés, it is often the only obvious first course.

The list of ingredients may not sound wildly inspiring, but the final result is a comfortable, warming soup that is wonderfully welcome on a day when there's a nip in the air. It is filling enough to take the place of a main course. Follow with bread and cheese and fresh fruit, and you've got a satisfying meal. Since the basic ingredients are so pleasingly cheap, it's worth splashing out on the best olive oil to season it. Buy oil marked 'extra virgin', which will have the rich olivey flavour that makes this soup so good.

SERVES 4

½ kg (1 lb) potatoes, sliced
salt and pepper
1 small onion, chopped
175 g (6 oz) kale, thinly sliced
4 tablespoons extra virgin olive oil

Place the potatoes in a large saucepan, add salt and enough water to cover. Simmer until tender. Liquidise and add extra water to give a thin consistency. Return to the pan and adjust the seasoning, adding plenty of pepper.

Bring the soup back to the boil. Stir in the onion and the kale (that's why you needed a large pan) and simmer for 10 minutes. Ladle into bowls, pour a tablespoon of olive oil on to each one, and serve.

Pear and Stilton Soup

Pears and stilton, apples and cheddar, simple companions but real soulmates. Here is that marvellous balance of salt and sweet, the flavour of the cheese highlighting that of the fruit and vice versa. Hard to beat.

This soup is lighter and less cloying than the classic stilton soup, which I love but find terribly rich. To add a contrasting crunch to the soup, serve with tiny baked croûtons*.

SERVES 4

1 onion, chopped
15 g (½ oz) butter
4 medium sized ripe pears, cored, quartered and chopped
¾ litre (1½ pt) chicken stock
salt and pepper
125 g (4 oz) stilton
juice of ½–1 lemon
fresh chives, chopped

In a large pan, cook the onion gently in the butter, without browning. Add the pears and the stock, and a little salt and pepper. Simmer until the pears are very tender. Pass through the fine blade of a *mouli-légumes*, or liquidise and sieve. Return to the pan and reheat, without boiling. Add the stilton and stir until dissolved.

Sharpen with lemon juice to taste, and adjust the seasoning. Sprinkle the chives over the top and serve.
If you make this soup in advance, reheat without boiling.

Widow's Soup

Malta is a very peculiar place; a small, hot, dry, dusty Mediterranean island, overlaid with the legacy of years of British rule: red telephone boxes in the corners of medieval squares; 'John the Butcher' emblazoned on a sign above a shadowy entrance in a maze of narrow backstreets; bottles of tomato ketchup and brown sauce and cups of thick tea under the parasols of a pretty sun-trap of a southern square.

The traditional cooking of these islands, hard to find behind the hamburgers and dismal 'iced fancies', is that of a poor people making the best of limited resources, drawing in and adapting dishes from a succession of conquerors. This soup is said to have earned its name from the cheapness of the ingredients – with a hunk of good bread (and proper Maltese bread, baked in wood-fired ovens, is terrifically good) it makes a filling meal. Vary the vegetables according to availability.

SERVES 4–6

1 large onion, chopped
1 tablespoon olive oil
1 large potato, chopped
175 g (6 oz) cauliflower florets, quartered
175 g (6 oz) carrots, sliced
1 small lettuce, shredded
175 g (6 oz) shelled fresh peas or thawed frozen peas
250 g (8 oz) tomatoes, skinned and roughly chopped, or half a 400 g (14 oz) tin chopped tomatoes
1½ tablespoons tomato paste
1 teaspoon sugar
½ teaspoon red wine vinegar
salt and pepper
6 eggs
250 g (8 oz) ricotta cheese, or firm young goats cheese

Fry the onion in the oil in a large pan, without browning. Add the potato, cauliflower, carrots, lettuce and peas if fresh. Stir, then add the tomatoes, tomato paste, sugar, vinegar, salt and pepper and enough water (or stock) to cover generously. Bring to the boil and simmer until the vegetables are tender. Add the thawed frozen peas now. Taste and adjust the seasoning.

Turn down the heat so that the surface of the water is barely trembling. Break the eggs one at a time on to a saucer, and slip them into the soup. Cut the cheese into 6, and tuck the pieces between the eggs. Poach the eggs until the white has just set – about 8–10 minutes.

Carefully place an egg and a piece of cheese in each serving bowl, and ladle the soup around them.

Pea Soup With Rouille

Pea soup and pease pudding are good English traditions – hearty, warming food to stave off the cold and damp. Jazz up the basic soup with the sharpness of thick yoghurt and the heat of chillied *rouille* sauce, and not only is it bright and pretty to look at, but it tastes terrific.

SERVES 4–6

350 g (12 oz) split green or yellow peas
3 carrots, sliced
2 onions, sliced
3 sticks of celery, sliced
2 whole cloves of garlic
1 bay leaf
1 sprig of thyme
3 sprigs of parsley
chicken or vegetable stock (optional)
salt
125 g (4 oz) thickly cut ham, chopped
4–6 tablespoons Greek sheep's yoghurt

Rouille:
2 small fresh or dried red chillis
1 red pepper, skinned and chopped
2 cloves of garlic, chopped
1 tablespoon soft breadcrumbs
pinch of salt
4 tablespoons olive oil

Place the peas, carrots, onions, celery and garlic in a large pot. Tie the bay leaf, thyme and parsley together with a piece of string and add to the pan with enough stock or water to cover by 2–3 cm (1 in). Bring to the boil and simmer gently for 50-60 minutes until the peas are soft. Remove the herbs and liquidise or pass through a *mouli-légumes*, adding extra stock or water to thin down if necessary, though the soup should be substantial. Stir in the ham.

Meanwhile, make the *rouille*. If using dried chillis, cover with boiling water and soak for 30 minutes. Halve the fresh or soaked chilli and remove the seeds. Chop. Grill the pepper skin-side up, until blackened. Skin and chop. Liquidise the red pepper and chillis with the garlic, breadcrumbs and salt. Keep the liquidiser running and trickle in the oil as if making mayonnaise.

Reheat the soup and adjust the seasoning. Ladle it into bowls and place a tablespoon of yoghurt in the centre of each, topped with a teaspoon of *rouille*. Serve immediately, with the remaining *rouille* served separately.

Thick Fish Soup

I love thick tomatoey fish soups, packed with bits and pieces, and this is just that. It is hearty enough to be served as a main course.

SERVES 4–6

500 g (1 lb) squid*, cleaned
500 g (1 lb) cod or other firm white fish
1 large onion, chopped
1 carrot, very finely chopped
½ kg (1 lb) tomatoes, skinned* and chopped
2 cloves of garlic, chopped
2 teaspoons coriander seeds, roughly crushed
1 bouquet garni
2 tablespoons olive oil
350 g (12 oz) potatoes, thinly sliced
1 tablespoon tomato paste
15 g (½ oz) flour
15 g (½ oz) butter
salt and pepper

Cut the squid sacs into rings, and chop the tentacles roughly. Set aside 2 of the black ink sacs. Cut the cod into large chunks. Place the onion in a large pan and add the carrot, tomatoes, garlic, coriander seeds and bouquet garni. Sprinkle with olive oil. Lay the potatoes on top, and finally add the fish.

Mix the tomato paste with 300 ml (½ pt) water. Add the reserved ink sacs, crush and stir well. Pour into the pan and top up with enough water to cover. Season. Bring to the boil and simmer for 10 minutes. With a slotted spoon, lift out as much of the fish as you can find, and the potato slices if cooked through. Turn up the heat and boil hard for a further 10 minutes. Mash the butter with the flour to form a *beurre manié*. Turn down the heat, so that the liquid is almost simmering, and add the *beurre manié* bit by bit. Stir and cook for a further 5 minutes without boiling. Return the fish to the pan to heat through, and serve.

D'La Soupe D'Andgulle (Fish Soup)

Jersey. What kind of image does the name conjure up for you? There's Bergerac, I suppose, but apart from the dashing hero of the TV screens, what other pictures spring to mind?

Until a few years ago, I imagined that Jersey was just a dull, sleepy island, far enough away from the mainland for the unadventurous to feel that they were travelling, and yet stolidly British – a fuddy-duddy kind of a place.

How wrong can one be? I've been lucky enough to visit Jersey in the spring several years in a row now, when it is at its most enchanting, relatively unencumbered with tourists. April is the perfect time to enjoy the tiny, hidden valleys and the dramatics of the rocky, crashing northern coasts.

This is a filling main course Jersey soup, flecked by rights with yellow marigold petals – though it tastes just as good without.

SERVES 6–8

1 kg (2 lb) tail piece of conger eel
½ cabbage, shredded
1 onion, chopped
1 large carrot, chopped
125 g (4 oz) shelled fresh peas or thawed frozen peas
2 tablespoons fresh parsley, chopped
2 sprigs of thyme
salt and pepper
2 tablespoons flour
1 litre (2 pt) full-cream milk
marigold leaves and petals (optional)

Wash the fish and put into a large saucepan. Add 1¾ litres (3 pt) water, covering the conger completely. Bring to the boil and simmer for 1 hour, skimming off any scum that rises to the top. Strain off the liquid. Pick out the edible flesh left on the conger bones.

Return the liquid to the cleaned saucepan and add the cabbage, onion, carrot and peas – if you are using frozen peas leave them out for the moment – and the herbs, including the marigold leaves if using. Season with salt and pepper. Simmer until the vegetables are tender, adding the thawed frozen peas right at the end.

Mix the flour with a couple of spoonfuls of the hot soup, then pour into the soup and stir. Simmer gently for 5 more minutes. Add the milk and reheat until it is almost boiling. Taste and adjust the seasoning, then throw in the marigold petals and the reserved fish, and serve.

Smoked Haddock and Onion Soup

A smoked haddock soup may sound a touch perverse, but don't let yourself be put off by that. There's just enough fish to give a mild smokiness. Try your very best to find undyed smoked haddock.

SERVES 4

250 g (8 oz) smoked haddock, skinned and chopped
½ kg (1 lb) onions, chopped
2 cloves of garlic
1 sprig of thyme
45 g (1½ oz) butter
¾ litre (1½ pt) milk
salt and pepper

Melt the butter in a pan large enough to take all the ingredients. Add the onion, whole garlic cloves and thyme. Stir and cover. Cook over a very gentle heat until the onions are meltingly tender – this should take at least 30 minutes, and is even better if cooked really gently for 45 minutes. Stir occasionally.

Add the haddock to the onions, and cook for a further 5 minutes. Pour in the milk, and add a little salt and plenty of freshly ground pepper. Bring to the boil and simmer for 10 minutes. Pass through a *mouli-légumes*, or liquidise and sieve. The soup should be fairly thick, but if necessary add a little extra milk. Taste and adjust the seasoning. Reheat and serve with toast or croûtons*.

Manhattan Clam Chowder

Until I visited New York, I had always thought of clam chowder as a creamy pale soup. This, it turns out, is a New England clam chowder. Lunch at the Oyster Bar in Grand Central Station, sitting on a high stool at the counter, introduced me to the Manhattan Clam Chowder, steaming hot and tomatoey.

In America they use giant meaty quahog clams. You do occasionally find these at the fishmonger in Britain, but not too often. Tiny venus clams are much more common and make a good alternative. Mussels* can also be used, although they will need to be scrubbed and de-bearded first (page 259).

This soup is filling and hearty. All you need to complete the meal is cheese, salad and some fresh fruit.

SERVES 4

1–1½ kg (2–3 lb) venus clams
¾–1 litre (1½–2 pt) fish stock*, or 1 glass dry white wine
125 g (4 oz) streaky bacon, chopped
1 tablespoon olive oil
1 large onion, chopped
2 sticks of celery, chopped
1 large baking potato, chopped
2 leeks, thickly sliced
1 sprig of thyme
1 bay leaf
1 × 400 g (14 oz) tin chopped tomatoes
3 tablespoons fresh parsley, chopped
salt and pepper

Rinse the clams well under the cold tap. Pour a 1 cm (½ in) layer of water into a pan large enough to take all the clams. Bring to the boil, and tip them in. Cover tightly and shake over a high heat until they have all opened. Discard any that stay stubbornly shut. Strain the cooking juices to remove any grit, and add enough fish stock, or wine and water, to make up to 1 litre (2 pt). Remove the clams from their shells.

Fry the bacon over a high heat in a small non-stick frying pan, until crisp and browned. Remove from the heat, and lift out the bacon with a slotted spoon. Drain on kitchen paper and set aside. Pour the fat into a large pan and fry the onion and celery in it until soft and lightly browned, adding a little extra oil if necessary. Add the potato, leeks, thyme and bay leaf, and stir for a further minute.

Then add the shellfish liquid, tomatoes, parsley, salt and pepper. Bring to the boil and simmer gently until the potato is tender. Taste and adjust the seasoning.

Just before serving, stir the clams into the soup. Simmer for about 1 minute, to heat them through. Serve the crisp bacon separately to scatter over the top.

FIRST COURSES AND LIGHT MAIN COURSES

Dukkah

Dukkah is a heavenly Egyptian mixture of toasted nuts and spices. It is one of those recipes that is slightly different in every Egyptian household – some may use roast chickpeas instead of hazelnuts, others may prefer dried mint to cumin, and the balance of the other spices varies according to personal preference.

I like recipes of this kind – you can have such fun developing your own favourite combination, and it is hardly the end of the world if you are a teensy bit short on one of the ingredients.

In Egypt, you might take a piece of rough bread, drizzle olive oil over it and then sprinkle it with *dukkah*. You can do it in England too, and quite delicious it is – it's also good if the bread is toasted. But there is more to it than that.

Make up a batch for picnics and parties (it lasts well kept in an airtight jar). Serve a small bowl of *dukkah* with hard-boiled eggs and crudités – so that picnickers can dip their food into it – or sprinkle it over grilled meats as a seasoning – salt and pepper, but even more so.

30 g (1 oz) hazelnuts
4 tablespoons sesame seeds
2 tablespoons coriander seeds
1½ tablespoons whole cumin seeds
½ tablespoon black peppercorns
2 teaspoons ground cinnamon
½ tablespoon salt

Roast the hazelnuts* and chop roughly.

Heat a small, heavy frying pan over a medium heat and add the sesame seeds. Shake gently until they turn a shade darker and give out a nutty smell. Tip them into a bowl. Repeat with the coriander and cumin seeds. Place the roast spices, sesame and peppercorns in a clean coffee grinder and whizz quickly to give a coarse dry powder. Mix with the cinnamon and salt.

Crush the hazelnuts in the grinder – be particularly vigilant not to whizz them for too long, or you will end up with a hazelnut butter instead of very finely chopped nuts. Mix in with the rest.

Anchoïade With Tomatoes

Anchoïade is one of those pungent, salty southern pastes, not dissimilar to *Tapenade*, with its base of olives, or the Piedmontese *Bagna Cauda*, also made with anchovies. Like *Tapenade* it comes from Provence.

Serve as an hors d'œuvre, or cut into fingers or small squares to eat with drinks before a meal. It can also make part of a light lunch, with a hard-boiled egg and a green salad.

Anchoïade can be kept in a covered jar in the fridge for several days.

2 tins anchovies in oil, chopped
4 cloves of garlic, chopped
2 tablespoons fresh basil, chopped
5 tablespoons extra virgin olive oil
2 teaspoons red wine vinegar
2 teaspoons tomato paste
freshly ground black pepper
slices of rough country bread
the best, sweetest tomatoes you can find, sliced

The simplest way to make *anchoïade* is to throw the first seven ingredients (including the oil from the anchovies) into a processor or liquidiser and whizz to a paste. Finito.

If you haven't got either, then it's pestle and mortar time. Pound the garlic to a paste, then add the anchovies. Pound again, and then in with the basil. Pounding constantly, add the olive oil in a slow trickle, then stir in the remaining ingredients.

To serve, grill the bread on one side only, then spread the untoasted side thinly – it is strong stuff – with *anchoïade*. Bake in a

hot oven (230C/450F/Gas 8) for about 5 minutes, until crisp.
Meanwhile, slice the tomatoes – if they're a bit short on flavour,
sprinkle with an extra pinch of sugar and a few drops of red wine
vinegar.

Lay cool tomato slices on the hot bread, and eat immediately.

Home Made Cream Cheese With Herbs and Garlic

There's something immensely satisfying about making your own
cream cheese. Funny really, because it is one of the simplest things
to make – all you are doing is putting one liquid into another and
then leaving the pair of them alone to get on with the real work.

The curds that you end up with are bland and definitely need
some pepping up. The double cream (or you might use soured
cream) gives a good consistency, and the rest of the ingredients add
flavour.

You could also mould your own small, fresh cheeses. Salt the
drained curds and then pack into perforated yoghurt pots, or
smaller containers. Cover and weigh them down with a small
weight, and leave overnight to drain further. Turn them out next
day, and roll them in finely chopped herbs. Eat within a day or so.

SERVES 4

1 litre (2 pt) milk
2 tablespoons essence of rennet
3 tablespoons thick double cream
2 tablespoons fresh herbs, finely chopped
1–2 cloves of garlic, crushed
2 spring onions, finely chopped
salt and pepper
paprika

Heat the milk to blood temperature (approx. 38C/100F). If you
don't have a thermometer, test for the correct heat by dipping your
finger into the warm milk. When you can hold it there for just 10
seconds, it is the right temperature. Stir in the rennet, cover and
leave for 1 hour, to set.

Line a sieve with muslin, and tip in the set milk, breaking it up
with a spoon. Leave it to drain for two hours, turning and breaking
up the curds from time to time, so that the whey can escape.

When it is well drained, stir in the cream, herbs, garlic, spring
onions, salt and pepper. Taste and adjust the seasoning. Pile into a
serving bowl and sprinkle with a little paprika.

Serve with hot melba toast or crisp rusks. Alternatively, serve with crudités – sticks of raw vegetables, celery, carrot, green and red peppers, fennel and so on.

Tahina Salad

Tahina salad, a rich thick sesame cream, eaten, like houmus, with warm pitta bread as part of a mixed hors d'œuvre, is a regular feature on menus from Greece, right through the Middle East, to Morocco.

In early 1988, a group of food writers were whizzed off on a fascinating press trip to Israel. We stayed in Tel Aviv, a strange, ugly town with a raw appeal which I fell for, although many would hate it. Although the city itself, less than eighty years old, may seem an eyesore with its myriad high rise blocks, it does boast a beautiful long sandy beach. On a sunny day in February, the sea glitters, the scene is peaceful – a few people walking dogs, jogging, sunbathing and a handful of hardier specimens taking the plunge.

Four of us gave in to the warmth, and a welcome slothfulness drew us to a beach café, while the rest of the party continued the seven-day whistle-stop tour of Israel's sites. We ate houmus, aubergine with *tahina*, flaky fried yemenite breads, cooling finely-chopped salads of tomato and cucumber, filo pastry cigars stuffed with spiced meat, olives, pickled chillis, warm pitta bread and this *tahina* salad. You can buy *tahina* paste from Greek or Middle Eastern shops and some supermarkets.

SERVES 4–8

2 cloves of garlic
juice of 1½–2 lemons
150 g (5 oz) *tahina* paste
salt
2 tablespoons parsley, chopped, plus a little extra
olive oil

Crush the cloves of garlic into a medium sized mixing bowl. Mix in the juice of half a lemon. Spoon the *tahina* into the bowl and beat it into the lemon juice. Add the juice of 1 more lemon in 3 batches, mixing in well each time. Now add cold water, beating in a couple of tablespoons at a time until you get a thick cream. You will find that at first the *tahina* will thicken until it becomes dry and lumpy, then as you continue adding lemon and water, the mixture will slacken, turning pale, creamy and unctuous.

Taste the cream and add more lemon juice if necessary – remember it is very rich, so needs an adequate sharpness, to balance – and salt. Stir in the chopped parsley and, just before serving, trickle a teaspoon or 2 of good olive oil over the top and sprinkle with a little more fresh parsley. Serve with warm pitta bread.

Baked Anchovy and Brie Sandwiches

The Anchovy and Brie Sandwich is a delicacy I came to appreciate when I was beavering away rather nervously at my first grown-up job. It sustained me through worrying times, when I didn't have the foggiest idea if I was doing the right thing.

In those days, the sandwich was provided by the little sandwich shop around the corner. I've long forgotten all my shorthand and the precise location of the shop, but the combination of buttery cheese and salty anchovy is one I return to with some frequency. Every now and then I treat myself to an embellished version made by my own fair hand, and it still bucks me up no end.

Baked in the oven so that the outer layer of bread becomes crisp and crunchy and the brie melts into the anchovy, this sandwich makes a terrific quick lunch or light supper, accompanied by a green salad.

SERVES 1

2 large slices of bread (brown or white)
olive oil or butter
30 g (1 oz) brie, thinly sliced
2–3 anchovy fillets
3–4 slices of tomato
2 basil leaves or 1 teaspoon chopped chives
freshly ground black pepper

Cut the crusts off the bread and butter or brush with oil on both sides. Lay one piece on a baking sheet. Arrange the brie on the bread, leaving a 1 cm (½ in) border. Season generously with pepper. Cut the anchovy fillets in half lengthways and arrange on the brie, then top with the herbs and tomato. Cover with second slice of bread, and press the edges firmly together with the handle of a fork or spoon.

Heat the oven to 200C/400F/Gas 6 and bake the sandwich for 15 minutes, or until golden brown. Eat immediately with a green salad.

Fried Aubergine Slices With Lebne and Pine Kernels

This dish can either be served on its own as a first course for a small number of people, or as one of a collection of little dishes to form part of a *meze*, or mixed hors d'œuvre, or even a whole meal.

I ate it in a restaurant in the back streets of Tel Aviv's old port. It was a Friday night, the start of the Jewish sabbath. From sundown on Friday to sundown on Saturday, quiet falls on the city streets and many restaurants are shut. We had been searching the area, renowned for its wealth of restaurants, for half an hour or more, looking for somewhere open and alluring. The Sea Dolphin was the final possibility and, fortunately, turned out to be an excellent choice.

One small variation of the dish is to flavour the cooking oil with chopped garlic and/or chilli. Just add them to the oil, and infuse over a very low heat for 10 minutes. Strain the oil to remove the bits, then fry the aubergine in it.

SERVES 4

450 g (15 oz) yoghurt, or 1 × 225 g (8 oz) tub of strained Greek
    yoghurt
1 tablespoon chopped chives
1 large aubergine
salt
oil
3 tablespoons pine kernels

If you are using ordinary yoghurt, line a sieve with a double layer of muslin and tip the yoghurt into this. Leave to drain, over a bowl or the sink, for around 8 hours, until it is very thick. If you use strained yoghurt, and are short of time, you could leave it as it is, but if possible drain as above for 1–2 hours. This drained yoghurt cheese is called *lebne*. Mix in the chopped chives.

Slice the aubergine into 8 thick discs and sprinkle with salt and set aside for 30 minutes–1 hour, to draw out the juices. Pat dry with kitchen paper.

In a small frying pan, dry fry the pine kernels, tossing so that they cook evenly, until golden brown. Fry the aubergine in oil on both sides, until brown and tender. Season with salt. Either serve hot immediately, topping each slice with a generous dollop of the *lebne* and sprinkling with pine kernels, or leave the aubergine to cool, draining on kitchen paper, and serve with *lebne* and pine kernels at room temperature.

Carrot and Rice Timbales

These little green mounds look so pretty and taste so good that it's hard to believe that all they're made of is boring old carrots, tiresome floppy lettuce and a bit of rice. But it's true.

It's a very satisfying moment as they slip smoothly out of their moulds and on to a plate, well-mannered and well-kitted out as they are. They are simple to concoct, and can be either a first course or a vegetable accompaniment to a main course.

There's no reason at all why you shouldn't adapt the recipe to other vegetable purées (such as celeriac, pea, broad bean) with considerable success.

SERVES 6 as a first course or side-dish

½ kg (1 lb) carrots
2 eggs
1 tablespoon double cream
lemon juice
salt and pepper
1 sprig of tarragon
60 g (2 oz) rice
1 round lettuce

Slice and cook the carrots until tender. Drain well, and put in a blender with the eggs, double cream, a squeeze of lemon juice, salt, pepper and tarragon. Blend, and adjust the seasoning.

Cook the rice, drain and stir into the carrot mixture. Pluck 16 untorn leaves from the lettuce. Bring a large pan of water to the boil, drop the lettuce leaves in and bring back to the boil. Remove the leaves about 10 seconds later, rinse under the cold tap, and drain well.

Brush 6 small ramekins or dariole moulds with a little oil, and line with 1 or 2 lettuce leaves as necessary. Throw away any left over leaves. Fill the moulds with carrot mixture, and flip any overhanging lettuce over the mixture. Cover each one with foil.

Stand the moulds in a roasting tray, filled to a depth of 2–3 cm

(1 in) with water, and bake at 190C/375F/Gas 5 for 15 minutes. Lift out of the roasting tray and turn out on to individual dishes, or one large dish – in which case it's best to turn them out first on to a greased saucer, then slip on to the serving dish.

Turineisa – Stuffed Courgettes

There is more to Turin than a shroud and Fiat – although a visit to the inner sanctum of the shroud is quite an experience, housed in its temple of black marble, and not a word about you know what . . .

But Turin itself, the first capital of united Italy, is an elegant city, with its arcaded streets, turn-of-the-century cafés and superb food. Autumn is the best of seasons for Piedmont food, which comes into its own with the first crops of wild mushrooms, the muskiness of white truffles, the wide choice of game, the first chills and frosts.

The cooking overlaps here and there with that of the south, but it is essentially a northern country cuisine, refined by the French and the affluence of the city. One favourite first course is a dish of hot hors d'œuvres: *caponet* (stuffed cabbage), vol-au-vents filled with *fonduta* (Piedmontese fondue) and *Turineisa* (stuffed courgettes) are sure to be on the plate.

SERVES 4–6

275 g (9 oz) minced pork or veal
60 g (2 oz) butter
90 g (3 oz) high quality sausagemeat
a handful of fresh parsley, finely chopped
1 large clove of garlic, finely chopped
6 basil leaves, finely chopped
1½ tablespoons grated parmesan
ground nutmeg
salt and pepper
2 eggs
4 plump courgettes
1 small glass dry white wine

Cook the minced pork in half the butter until opaque, breaking up the lumps. Add the sausagemeat, parsley, garlic and basil, and cook until all the pink has disappeared. Mince or process to a fine paste, then mix in the parmesan, nutmeg, salt and pepper, and finally beat in the eggs.

Trim the courgettes and halve lengthways. Using an apple corer, scoop out the centre of each half to form a boat-shape. Fill with the meat mixture – I find it easiest to use a piping bag – and sit snuggly in a buttered baking dish. Dot with the remaining butter, and pour over the wine. Bake at 190C/375F/Gas 5 for 45–50 minutes, basting occasionally with their own juices, until the filling is well browned.

Water-chestnuts On Horseback

Outside the Chinese greengrocers of Newport Court and Gerrard Street in Soho, stacked up on the pavements, are boxes and baskets of mysterious fruit and vegetables. Bunches of green-leaved *pak choi* and mustard greens, the hard horny hulks of the durian, winter melons, *chayotes*, ridged and bitter gourds, arrowhead and lotus root.

In among this unfamiliar collection, you may notice heaps of purplish mahogany-coloured corms with flaky brown scales, 2–5 cm (1–2 in) in diameter – these are Chinese water-chestnuts, with a crisp juicy flesh hidden inside the dull exterior. Pick out corms that are unblemished and firm.

They can be eaten raw and very nice they are – nutty and juicy. Peel a bowlful and then nibble away at them, serve them with drinks instead of salted nuts, or you might add them, roughly chopped, to a green salad.

When you cannot find fresh ones, the alternative is to search out tinned water-chestnuts instead. They tin well, and are sold not only in Chinese food stores, but also in many Western supermarkets and delicatessens. A tin of water-chestnuts makes an excellent store cupboard standby – to give a fresh crispness to salads and other dishes; try stir-frying slices of water-chestnut with strips of chicken breast, spring onions, garlic and fresh ginger, a dash of sesame oil, and soy sauce.

Fresh water-chestnuts can be kept for a week in the salad drawer of the fridge. Once peeled, they should be submerged in a bowl of lightly salted water, and stored again in the fridge.

SERVES 4

16 water-chestnuts, tinned or fresh
8 rashers of streaky bacon
16 wooden cocktail sticks

If you have fresh water-chestnuts, wash them well and peel. If they are tinned, drain them and rinse. Cut the rind off the bacon and stretch each piece with the back of a knife: hold one end down with your fingers, and drag the back of the knife down the rasher. Cut the elongated slices in half in the centre. Wrap each half around one of the water-chestnuts and secure with a cocktail stick.

Grill under a hot grill, until the bacon is beginning to brown and the water-chestnut is piping hot. Alternatively, arrange on a baking tray and bake in a hot oven (230C/450F/Gas 8) for 10–15 minutes.

Bananes Gratinées

I think I actually prefer cooked bananas to fresh ones, which by and large tend to be rather dull and stodgy unless you get one that is perfectly ripe. Baking them or frying them, on the other hand, can bring out that true banana flavour, and melting texture.

As a child, I often used to bake bananas wrapped in thin slices of bacon and, much as I love them done this way, I still have a tendency to think of it, quite wrongly, as a childish recipe.

You cannot fiddle too much with bananas when you cook them, but a little something extra to emphasise their sweetness (such as the salt of bacon) is a good idea. When Marcel Boulestin was writing in the London *Evening Standard*, back in the 1930s, he gave a couple of delicious ways of cooking them. The *Bananes Gratinées*, below, is my favourite, with its contrasting sweet and savoury, crunch and soft. It makes a good first course.

At the other end of the meal, but not the same one of course, you might like to try Bananas Creole. Place 4 peeled bananas in a fire-proof dish, sprinkle with demerara sugar, 2 tablespoonfuls water and a generous squeeze of lemon juice. Bake in a medium-hot oven (220C/425F/Gas 7) until brown, pricking and basting the bananas occasionally. And, as Boulestin says, a little drop of rum improves this sweet no end . . .

SERVES 4

4 bananas, peeled
75 g (2½ oz) butter
¼ teaspoon paprika
30 g (1 oz) dry white breadcrumbs
60 g (2 oz) farmhouse cheddar, grated
salt and pepper

Melt 1 oz of the butter in a saucepan, and gently fry the bananas, sprinkled with the paprika, for about 2 minutes.

Arrange them in a heat proof dish, pouring the butter over the top. Mix the breadcrumbs with the cheese, salt and pepper, and spread over the bananas. Dot with the remaining butter and bake in the oven at 220C/425F/Gas 7 for 20 minutes or so, until nicely browned.

Crudités With Crab Mayonnaise

There's little I like better for my supper than a dressed crab with thin slices of brown bread and butter and homemade mayonnaise. Now this is fine if it's just me, but if I'm feeding a crowd of people it works out at a terrible price. Compromise is called for. This mayonnaise will stretch a smaller amount of crab meat (use brown or white or a mixture) around a full dining table. Don't waste time and money on frozen crab meat – it's tasteless. When there's no fresh crab available, make something else.

SERVES 6–10

Mayonnaise:
125–175 g (4–6 oz) fresh crab meat*
2 teaspoons wholegrain mustard (such as Moutarde de Meaux)
a few drops of tabasco
a few drops of soy sauce
7 tablespoons mayonnaise
3 tablespoons whipping cream, whipped
salt

Crisp fresh vegetables: radishes, peppers, cucumber, spring onions, fennel, celery.
And/or lightly cooked vegetables: asparagus, green beans, new potatoes, salsify.
And/or cooked shellfish: prawns, scallops, lobster.

Mix all the mayonnaise ingredients together. Taste and adjust the seasoning. Pile into a bowl. Serve at room temperature.

For a simple first course, serve with crisp raw vegetables, trimmed as appropriate, so that they can be dipped into the mayonnaise.

For a more elaborate first course, or as the centre-piece of a lazy summery meal, add lightly cooked vegetables, warm or cold, and lightly cooked shellfish, or hard-boiled quails' eggs.

Shrimp Beignets

These crisp puffy little fritters are really out of this world, though I say so myself. I ate far more of them than was at all good for me when I was trying out the recipe, and in the end had to tip the remaining half of the batter out to prevent myself making just 1 or 2 more. Wasteful, I know, but I'd got to the stage where drastic measures did have to be taken, and fast.

SERVES 6

135 g (4½ oz) flour
¼ teaspoon salt
1 tablespoon oil
1 egg, separated
150 ml (¼ pt) lager
350 g (12 oz) peeled shrimps
¼ teaspoon cayenne pepper
oil
lemon wedges

Sieve the flour with the salt into a mixing bowl. Make a well in the centre and add the oil, egg yolk and lager. Gradually beat in enough warm water to form a batter with a consistency of double cream – you'll probably need between 200–300 ml (⅓–¼ pt). Beat until smooth. Add the shrimps and cayenne pepper, and set aside until you are ready to use.

Fill a frying pan to a depth of 2–3 cm (1 in) with oil and heat, or use an electric deep fryer. While the oil is heating, whisk the egg white until stiff, then fold into the shrimp batter. Drop a dessertspoonful at a time into the hot oil, and fry until the top surface has just set and the underneath is lightly browned. Turn and brown the other side. Drain quickly on kitchen paper, and serve with the lemon wedges.

Bocconcini of Asparagus and Duck

Bocconcini means little mouthfuls, and these are the most enticing little mouthfuls of piping hot asparagus and duck breast, and a good way of making those two fairly pricey ingredients go a long way, without seeming mean.

Serve them either as a first course for 4, or as superior canapés with drinks – one up on soggy crackers with a smear of cream cheese and a fluorescent flash of red lumpfish caviar.

MAKES 15–20

8 fresh asparagus spears*
1 duck breast
Dijon mustard
oil
salt and pepper

Trim the woody ends off the asparagus spears and then tie them together in one bundle. Fill a deep, narrow saucepan to a depth of about 8 cm (3 in) with lightly salted water. Bring to the boil, and stand the asparagus upright in the saucepan. Cover tightly with a lid, or a dome of silver foil if the asparagus is waving over the top. Keep the water at a generous boil, and cook for 5–10 minutes until the tips are just tender and the stems barely so. Alternatively, steam in a steamer. Drain immediately and plunge into a bowl of iced water to cool. Drain.

Put the duck breast in the freezer and chill until firm. Place skin-side down, cut the thinnest slices across the grain at a slant, using a sharp knife, as if you were slicing smoked salmon.

Cut each asparagus spear into 3, or 4, 5 cm (2 in) lengths. Smear one side of each slice of duck with a dab of mustard, then roll around a piece of asparagus, mustard-side in. Secure with a cocktail stick, and season lightly with salt and pepper. Brush with oil.

Grill under a thoroughly pre-heated hot grill, for 1–2 minutes on each side, and serve immediately.

To serve as a first course, toss leaves of frisée and bronzed batavia or Lollo Rosso lettuce, or other lettuce leaves, in a light French dressing, and arrange on individual plates or one large plate. Arrange the grilled *bocconcini* on them and scatter a few chopped chives over the top.

Finnish Rye Tartlets

To be truthful, these delicious tartlets are not the common fare of your average Finn, nor, I imagine, have they ever been made in Finland. Let me explain, then, why I've called them Finnish Rye Tartlets. When I was checking out a recipe for Scandinavian Christmas rice pudding, I spent some time reading about Scandinavian Christmas celebrations. They make it a grand festive occasion, a holiday of feasting and revelry to set them up for the dark months ahead.

In Finland, they may bake a whole ham in a rye crust. I didn't think I could really suggest that you, too, should try this one out, but it did seem like a good combination. Adding soured cream and caraway seeds led ultimately to these 'Finnish Rye Tartlets'.

SERVES 6

Pastry:
90 g (3 oz) rye flour
90 g (3 oz) plain flour
½ teaspoon salt
125 g (4 oz) butter

Filling:
30 g (1 oz) butter
¾ kg (1½ lb) onions – sweet red onions if available – very thinly sliced
175–250 g (6–8 oz) thickly sliced cooked ham, cut into strips
1½ teaspoons caraway seeds
300 ml (10 fl oz) soured cream
2 tablespoons parmesan, finely grated
salt and pepper

Sift the flours with the salt. Rub in the butter and add enough water (2–3 tablespoons) to form a firm dough. Roll out 3 mm (⅛ in) thick, and line 6 11 cm (4½ in) tartlet tins or one 25 cm (10 in) tart tin. Prick the bases with a fork, and chill for 30 minutes. Bake blind*, returning to the oven for 10–15 minutes until browned.

Beat the soured cream with the cheese, salt and pepper. Reheat the cases in the oven if necessary. Set the grill to heat up. Pour boiling water over the onions and leave for 5 minutes. Drain thoroughly. Fry the ham, caraway and onions quickly in the butter to heat through. Divide among the cases, spoon over the cream and brown under the grill. Serve quickly.

EGGS AND CHEESE

―――――― ❧❧ ――――――

Baked Eggs With Tomato and Mozzarella

Baked eggs, on their own or on a bed of vegetables, or with cheese, or cream and herbs, or whatever, are a great favourite of mine. Quick to prepare, quick to cook and, by and large, popular with everyone. The only tricky thing is getting the eggs cooked just right. The yolk should still be runny, the white opaque. The leathery skin formed on an overcooked egg is as unpleasant as pockets of gluey undercooked white. In the end you must rely on your own judgement. If you are not sure whether they have been in the oven long enough, test as neatly as possible with a skewer or the tip of a knife, scratching along the surface of the white surrounding the yolk.

SERVES 8 as a first course, 4 as a main course

8 eggs
1 mozzarella
¾ kg (1½ lb) tomatoes, skinned*, seeded and chopped
4 shallots, finely chopped
1 sprig of marjoram
1½ tablespoons olive oil
salt and pepper
1 or 2 teaspoons sugar
30 g (1 oz) butter

Drain the mozzarella, and cut into 1 cm (½ in) cubes. Mix together the mozzarella, tomatoes, shallots, marjoram and olive oil in a bowl.

28

Add salt, pepper and sugar to taste. Leave to stand for 15 minutes, for the flavours to mingle.

Lightly grease a large, shallow oven-proof dish. Spread the tomato and mozzarella mixture in a smooth layer on the base of the dish. Heat the oven to 180C/350F/Gas 4, and prepare a *bain-marie* – fill a roasting tray with boiling water to a depth of 2 cm (¾ in). Place in the oven.

Heat the dish with the tomatoes and mozzarella in the oven for 5 minutes. Take it out, and quickly and carefully break the eggs on top of the mixture. You may find it easier to break them on to a large plate or shallow bowl first, and just ease them gently on. Dot with butter, and whip straight back into the oven. Bake for 10 to 12 minutes, until the white is just opaque but the yolks are still runny.

Huevos A La Flamenca

Huevos a la Flamenca, baked eggs with tomato, chorizo and green beans, is one of the standard dishes in southern Spanish tapas bars. I first tasted it in a seedy-looking place in Seville. It was love at first mouthful, in fact the beginning of my love-affair with Spanish cooking.

Buy chorizo, the essential Spanish sausage, from good delicatessens. You should be offered the choice of mild or *piccante* – hot and spicey. Choose whichever suits your palate. Take the thicker, slicing sausage, 5 cm (2 in) or so in diameter, if available. Otherwise, slice the thinner chorizo into as many slices as seems reasonable and necessary. When asparagus is in season, try substituting it for the green beans.

SERVES 4 as a first course, 2 as a main course

4 eggs
125 g (4 oz) green beans
90 g (3 oz) shelled fresh peas, or thawed frozen peas
1 onion, chopped
2 cloves of garlic, chopped
scant tablespoon fresh parsley, chopped
2 tablespoons olive oil
125 g (4 oz) ham, roughly chopped
600 g (1¼ lb) tomatoes, skinned* and chopped
125 g (4 oz) chorizo
salt
paprika

Top and tail the green beans, cut into 2½ cm (1 in) lengths and parboil for 5 minutes. If you use fresh peas, do the same with them.

Fry the onion, garlic and parsley in the olive oil until translucent. Stir in the ham, then add the tomatoes and fresh peas, if using. Simmer together for 10 minutes, stirring occasionally to make sure it does not catch. Add the green beans and the chorizo, whole, and continue to cook for 5 minutes. Stir in thawed frozen peas at this point, and simmer until the beans are just tender. Add a little extra water or stock if it becomes too thick and dry. Season with salt and paprika. Keep the sauce simmering very gently on the heat, and dredge out the piece of chorizo sausage. Cut into 4 thick slices.

Pre-heat the oven to 230C/450F/Gas 8. Take 4 oven-proof bowls, or 1 large one if you are serving it as a main course, and quickly divide the very hot sauce between them. Make a depression in the centre of each, and break the egg into it, letting the white flow across the surface. Cover the yolk with a slice of chorizo, and whip the bowls quickly into the oven. Bake for 8–12 minutes, until the white has barely set.

Serve quickly, with plenty of bread to mop up the juices.

Leek and Carrot Kuku With Stilton

A *kuku* is a Middle Eastern baked omelette, thick with vegetables. Like the Spanish *tortilla*, it can be eaten hot, warm (best of all) or cold, cut into wedges or squares. Stilton is about as un-Middle Eastern as you can get, I know, but the thin vein of cheese running through the centre adds a welcome hint of salt. The *kuku* is excellent as either a main course or part of a buffet, and it makes a perfect picnic dish.

SERVES 6–8 as a main course

9 eggs
3 leeks, trimmed
½ kg (1 lb) carrots, coarsely grated
4 spring onions, finely chopped
3 tablespoons fresh parsley, finely chopped
salt and pepper
butter
175 g (6 oz) stilton, crumbled

Cut the leeks into 5 cm (2 in) lengths and shred. Drop into boiling water, bring back to the boil, then drain thoroughly. Cool. Break the eggs into a large bowl and beat well. Stir in the leeks, carrots, spring onions, parsley, salt and plenty of pepper.

Generously butter an oven-proof dish (a gratin dish, 5–8 cm (2–3 in) deep, 30 cm (12 in) in length is ideal) and spoon half the mixture into it. Sprinkle stilton evenly over it, and cover with the remaining egg mixture. Cover with foil and bake at 160C/325F/Gas 3 for 30 minutes. Remove the foil and bake for a further 15–20 minutes, until the eggs have set and the top is golden brown.

Cut into squares, and serve hot or warm from the dish, with buttered chicory and a baked sweet or plain potato. Or serve cold with salads.

TWO GOATS CHEESE OMELETTES

An admission: I find plain omelettes and even omelettes *aux fines herbes*, however perfectly made, boring and unsatisfying. I like bits and bobs in my omelettes, things that give that extra edge and interest. These two, both speckled with goats cheese, fulfill my concept of the ideal omelette.

Apple and Goats Cheese Omelette

SERVES I

3 eggs
30–45 g (1–1½ oz) goats cheese
1 sprig of thyme
1 small eating apple, peeled, cored and chopped
salt and pepper
15 g (½ oz) butter

Crumble the goats cheese (or chop it finely if it's quite moist). Beat the eggs vigorously with the thyme, salt and pepper. Melt the butter and heat in a frying pan. When frothing, throw in the chopped apple. Sauté until beginning to brown. Distribute the cubes fairly evenly around the pan.

Give the eggs a final quick whisk and pour into the hot pan, tilting from side to side to ensure that the egg is evenly distributed. As the edges begin to set, scrape gently towards the centre, allowing the still liquid egg to fill the gaps. Continue to cook over a high heat, until the omelette is set underneath and *baveuse* on top – that is thick and creamy, but not yet solid.

Scatter the crumbled goats cheese in a wide band along a diagonal. Flip one side carefully over the cheese, then quickly flip the entire omelette out on to a warm plate, waiting patiently at the side. The omelette should be neatly folded in 3. Eat immediately.

Goats Cheese and Croûtons Omelette

SERVES I

3 eggs
30–45 g (1–1½ oz) goats cheese
1 sprig of thyme
salt and pepper
1 cm (1½ in) thick slice of light rye bread (though ordinary white or
  wholemeal could be used)
30 g (1 oz) butter

Prepare the eggs, goats cheese and seasoning as above. Cut the crusts off the bread, and cut into 2 cm (1 in) cubes. Melt the butter in a frying pan and heat until frothing. Add the cubes of bread, and sauté until a light golden brown. Very quickly, pour in the beaten eggs and cook as above.

Scrambled Eggs With Lemon

I once made these scrambled eggs with lemon for my father. I love them, but he wasn't highly complimentary. It was, he explained, the principle of the matter. He felt that properly made scrambled eggs (made with good free-range eggs) were so delicious, that one didn't need to add anything else.

Well, I don't agree, and I would like to add that the principle didn't seem to affect his appetite. It's not, after all, as if eggs were a great rarity. Scrambled eggs, like many other egg dishes, take well to other flavours – herbs, mushrooms, ham and so on. Lemon juice is a less orthodox but very successful addition.

Scrambled eggs with lemon can be eaten hot, but are better left to cool and served as a first course. When scrambling the eggs, err on the side of undercooking, as the eggs will continue to cook in their own heat as they cool.

You can serve this on its own, as a starter, with lots of hot toast or crusty bread, or maybe in crisp small pastry cases for a smarter hors d'œuvre. It is particularly good with smoked salmon, trout, or eel, and so can be used to make a rather small amount of expensive smoked fish stretch to feed a large number of people.

SERVES 4 as a starter

6 large eggs
2 tablespoons double cream
zest and juice of 1 lemon
salt and pepper
fresh parsley or chives, finely chopped

Pare the zest from the lemon in strips and shred. Blanch for 1 minute in boiling water. Drain and set aside.

Break the eggs into a bowl and whisk well with the cream, half the lemon juice, salt and pepper. Either place the bowl over a pan of simmering water (they will take longer to cook, but will taste marvellous), or pour the eggs into a pan and set over the lowest of flames. In either case, stir constantly, scraping the egg from the base and sides as it sets. Remove from heat *when it is still creamy*, taste and add more lemon juice, salt and pepper if necessary. Leave to cool. Scatter with the parsley or chives and the reserved strips of lemon zest, and serve at room temperature.

Asparagus and Brie Envelopes

Although you can buy asparagus almost all year round now, flown in from unlikely sounding corners of the world, I still look forward to the British asparagus season, heralding the beginning of summer. You cannot improve much on the minimal delights of a plate of freshly cooked spears of asparagus, tips bathed in a pool of golden melted butter.

However, man or woman cannot live on asparagus alone. The advantage of this recipe is that it stretches a few spears of asparagus elegantly to provide an ample first course for 4.

SERVES 4 as a first course, 2 as a main course

8 spears of green asparagus*
salt
250 g (8 oz) firm brie, chopped
1 teaspoon red (or green) peppercorns
8 sheets filo pastry*
90 g (3 oz) butter, melted

Trim the woody ends off the asparagus then tie together in one bundle. Fill a deep, narrow saucepan to a depth of about 8 cm (3 in) with lightly salted water. Bring to the boil, and stand the asparagus upright in the saucepan. Cover tightly with a lid, or a dome of silver foil if the asparagus is waving over the top. Keep the water at a generous boil, and cook for 5–10 minutes until the tips are tender and the stems barely so. Drain immediately and plunge into a bowl of iced water to cool. Drain again, and cut each spear in 3.

Mix the brie with the peppercorns. Cut the sheets of filo pastry in half lengthways, and pile on top of each other. Cover with a sheet of greaseproof paper and a damp tea-towel, to prevent their drying out. Take 1 piece and brush generously with melted butter. Lay a second piece on top and brush with butter. Lay 2 bits of asparagus along a narrow end, trimming so that they are about 4–5 cm (1½–2 in) shorter than the width of the pastry. Cover with one eighth of the brie and peppercorn mixture. Flip the long edges over on to the filling, then roll up neatly, so that the filling is completely enclosed. Lay on a baking sheet, and repeat with the remaining ingredients.

Brush the tops of the rolls with any remaining butter. Bake at 230C/450F/Gas 8 for 10–15 minutes, until golden brown. Serve immediately.

Camembert Croquettes

Camembert is probably the best known of all the Normandy cheeses, but it is not at all the oldest. Camembert as we know it only appeared on the scene at the beginning of the nineteenth century, unlike the Livarot, Pont l'Evêque and Pave d'Auge cheeses, which have a long ancestry.

Crisp-coated camembert croquettes have also become part and parcel of Normandy cooking, rich and melting and irresistible.

SERVES 4–6

1 camembert, chopped
150 g (5 oz) fromage frais
60 g (2 oz) softened unsalted butter
60 g (2 oz) flour, sifted
pepper
2 egg yolks
flour
2 whole eggs, beaten
60 g (2 oz) cream crackers
oil

Put the camembert into a mixing bowl and mash with a fork. Drain off any whey from the fromage frais and add to the camembert.

Mix, and add the butter, flour and pepper. Beat well. Heat a pan of water until hot, but not bubbling, and place a bowl over it. Beat the mixture vigorously until smooth – this will take about 4 to 5 minutes. Take the bowl off the heat, and beat in the 2 egg yolks. Leave the mixture to set in the fridge for a minimum of 2 hours.

Crush the cream crackers to fine crumbs. Form tablespoons of the cheese mixture into small rissole shapes, roll them in flour, dip them in the beaten egg, then coat them in the crumbs.

Fill a high sided frying pan to a depth of 2 cm (¾ in) with oil and heat. Fry the rissoles until golden brown, 2 or 3 at a time (or use an electric deep fryer). Drain on kitchen paper, and keep warm while you fry the remaining rissoles. Serve with a green salad and apple or cranberry sauce, or other sharp conserve.

Deep-Fried Radicchio With Goats Cheese

In winter months, when I want a quick, light lunch, I often toss a few radicchio leaves in French dressing, lay a slice of goats cheese or crumbly Lancashire on top and whip it under the grill. The heat turns the pretty maroon colour of the leaves to a less prepossessing brown, but it tastes wonderful.

Deep-fried radicchio, clasped in crisp layers of breadcrumbs, is even better, though it takes more time. Still, you can do most of the work in advance, leaving only the frying until the last minute.

SERVES 4

1 head of radicchio
seasoned flour
2 eggs, beaten
fine dry breadcrumbs
oil

Sauce:
60 g (2 oz) goats cheese
150 ml (5 fl oz) soured cream or fromage frais
salt and pepper
1½ tablespoons fresh chives, finely chopped

To make the sauce, cut the rind off the goats cheese and crumble. Beat or liquidise with the soured cream. Season to taste with pepper and a little salt, and stir in the chives.

Separate the leaves of the radicchio, wash and dry. Dust each leaf with flour, then dip in the beaten egg and coat thoroughly in breadcrumbs. The leaves can be prepared up to 4 hours in advance and kept in the fridge, covered loosely, until required.

Heat a large pan of oil to 190C/375F and fry the radicchio leaves until golden brown. Drain briefly on kitchen paper, and serve immediately with the sauce.

Glamorgan Sausages

If this is your first encounter with Glamorgan Sausages, let me tell you that they have no meat in them at all, and make one of the best supper dishes, sure to please grown-ups and children alike, and vegetarians too.

They are usually fried, but I prefer them grilled. They are less greasy, dry and crisp on the outside and wonderfully melting and savoury inside.

SERVES 4

150 g (5 oz) fresh breadcrumbs
150 g (5 oz) caerphilly
½ leek, very finely chopped
1 tablespoon fresh parsley, chopped
1 sprig of thyme
salt and pepper
2 eggs, beaten
1½ teaspoons English mustard
milk
extra breadcrumbs to coat
lard, dripping, butter or oil

Mix the breadcrumbs with the cheese, leek, parsley, thyme and plenty of salt and pepper. Beat the eggs with the mustard. Set aside 2 tablespoons of this mixture. Mix the remainder into the crumbs and cheese with just enough milk (about 3 tablespoons) to bind the mixture together.

Divide into 8 and shape into sausages 2–3 cm (1 in) in diameter. Dip each one into the reserved egg, and roll in breadcrumbs to coat. If you have time, chill for 30 minutes before cooking.

Either fry in lard, dripping, or a mixture of butter and oil, briskly at first to brown, and finish at a gentler temperature for a final 2–3 minutes, or else brush with oil or melted butter and grill, turning every 1–2 minutes, until well browned on all sides.

PASTA, PANCAKES AND RICE

Cornmeal Pasta With Red Pepper and Goats Cheese

The cornmeal noodles, with their grainy texture, are easy to make, but allow plenty of time for the rolling and cutting. When time is in short supply, use shop-bought tagliatelle.

SERVES 4

Noodles:
175 g (6 oz) plain strong flour
¼ teaspoon salt
175 g (6 oz) fine cornmeal or polenta*
4 large eggs, lightly beaten
olive oil

Sauce:
2 red peppers, cut into strips
4 cloves of garlic, quartered
1 small onion, chopped
5 tablespoons olive oil
salt and pepper
60 g (2 oz) goats cheese

To make the noodles, sift the flour with the salt, and mix it with the cornmeal or polenta in a large bowl. Make a well in the centre and pour in the eggs. Begin to stir the flour into the eggs with a fork, graduating to your bare hands when it becomes too thick. When it is all worked in you should have a firm dough – if it seems sticky and crumbly, add extra flour, a tablespoon at a time. Knead the dough for 10 minutes, until smooth and elastic.

If you have a food processor, mix and knead the dough in that, using the bread paddle – it will only need a couple of minutes' kneading. Once kneaded, return the dough to the bowl and brush the upper surface with oil. Cover with cling film and leave to rest for 1 hour.

Divide the dough into 3 parts, and roll each out quickly and as thinly as possible on a floured board. Leave each of the sheets of noodles on a clean tea-towel for 30 minutes to dry out, then roll up loosely, and cut into ribbons 5 mm (¼ in) wide. To cook, drop into a large pan of boiling salted water. Bring back to the boil. Test the pasta immediately – it may take only a few seconds to cook. Cook until *al dente*, and drain.

For the sauce, cut the pepper into strips, and place in a pan with the onion, garlic and olive oil. Cover and stew over a low heat until the pepper, garlic and onion are meltingly tender – about 30 minutes. Season and keep warm, or reheat when needed. To serve, pour over the hot cornmeal noodles and sprinkle the crumbled goats cheese over the top.

Crab and Avocado Sauce For Pasta or Spaghetti Squash

This sauce is excellent with spaghetti or tagliatelle, but I particularly like it with the remarkable spaghetti squash, whose flesh falls into long strands when you dig your fork into it. The combination of soft avocado and gingery crab with the crisp vegetable threads is very appealing. Turn to the vegetable chapter for more on spaghetti squash.

SERVES 4

1 small onion, chopped
1 teaspoon fresh ginger, grated
½ tablespoon oil
150 ml (¼ pt) fish stock*
3 tablespoons dry sherry
250 g (8 oz) crab meat, *half brown, half white*
salt and cayenne pepper
1 avocado, peeled and cut into 1 cm (½ in) cubes
juice of 1 lemon

Fry the onion and ginger in the oil until tender. Add the fish stock and the sherry and simmer together for 5 minutes. Stir in the brown crab meat, salt and cayenne pepper.

Toss the avocado in half the lemon juice, to prevent discolouration. When the sauce is ready, add the avocado and the white crab meat. Stir well, and cook for about 30 seconds, to heat through. Taste and adjust the seasoning, adding more lemon if necessary. Pour over the hot pasta, or cooked spaghetti squash.

Baked Red Pepper Sauce For Pasta

A fiery dark red sauce for pasta. The long, slowly baked tomatoes and peppers develop a rich caramelised flavour, melting down to a thick purée, that keeps in the fridge for up to a week, or can be frozen.

Those spindly little red chillis, remarkably powerful, are the best for the sauce. If you cannot get these, substitute dried red chillis, or 2–3 larger fresh green ones, or 2 of the round crinkled Scotch Bonnet chillis.

SERVES 6–8

6 tablespoons olive oil
3 red peppers, seeded and cut into strips
375 g (12 oz) tomatoes, quartered
6 cloves of garlic (do not peel)
5 tiny red chillis, halved
5 pieces of dried tomato, cut into strips (optional)
salt
pinch of sugar

Put a tablespoon of the olive oil into a shallow oven-proof dish large enough to take the prepared ingredients, and tilt and swing the dish to coat with oil. Spread the peppers in the dish, then cover with the tomato quarters. Tuck the garlic, chillis and dried tomato pieces down among the pepper and tomato. Pour the remaining oil over the filled dish and sprinkle with a little salt.

Bake at 180C/350F/Gas 4, uncovered, for about 1½ hours, stirring and turning occasionally so that it cooks evenly. When the tomatoes, peppers and garlic are soft and melting, remove from the oven. Sieve the contents of the dish, pressing through as much purée as you can and leaving just the skins and seeds behind. Taste the purée and add extra salt and a pinch of sugar if necessary. The seasoning should be on the strong side, but not overpowering. Pack the mixture into a jar and cover.

To use the sauce, heat it gently with either a little extra oil or butter or 150 ml (¼ pt) cream, and pour over steaming hot pasta. It can also be used to add extra flavour to ordinary tomato sauces, spread thinly on croûtons* for soups or added to lasagne.

Pasta With Anchovy Sauce and Poached Eggs

For years I accepted, sadly, that I was never going to master the art of poaching eggs. I tried this way and that, but it never really worked. After a year of full-time food writing, I decided that this state of affairs couldn't go on. How could I call myself a food writer if I couldn't even poach an egg?

Armed with a dozen eggs, a dozen pans and about as many basic cookery books, I set to. I intended to try out all the tricks that promise perfection, but first I would go absolutely by the book with the most basic method of all. It worked, perfectly. I suspect that my earlier catalogue of disasters may have been due to trying too many of those tricks at a time, and far too nervously.

Two tips for those of you still struggling. The fresher the egg the better the white holds together to give a nice, plump cushion surrounding the yolk. Use the widest non-stick frying pan you can find, then at least you don't run the risk of your eggs sticking to the bottom.

To celebrate my new found skill, I ate my poached eggs on a bed of pasta laced with a rich anchovy sauce. Wow, was I pleased with myself that evening!

SERVES 2

250 g (8 oz) green tagliatelle
30 g (1 oz) butter
8 anchovy fillets, chopped
4 tablespoons double cream
pepper
2 eggs

Bring a large pan of water to the boil. If your pasta is dried, throw it in before you start making the sauce so that it has plenty of time to cook. If it is fresh, add it once you've got the sauce going. Cook the pasta until *al dente*, and drain well.

Meanwhile, melt the butter in a small frying pan and add the anchovies. Fry gently, mashing the fillets into the butter until they have dissolved. Lower the heat and stir in the cream and pepper to taste. Leave this over a very gentle heat until needed.

Poach the eggs, drain well and trim off any ragged edges. Toss the hot cooked pasta with the anchovy sauce. Pile on to a serving dish and nestle the eggs on top. Serve immediately.

Socca – Chickpea Pancakes

The spirited bountiful food markets of Nice are sure to send any cook into ecstatic delight. When I first walked through the fruit and vegetable market, I longed to buy everything and rush home to put together a huge lunch for all the nicest people I know – not very practical, since I was staying in a frighteningly grand hotel and they wouldn't have appreciated me turning my room into an impromptu kitchen/diner.

So purchases were limited to those things that would survive the journey back to England, and those that I could eat on the spot. Peaches and figs . . . and then I found the *socca* maker. *Socca* is a crisp and soft, smokey-tasting pancake, made with chickpea flour. It's cooked in a circular metal tray, a metre or so across, set over a rough tin-drum stove. Pay your money, and the vendor tears off a good portion of hot *socca*, wraps it in paper and hands it to you to eat as you walk along.

Cooking real *socca* at home is, of course, quite impossible without the proper equipment, and Mediterranean surroundings. But I reckon that smaller, pan-fried chickpea pancakes are still pretty good. Serve them as part of a meal, with ratatouille, perhaps, and fried eggs and ham, or on their own.

Chickpea flour is easy to come by when you know where to look and what to look for. Most wholefood shops and Asian food stores should be well supplied, but it is likely to be labelled either *gram* flour or *bessan*.

MAKES about 10

250 g (8 oz) chickpea flour
½ teaspoon salt
2 tablespoons virgin olive oil
600 ml (1 pt) water

Mix the chickpea flour with the salt in a bowl. Make a well in the centre and pour in half the water. Stir, drawing in the chickpea flour to form a thick batter. Beat in the olive oil, then gradually enough water to give a batter with the consistency of single cream – you may need a little more than 600 ml (1 pt). If you have any lumps, sieve or process quickly. Let it stand for 20 minutes.

Coat the base of a heavy frying pan with a thin film of olive oil and heat thoroughly. Stir the batter and then pour in enough to form a pancake 3 mm (⅛ in) thick. Cook until browned underneath then turn over and cook just long enough to seal the upper side. (If you cannot get the first pancake thin enough, then your batter is probably too thick – let it down with a little more water.) Repeat until all the mixture is used up, greasing the pan between pancakes.

Couscous With Apricots and Nuts

Moroccan couscous is really a type of pasta, fine grains of semolina rolled in a thin coating of flour. Most of the couscous sold in this country is pre-cooked and requires no more than moistening and reheating, an ideal standby to accompany stews of all kinds. Serve it plain with just a couple of spoonfuls of oil or butter to lubricate, or dress it up with dried fruit and nuts.

SERVES 6–8

375 g (12 oz) couscous
60 g (2 oz) dried apricots, soaked if necessary, and finely chopped
60 g (2 oz) chopped toasted* nuts (almonds, pine kernels and/or
    hazelnuts, but not peanuts!)
salt and pepper
3 tablespoons olive oil

Measure the volume of the couscous, and pour over the same volume of water. Set aside for 15 minutes, stirring occasionally until all the water has been absorbed. Half an hour before serving, mix in the remaining ingredients with your hands, breaking up any lumps. Either steam in a sieve lined with muslin, set over a pan of simmering water, or pile into a serving dish, cover with foil, and reheat in a moderate oven (190C/375F/Gas 5) for 20–30 minutes, until piping hot.

Russian Buckwheat Pancakes

Buckwheat flour, from delicatessens and wholefood shops, has a soft smokey flavour. It's one of the staples of Breton cooking, in *crêpes*, big dumplings and thick porridges. It resurfaces again in central and eastern Europe for making pancakes, especially the delicious yeast-raised *blini*.

These puffy little pancakes are raised with baking powder, not yeast. They are delicious with no more than a squeeze of lemon and a dusting of sugar, better still with sour cream and one of the 3 suggested combinations at the end of the recipe.

MAKES about 10

90 g (3 oz) buckwheat flour
90 g (3 oz) plain white flour
½ teaspoon baking powder
pinch of salt
300 ml (½ pt) milk
30 g (1 oz) butter, melted
1 egg, separated

Sift the flours with the baking powder and salt. Make a well in the centre and add the egg yolk, melted butter and half the milk. Whisk together gradually drawing in the flour and adding the remaining milk little by little.

When you are ready to cook the pancakes, whip the egg white until stiff, and fold into the pancake mixture. Heat a greased heavy bottomed frying pan over a medium heat, and drop half a ladle (2–3 tablespoons) of batter on to it. Cook until browned underneath and puffed. Turn over and brown the other side and then keep warm. Repeat with the remaining batter, greasing the pan between pancakes.

Serve with lemon wedges, soured cream and one of the following: smoked trout, or salmon, and fresh coriander leaves; fried mushrooms, with dill and crumbled hard-boiled egg; keta (salmon caviar), lumpfish caviar, or better still real caviar, and chives.

American Buttermilk Pancakes

Don't balk at the thought of eating pancakes with sausages, bacon *and* maple syrup. We eat apple sauce with pork, and redcurrant jelly with lamb, after all. It's an excellent if unexpected combination. If it really doesn't appeal to you, try one of the all sweet combinations instead, or plain lemon and sugar.

Do be careful not to buy maple-*flavoured* syrup by mistake. It's easy to confuse the bottles if you are in a hurry, and no doubt that is the intention. It's not particularly nice, or particularly similar to the real thing. Real maple syrup may be expensive, but a little goes a long way.

MAKES 10 small, 5 large pancakes

125 g (4 oz) self-raising flour
pinch of salt
¼ teaspoon bicarbonate of soda
1 tablespoon sugar
1 egg, beaten
300 ml (½ pt) buttermilk

Sift the flour with the salt and the bicarbonate of soda. Add the sugar. Make a well in the centre and add the egg and half the buttermilk. Beat, gradually drawing in the flour and adding the remaining buttermilk.

Heat a greased heavy bottomed frying pan over a medium flame. Pour half or a whole (depending on what sized pancakes you want) small ladle of pancake mixture into the pan. Cook until browned underneath and puffed. Turn over and brown the other side, and then keep warm. Repeat with the remaining mixture, greasing the pan between pancakes.

Serve with one of the following: soft unsalted butter, whipped until light and fluffy, and maple syrup; grilled bacon and sausages, and maple syrup; vanilla ice cream, grated chocolate and toasted hazelnuts (and maple syrup, if you like!).

Persian Chilau Rice With Herbs

There's a desperate mystique about cooking rice, but it really isn't that difficult, and most people have a good method that suits them. If the worst comes to the worst, and your rice turns out far from light and fluffy, busk it: if it's sticky, then it's Chinese style, and if there's not enough water and it catches on the base, insist that this is Persian style rice.

Actually, you would do better to learn the proper way to cook Persian *chilau* which is one of the very best ways of preparing rice – the bulk of it *is* light and fluffy, steamed for the last 20–30 minutes, while at the bottom of the pan is the most wonderfully crisp and crunchy brown crust, the crowning glory of the dish. You must use a heavy based pan – a cast iron one is ideal. Practise a few times before serving it up at a dinner party – I find that it comes out best when I use a low heat, but not quite the lowest my gas hob can offer. However, exact timing and temperature will vary from hob to hob, and pan to pan.

SERVES 6

375 g (12 oz) basmati rice*
salt
60 g (2 oz) melted butter, or 4 tablespoons olive oil
3–4 tablespoons chopped fresh herbs: dill, parsley, coriander, mint, chives

Soak the rice in a generous amount of water with 1 tablespoon of salt, for 1–8 hours (the longer the better). Drain and rinse.

Bring a large pan of salted water to a rolling boil, and add the rice. Simmer for between 3 and 8 minutes (depending on the length of soaking time and the age of rice) until the rice is almost, but not quite, cooked. Drain and rinse with hot water. Mix in the herbs.

Melt half the butter in the base of a *heavy* pan, add the rice, smoothing down loosely, and dot the remaining butter over the surface. Fold a clean tea-towel in half and lay it over the pan. Settle the lid snugly over the tea-towel, and lift the trailing ends on top of the lid to prevent them burning. Place the pan over a low heat, and cook for 20–25 minutes.

Spoon the rice into the serving dish, and scrape the brown crusty bits from the base of the pan. Scatter them over the rice. Top with a dollop of yoghurt, and serve with flaked almonds, fried in butter or oil, or chopped onion, browned in butter or oil.

Mushroom Risotto With Marsala

The beefing up of plain commercial mushrooms with dried *porcini* (*cèpes*, or boletus mushrooms, from delicatessens) is a trick I often resort to. A mere 15 g (½ oz) of dried mushrooms brings an earthy, meaty flavour to reinforce the mildness of cultivated mushrooms.

This risotto, with its hint of winey sweetness, has a unique sombre drama to it, dark creamy brown, flecked with green parsley. There are 2 keys to making a good creamy risotto. The first is the rice. It must be a high quality Italian risotto rice*. *Arborio* is one of the best – its medium length, fat, almost square grains, absorb a tremendous amount of liquid without collapsing – but there are others. The second is patience. Never try to rush it by chucking in all the liquid at one fell swoop and leaving it to cook all on its own. The final result pays ample reward for the constant vigil over the hot stove.

SERVES 4 as a side-dish, 2–3 as a main course

1 × 10 g (½ oz) packet dried *porcini*
60 g (2 oz) butter
1 onion, chopped
1 sprig of thyme
250 g (8 oz) *arborio* rice
250 g (8 oz) mushrooms, coarsely chopped
salt and pepper
1 small glass marsala
600 ml (1 pt) of light chicken stock, or water
2 tablespoons fresh parsley, finely chopped

Pour enough hot water over the *porcini* to cover generously. Leave to soak for 30 minutes, then drain. Strain and save the soaking water. Chop the *porcini*. Melt the butter in a large, heavy bottomed pan, and sweat the onions and thyme in it until tender, without browning. Bring the stock or water to the boil in a separate pan, turn the heat down low and half cover. Add the rice to the onions and stir until translucent. Stir in both kinds of mushroom, the *porcini*'s soaking water and 150 ml (¼ pt) of the hot stock or water. Simmer gently without stirring, until the liquid is absorbed.

Stir in another 150 ml (¼ pt) of hot stock or water, and again simmer until the liquid is absorbed. Repeat until the rice is almost cooked – it should absorb around 500 ml (¾ pt) stock or water in all. Now stir in the marsala. Simmer again until absorbed. By now the rice should be tender but still just firm, thick and creamy. If it is still a little too chewy, add a smidgen more stock or water and carry on simmering. When it is done, stir in the parsley, adjust the seasoning and serve.

Tomato Risotto

A recipe born out of necessity and past experience. It was Sunday, three out of five tomatoes were old and mouldy. But I did have proper risotto rice, an onion, garlic, a chip of forgotten parmesan and a small trickle of vermouth at the bottom of the bottle. So risotto it was, and it turned out to be just the thing – the gentle zing of the vermouth made it especially good.

I was lucky to have that *arborio* rice*. It honestly isn't an affectation or food snobbery to insist that you should use the proper kind of rice to make risotto. This risotto is simple enough to serve as a side-dish, but carries enough flavour to stand on its own with a sprinkle of grated parmesan.

SERVES 4 as a side-dish, 2–3 as a main course

1 onion, chopped
2 cloves of garlic, finely chopped
1 generous tablespoon olive oil
¾ litre (1½ pt) light stock or water
250 g (8 oz) *arborio* rice
250 g (8 oz) tomatoes, skinned* and roughly chopped
2 tablespoons dry vermouth
salt and pepper
¼ teaspoon ground nutmeg
125 g (4 oz) defrosted frozen peas (optional)
grated parmesan, or other hard cheese

Cook the onion and garlic gently in the olive oil until translucent and soft, without browning. While the onion is cooking, bring the stock or water to the boil in a separate pan. Turn the heat down low, and half cover. Tip the rice into the onion and garlic, and stir for a minute or so. Add the tomatoes and vermouth. Stir, and simmer for a further 2 minutes.

Now stir in 150 ml (¼ pt) hot stock or water, the salt, pepper and nutmeg. Simmer until almost all the water has been absorbed. Repeat until the rice is tender, but still firm. You will probably need about 600 ml (1 pt) liquid, maybe a little more. Add the peas and cook gently for a further 2–3 minutes, to heat them through. The risotto should be moist and creamy, but not swimming in liquid. Serve sprinkled with parmesan.

VEGETABLES

———— 🌿🌿 ————

Asparagus With Pistachio and Egg Dressing

In May and June, when the English asparagus season reaches its
height and prices drop, I revel in asparagus, hot or cold, with
melted butter, olive oil and a dusting of parmesan, a simple mild
vinaigrette, or this pistachio and egg dressing. Use the dressing on
hot or cold asparagus.

SERVES 4 as a first course

1 kg (2 lb) asparagus
2 tablespoons shelled pistachios
1 egg, hard-boiled and finely chopped
4 tablespoons olive oil
1 tablespoon rice vinegar (from Chinese or Japanese shops) or
   1½ tablespoons lemon juice
salt and pepper

Trim and cook the asparagus in the usual way (page 253). Drain
thoroughly and arrange on a serving dish.

Pour boiling water over the pistachios, and leave for 1 minute.
Drain, and rub off any brown skin. Chop finely, and mix with the
egg. Beat in the olive oil, vinegar or lemon juice, salt and pepper.
Taste and adjust the seasoning.

Pour a little of the dressing over the tips of the asparagus, and
serve the remainder separately.

Caponata

Caponata is one of the classic Sicilian aubergine dishes, of which, it should be said, there are many. *Caponata*, though, is the best known of them all, which is quite as it should be since it is as delicious as it is unusual.

It is sometimes referred to as a variation on the French ratatouille, which isn't terribly accurate. *Caponata* is punchier and wilder than ratatouille, and hasn't been spoiled by over-exposure and negligent commercial cooking.

SERVES 4

1 large aubergine, chopped
salt
6 tablespoons olive oil
6 sticks of celery, chopped
1 onion, chopped
1 × 400 g (14 oz) tin chopped tomatoes, or ½ kg (1 lb) tomatoes, skinned*
  and chopped
2 tablespoons caster sugar
4 tablespoons red wine vinegar
1 teaspoon ground nutmeg
1 teaspoon capers, rinsed
salt and pepper
12 black olives, pitted and roughly chopped
2 tablespoons fresh parsley, chopped

Spread out the aubergine in a colander, sprinkle with salt and set aside for 30 minutes–1 hour. Press gently to extract as much water as possible, then dry on kitchen paper or a clean tea-towel.

Heat 4 tablespoons olive oil in a heavy based frying pan. Sauté the celery until browned. Scoop out and set aside. Fry the aubergine in the same oil, until browned and tender, adding a little extra oil if necessary. Leave to cool.

Add the remaining oil to the pan, and sauté the onion until golden. Add the tomatoes, and simmer for 15 minutes until thick. Add the sugar, vinegar and nutmeg, and cook for a further 10 minutes, until you have a rich sweet and sour sauce. Add a little salt and plenty of pepper. Stir in the capers, olives, parsley, aubergine and celery. Taste and adjust the seasoning, then pour into a serving dish. Leave to cool.

Serve as an hors d'œuvre with salamis, hams, radishes, tomato, basil and onion salad, and big chunks of rough country bread. Alternatively, offer it as a half-way house between a vegetable side-dish and a relish, with plain grilled or barbecued meats.

Grilled Aubergine and Mozzarella Sandwich

This is a favourite sandwich of mine, based on one I ate in a diner in
New York. There is enough here to make 3 or 4 substantial
sandwiches, but if you are cooking for 2 people only, toss the extra
grilled vegetables in a spoonful of French dressing to make a salad
for the next day.

SERVES 3–4

6 tablespoons olive oil
juice of ½ large lemon
2 cloves of garlic, finely chopped
salt and pepper
2 tablespoons fresh coriander, finely chopped or 2 teaspoons dried thyme
1 aubergine, sliced lengthways 1 cm (½ in) thick
2 small onions (red ones if you can find them), sliced into 2 cm (¾ in) rings
6–8 large thin slices of brown or rye bread
2 small tomatoes, thinly sliced
90–125 g (3–4 oz) mozzarella

Mix the oil, lemon juice, garlic, salt and pepper and two thirds of
the coriander or all the thyme. Turn the aubergine and onion slices
in this marinade, cover and set aside for at least 30 minutes, at most
4 hours, turning occasionally.

Remove the vegetables from the marinade, and grill until
browned and tender – about 5 minutes per side. Don't worry if they
burn slightly, as long as they are not charcoal through and through.
Keep them warm.

Toast half the bread on one side. Turn it over and arrange the
tomato slices on top. Season generously and top with slices of
mozzarella. Place the remaining bread on the grill rack as well. Grill
until the mozzarella has melted and the bare slices are brown.
Quickly top the mozzarella with the aubergine and onion, and any
remaining herbs, and cover with bare toasted bread, pressing down
gently.

Hot Beetroot and Apple With Sour Cream

I don't like bought ready-cooked beetroot. Most are sozzled with vinegar, and rather unpleasant vinegar at that. Even those that aren't are still disappointingly dull.

A good vegetable deserves better treatment, and whatever your personal feelings about beetroot, it *is* a good vegetable. Indeed, I would even go so far as to say that it is up there among the top ranks, as long as it is freshly and plainly cooked.

SERVES 6 as a first course or side-dish

2 large cooked beetroot*, peeled
2 eating apples
butter
salt and pepper
8 tablespoons soured cream, fromage frais or Greek strained yoghurt
2 tablespoons fresh chives or spring onion, chopped
6 slices of bread, crusts removed, or 30 g (1 oz) breadcrumbs

Cut the beetroot into 5 mm (¼ in) thick slices and halve. Quarter the apple and core, but do not peel. Slice the quarters thinly, so that they are about as thick as the beetroot. Arrange in a buttered gratin dish, or shallow oven-proof dish, in alternate overlapping bands. Season well and dot with 30 g (1 oz) butter. Cover with foil, and bake at 200C/400F/Gas 6 for 20–30 minutes.

Meanwhile mix the cream with the chives. To serve as a first course, cut the bread into triangles and fry in butter or toast until golden. For a side-dish, fry or grill the breadcrumbs until golden brown and keep warm.

When the vegetables are ready, either tuck the triangles of bread around the edges, or sprinkle the crumbs evenly over the top. Spoon the soured cream down the centre of the dish. Serve while still hot.

Millefeuilles of Baby Broad Beans

This is one of those perfect, simple combinations – use the smallest new broad beans and, if you want to make it extra special, skin the individual cooked beans as well. It takes time, but if you've got it it's worth it. Any coarseness of flavour is discarded with the greying skins.

SERVES 4 as a first course, 2 as a main course

250 g (8 oz) puff pastry*
1 egg, beaten

Filling:
375 g (12 oz) shelled small broad beans
1 carrot, sliced
1 tablespoon sugar
salt
1 sprig of basil, plus a few extra leaves to decorate
1 tablespoon olive oil
1 small onion, chopped
1 clove of garlic, chopped
½ kg (1 lb) tomatoes, skinned*, seeded and chopped
1 tablespoon tomato paste
1 teaspoon red wine vinegar

Roll the pastry out into a rectangle 30 × 23 cm (12 × 9 in). Trim the edges. Butter a baking tray and lay the sheet of pastry on it. Prick with a fork and chill for 30 minutes. Brush the surface with the egg. Bake at 230C/450F/Gas 8 for 10–15 minutes, until golden brown. Let it cool for 5 minutes then, with a sharp knife, cut into strips 8 × 23 cm (3 × 9 in). Halve each strip.

Place the broad beans in a pan with the carrot, half the sugar, the salt and a sprig of basil. Add enough water just to cover. Bring to the boil, and simmer until the beans are tender. Drain, reserving the cooking liquid. Discard the carrot and basil.

Soften the onion and garlic in the olive oil without browning. Add the tomatoes, tomato paste, remaining basil and sugar, vinegar, and 150 ml (¼ pt) of the cooking liquid. Simmer for 30 minutes, then pass through a *mouli-légumes*, or sieve. Stir the sauce – it should have the consistency of runny double cream, but if it seems watery, boil until reduced a little. Taste and adjust the seasoning.

To serve, mix the broad beans with the tomato sauce, and reheat. Reheat the pastry, too, if necessary, then place one piece on each plate, top with sauce and beans, letting it flow over, and cover with a second piece of pastry. Decorate with any extra basil leaves and serve immediately.

Szechuan Green Beans

I noticed this extraordinary-looking dish in a delicatessen in
Toronto, not that the recipe is remotely Canadian. I just couldn't
work out what the mass of glistening, brown-black strips, dramatic
against a plain white dish, actually consisted of.

It turned out to be the most sensational tasting, double-cooked
green beans – a Chinese, or rather Szechuan, recipe. I now serve it
cold, as part of an hors d'œuvre, making it a few hours, or even 24
hours, in advance. By the way, it's worth noting that deep-frying is
an excellent way of cooking green beans for a special occasion, even
if you don't go on to the second part of the recipe.

SERVES 4 as a first course

2 tablespoons dried shrimps
½ kg (1 lb) French beans, topped and tailed
oil
2 cloves of garlic, thinly sliced
½ teaspoon Szechuan or black peppercorns, coarsely crushed
2½ cm (1 in) piece of fresh ginger, peeled and cut into matchsticks
½ teaspoon salt
1 tablespoon sugar
1 tablespoon dark soy sauce
2 teaspoons rice or white wine vinegar
1 tablespoon sesame oil

Cover the shrimps generously with boiling water, and soak for 20
minutes. Drain and set the liquid aside. Chop the shrimps finely.
Heat the oil to 190C/375F and deep fry the green beans for 5
minutes, until tender and patched with brown. Drain on kitchen
paper.

In a wok or large high sided frying pan, heat 1 tablespoon oil until
it smokes. Add the garlic, pepper and ginger, and stir briefly. Then
add the shrimps and stir-fry for 30 seconds. Add the salt, sugar, soy
sauce and 5 tablespoons of the shrimp water. Stir to mix.

Finally add the green beans. Toss in the sauce to coat well, then
cover and, keeping the heat high, cook until virtually all the liquid
has been absorbed. Check after 1 minute – the sauce should have
caramelised, and the beans should be several shades darker, a few
may even be verging on black. Toss and, if necessary, cover again
for a further 20–30 seconds to finish cooking. Remove from the heat
and mix with the rice vinegar and sesame oil. Serve hot or, better
still, cold.

Smothered Broccoli

Instead of lightly cooking broccoli until it is just *al dente*, try it
'smothered' one day. This long, slow method of cooking vegetables
intensifies their natural sweetness and transforms the flavour. Add a
hint of garlic and the heat of red chilli, and the broccoli tastes
sensational.

SERVES 4 as a first course or side-dish

½ kg (1 lb) broccoli
olive oil
1–2 dried red chillis, seeded and crumbled (optional)
2 cloves of garlic, sliced
coarse sea salt

Divide the thick stems of broccoli – more than 2 cm (¾ in) in
diameter – in half or thirds down their length. Trim and rinse in
cold water.

Cover the base of a heavy based skillet or frying pan (big enough
to take the broccoli in a single close-fitting layer), with a generous
layer of olive oil. Add the chillis and garlic. Cook over a medium
heat until it sizzles. Add the broccoli, and coat in the oil. Reduce
the heat to its lowest setting. Season with salt, and add a scant 150
ml (¼ pt) water. Cover tightly. Cook gently for 1 hour, turning the
broccoli carefully 2 or 3 times.

The broccoli should be wonderfully tender, having absorbed
most of the water. If it still seems very liquid, uncover and raise the
heat to boil off some of the water. Serve hot or warm, with toast as a
first course, or as a side-dish.

Sautéed Butternut Squash With Chorizo

Over recent years, butternut squashes have eased their way on to
the supermarket shelves, and they are now regular occupants.
These hard, gourd-shaped squashes keep well. Their flesh is bright
orange, and they do have a nutty buttery taste. They can be
steamed, or simmered and lightly flavoured with marjoram or sage.
Cooked slices are delicious seasoned, scattered with parmesan,
dotted with butter and browned under the grill.

The squash can also be baked: halve, seed and bake with a little
butter or olive oil, salt and pepper for about 50 minutes at

180C/350F/Gas 4. You might like to bake an egg in the cavity of each half – 10 minutes or so before the squash is cooked, remove from the oven and carefully break an egg into each one. Dot with butter, and return to the oven. Remove when the white is just set, and season.

SERVES 3–4 as a main course

1 butternut squash
250 g (8 oz) piece of mild chorizo, skinned and thickly sliced
1 tablespoon butter
1 tablespoon oil
salt and pepper
fresh parsley, chopped

Peel the squash, discard the seeds, and cut into rough 2½ cm (1 in) cubes. Place in a small pan with 3–4 tablespoons water. Cover and cook over a moderate heat, stirring occasionally, adding a little extra water if necessary to prevent burning. Drain well.

Melt the butter and oil in a large frying pan, and sauté the squash for 4 minutes. Add the chorizo, and sauté until the squash and chorizo are beginning to brown. Tip into a warmed serving dish with the juices, season, and scatter with the parsley.

GREEN CAULIFLOWERS

Have you seen those beautiful green cauliflowers? There are two kinds. The first is just an ordinary cauliflower with a pea-green curd. The second is one of the most stunning-looking vegetables I know – the *romanesca* cauliflower, with its spiralling cones of green. To be honest, neither tastes wildly different from the white cauliflower – perhaps they do have a hint of broccoli to them – but they look enchanting. The 2 recipes that follow exploit their colour to the full, although they are just as good to eat when made with ordinary every day white cauliflower.

Purée Dubarry

This is nothing more than a cauliflower purée, made by mashing or blending 2 parts cooked cauliflower with 1 part cooked potatoes, a good knob of butter, some cream (or milk if you are watching the cholesterol), and lots of salt and pepper. When you use the green cauliflower, you end up with a delicious pale green creamy purée. I sprinkle a little chopped spring onion, chives, parsley, or fresh coriander leaf over the top, for the taste and for the contrasting greens.

Green Cauliflower Piedmontese

In this dish the cauliflower is cooked whole, half boiled, half steamed to preserve the colour and taste, then dressed with a quickly made anchovy, onion and chilli sauce.

SERVES 6 as a side-dish, 4 as a main course

1 green cauliflower, leaves removed

Sauce:
4 tablespoons olive oil
1 small onion, finely chopped
1 dried red chilli, crumbled
4 anchovy fillets, chopped
1 tablespoon fresh parsley, chopped
1 tablespoon red wine vinegar or sherry vinegar

Cut the stalk off the cauliflower so that it will sit firmly on its base. Fill a pan large enough to take the cauliflower to a depth of 2–3 cm (1 in) with salted water, and bring to the boil.

Take 2 strips of silver foil, about 8 cm (3 in) across and long enough to go round the cauliflower and a little bit more. Fold each one in 3 lengthways. Lay one at right angles to the other to make a cross and sit the cauliflower on the centre. Bring the ends up round the cauliflower to form a cradle, and lift it into the pan. Leave the silver foil straps flapping loosely, and cover. Simmer until the stalk is tender (test with a skewer), lift the cauliflower out with the foil straps and drain well.

While the cauliflower is cooking, cook the onion with the chilli in the oil until tender. Add the anchovies, mashing them into the sauce until they dissolve. Stir in the parsley and vinegar, and keep warm. Sit the cauliflower in a serving dish and pour the sauce over it.

Celeriac Purée au Gratin

If you've never tackled celeriac before, then this is an excellent way to start enjoying a delightful vegetable. Look out in supermarkets and grocers for a large roughly spherical object, 10–12 cm (4–5 in) across and slightly off-white. At one end there will be a tangle of gnarled stubby 'fingers'. This is not one of the world's most beautiful vegetables.

The flavour is similar to that of celery, though not the same and, in my opinion at least, really rather nicer. It has a sweetish edge to it that benefits from a dash of lemon juice to sharpen it up. A whole celeriac root will keep well, so if you haven't got a good local supply buy one when you do see it and use it within the next couple of weeks.

This celeriac purée is stretched and the flavour softened by the addition of an equal quantity of mashed potato – the end result is a welcome change to ordinary mashed potato.

SERVES 6 as a side-dish

1 celeriac
375 g (12 oz) potatoes
90 g (3 oz) butter
milk
2 tablespoons lemon juice
salt and pepper
60 g (2 oz) breadcrumbs

Slice off the celeriac roots, and trim off the rough skin. Cube, and drop the cubes into a bowl of water, acidulated with a couple of tablespoons of vinegar to prevent browning. Boil the celeriac in more acidulated water until tender. Drain. Boil the potatoes in their skins until tender. Drain and peel. Cut up roughly, then mash.

Process the celeriac with 60 g (2 oz) of the butter, or mash by hand. Mix well with the potato, adding enough milk to give a creamy purée. Season well, and add lemon juice to taste.

Smooth the purée into an oven-proof dish, cover with the breadcrumbs and dot with the remaining butter. Bake at 200C/400F/Gas 6 for 30 minutes until nicely browned.

Alternatively, if you are short of time or oven space, reheat the purée in a pan then spread in the dish, cover with breadcrumbs, dot with butter and whip under a very hot grill until browned.

Grilled Corn On The Cob With Herb Butter

I first encountered grilled corn on the cob in Athens. It was the
smell that hit me first, wafting down the street from the street-
vendors, turning the brown cobs on the smokey braziers. Whether
you use the kitchen grill or an outdoor barbecue, it's a marvellous
way to cook it – slightly crisp on the outside, sweet and juicy on the
inside.

SERVES 4

4 heads of sweetcorn
3 tablespoons salt

Herb butter:
90 g (3 oz) butter
2 sprigs of mint
½ tablespoon fresh parsley, chopped
½ tablespoon fresh oregano, chopped
1 dried red chilli

Strip the heads of corn of all their leaves and fibres. Dissolve the salt
in 2 litres (3 pt) water. Soak the sweetcorn in this brine for 1–4
hours, turning occasionally.

Melt the butter, and add the herbs and the chilli, broken or cut in
half. If you like it hot leave the seeds in, otherwise it may be best to
remove them. Leave the butter to infuse over a low heat for a few
minutes.

Heat the grill (or the barbecue) thoroughly. Drain the corn cobs,
and pat dry with kitchen paper or a clean tea-towel. Brush with
melted butter and grill for about 15 minutes, turning and basting
with more butter. The corn is cooked when it is well browned all
over. Serve with the remaining herb butter.

Mushroom and Brazil-Stuffed Cucumbers

Crisp cucumber, filled with rice, mushrooms and nuts in a sweet
and sour sauce is lovely hot as a main course, but also wonderful
cold, as a first course or part of a buffet.

SERVES 8 as a first course, 4 as a main course

Stuffing:
½ onion, chopped
60 g (2 oz) butter
375 g (12 oz) mushrooms, finely chopped
90 g (3 oz) rice
2 tablespoons white wine
150 ml (¼ pt) water or vegetable stock
salt and pepper
2 tablespoons fresh parsley, chopped
60 g (2 oz) brazil nuts, chopped

2 thick cucumbers
300 ml (½ pt) white wine
juice of 1 lemon
1 tablespoon tomato purée
4 tablespoons olive oil
60 g (2 oz) caster sugar
½ teaspoon coriander seeds, crushed
½ teaspoon cumin seeds, crushed
salt and pepper

Fry the onion in the butter until tender, then add the mushrooms. Sauté until just cooked, then add the rice. Stir until nicely coated, and pour in the wine and 150 ml (¼ pt) boiling water or vegetable stock. Season. Cover and simmer very gently for 10–20 minutes, until the liquid has all been absorbed and the rice is cooked. If necessary, add a little extra boiling water. When cooked, stir in the parsley and brazils.

Meanwhile, place all the remaining ingredients, except for the cucumbers, in a pan with a scant 150 ml (¼ pt) water. Bring to the boil and simmer for 10 minutes. Cut the cucumbers into 4 pieces each. Either halve lengthways and scoop out the seeds with a teaspoon to form boat-shapes, or halve each piece again, and hollow out the centre with an apple corer to form a cylinder.

Poach the cucumber in the syrup for 15 minutes. Drain well and arrange on a baking dish. Fill with the mushroom stuffing. Boil the syrup hard until reduced by half and pour over the stuffed cucumbers. Cover and bake at 200C/400F/Gas 6 for 10–20 minutes, until piping hot.

Sesame Roast Jerusalem Artichokes

Pick out Jerusalem artichokes that are firm and as smooth as you can find. There's nothing wrong with the really nobbly ones, it's just that they are harder to peel in one piece, even after they are half cooked.

Eat them plainly boiled or steamed, or cooked, drained well and then sautéed in butter until thoroughly reheated and beginning to brown. For smarter occasions, or when you feel in need of a serious treat, try this recipe, coating them first in sesame seeds, then roasting until the insides are meltingly tender and the outside is crisp and crunchy. The dish is good enough to eat as a first course on its own, or with the Sunday roast.

SERVES 4 as a first course or side-dish

½ kg (1 lb) Jerusalem artichokes
salt
5 tablespoons olive oil
2 cloves of garlic, chopped
2 dried red chillis, seeded and chopped
seasoned flour
1 egg, beaten
sesame seeds

Scrub the artichokes but do not peel. Parboil for 5 minutes in salted water. Drain and peel. While the artichokes are cooking, heat the oil with the garlic and chilli in a small pan set over a low flame for 5 minutes. Leave to infuse, then strain when ready to use.

Toss the artichokes in the flour, dip into the egg then roll in sesame seeds. They can be prepared a few hours in advance up to this point – chill, covered, in the fridge until needed. Pour the oil into an oven-proof dish large enough to take the artichokes in a single layer. Add the artichokes and coat in the oil. Roast at 200C/400F/Gas 6 for 30–40 minutes, turning and basting occasionally, until browned.

Tom Jackson's Curly Kale With Bacon

If the name Tom Jackson doesn't immediately ring a bell, cast your mind back a few years. Tom Jackson was the leader of the Post Office Workers' Union, and memorable too for his wonderful bushy mustachios.

He now runs a mail-order antiquarian and second-hand book service from his home in Yorkshire, specialising in books about food and drink. He is a wonderful cook. Roast beef and Yorkshire pudding is, of course, a favourite, but with his huge collection of cookery books in the basement, waiting to be sold, he has no shortage of new recipes to try out as well.

He cooks curly kale with bacon for extra flavour – not plastic-wrapped supermarket bacon plumped out with water, mind you. He's lucky enough to be able to buy local traditionally cured bacon. If you can find a source for yourself, you'll soon notice the difference. Apart from the taste, it won't shrink and ooze liquid into the pan.

SERVES 3–4

375 g (12 oz) curly kale, shredded
1 medium sized onion, chopped
8 rashers of streaky bacon
pepper

Cut the bacon into thin strips and fry in a large pan with the onion and a little extra lard if necessary, until softened.

Pack in the kale, and cover. Cook over a medium heat, turning occasionally, until the kale is cooked but still has plenty of bite to it. Season well with pepper and serve.

Smothered Leeks and Carrots

My wide, flat paella pan, with an upturned serving plate for a makeshift lid, has proved the ideal pan for cooking these smothered vegetables. If you don't have a single pan large enough to take all the carrots and leeks in one snug layer, it is best to use 2 separate frying pans, dividing the ingredients equally between them.

SERVES 8

1 kg (2 lb) leeks, trimmed and cut into 5 cm (2 in) lengths
1 kg (2 lb) carrots, cut into 5 cm (2 in) lengths
1 large onion, chopped
45 g (1½ oz) butter
2 tablespoons vegetable oil
salt and pepper

Melt the butter with the oil in a wide frying pan and brown the leeks, carrots and onion. Stand back and pour in 300 ml (½ pt) water at arm's length – it may spit at first.

Season well, and bring to the boil. Turn the heat down very low, cover and cook gently for 30 minutes, turning occasionally. (The vegetables can be cooked to this point in advance, and finished later.)

Remove the lid, turn up the heat and boil hard until the liquid is reduced to a thin layer on the base of the pan.

Tip into a warmed (serving) dish and serve immediately.

Leek and Mushroom Pie

This is a big hearty pie that will be welcomed by vegetarians and meat-eaters alike. Determined non-vegetarians can substitute bacon (no need to cook it first) for the mushrooms, or use both.

SERVES 6

Pastry:
500 g (1 lb) shortcrust pastry*
1 egg, beaten

Filling:
90 g (3 oz) butter
¾ kg (1½ lb) leeks, trimmed and sliced
1 onion, sliced
1 sprig of thyme
175 g (6 oz) mushrooms
150 ml (5 fl oz) double cream
1 egg
1 tablespoon flour
salt and pepper
4 hard-boiled eggs

For the filling, melt 60 g (2 oz) of the butter in a pan and add the leeks, onion and thyme. Stir to coat well, then cover and cook over a medium heat until tender. Remove the lid and, if there is a lot of liquid, continue to cook uncovered for a few more minutes until just moist. Remove from the heat. Meanwhile, cook the mushrooms separately in the remaining butter, then stir into the leeks. Cool slightly.

Beat the cream with the egg and flour, and stir into the leeks. Season with salt and pepper. Slice the hard-boiled eggs. Set the oven to 230C/450F/Gas 7, and place a metal baking sheet on the rack to heat through.

Roll out just over half the pastry, and line a 23 cm (9 in) deep pie tin with it. Place half the hard-boiled egg slices on the base, cover with the leek mixture and place the remaining egg on top. Roll out the remaining pastry. Brush the rim of the pie with the beaten egg and lay the lid on top, pressing gently to seal. Make a hole in the centre and use the remaining pastry to decorate. Brush the top with beaten egg.

Bake for 10–15 minutes, until the pastry is a golden brown, then turn down the heat to 180C/350F/Gas 4, and cook for a further 20 minutes.

Mushroom and Aubergine Moussaka With Gremolata

A no-meat moussaka, but just as filling and delicious as the standard kind. I forego the usual step of frying the aubergine, which can make the dish terribly greasy. They cook quite happily in the heat of the oven. Why make life more complicated by adding extra steps?

The final touch, a sprinkling of *gremolata*, the Italian mixture of very finely chopped parsley, lemon and garlic, gives the moussaka a zip of freshness to balance the mellow flavour of the slowly cooked vegetables.

SERVES 6–8 as a main course

1 kg (2 lb) aubergines, thinly sliced
salt
2 large onions, chopped
2 cloves of garlic, chopped
2 tablespoons olive oil
½ kg (1 lb) mushrooms, chopped
½ teaspoon ground cinnamon
1 × 400 g (14 oz) tin chopped tomatoes
1 tablespoon tomato paste
½ teaspoon sugar
pepper

Bechamel:
2 tablespoons olive oil
60 g (2 oz) plain flour
500 ml (¾ pt) milk
30 g (1 oz) grated parmesan or cheddar
salt and pepper

Topping:
2–3 tablespoons fresh parsley, very finely chopped
zest of 2 lemons, finely grated
1 clove of garlic, very finely chopped
2 large red peppers, grilled and skinned* (optional)

Sprinkle the aubergine slices with a little salt and set aside for 30 minutes while you make the sauces. Rinse and pat dry with kitchen paper or a clean tea-towel. Fry the onion and garlic gently in the olive oil in a large frying pan, until tender. Add the mushrooms and cinnamon and cook for a further 3 minutes. Pour in the tomatoes and paste, the sugar, salt and pepper. Simmer until fairly thick, for about 10–15 minutes.

While it is simmering, make the bechamel. Heat the oil gently in a medium saucepan and stir in the flour. Cook for 1 minute, remove from the heat and gradually blend in the milk to make a white sauce. Simmer gently for 10 minutes, then stir in the cheese, salt and pepper. Line a greased 25 cm (10 in) square baking dish (or similar) with the aubergine and season well. Spoon over half the mushroom sauce, cover with a layer of aubergine, salt and pepper. Repeat these layers. Pour the bechamel over the top layer of aubergine. Bake at 180C/350F/Gas 4 for 1 hour, until the aubergine is tender.

Meanwhile, mix the parsley, lemon zest and garlic to make the *gremolata*. Dice the red peppers. When the moussaka is cooked, sprinkle the parsley and lemon evenly over the surface, and dot with the red pepper. Return to the oven for 5 minutes (but no more), and serve immediately.

Stuffed Onions

Burghul in Arabic, *bulgar* in Turkish, *pourgouri* in Cyprus and cracked wheat in English (although it is usually sold under one of its other names) can be found on the shelves in healthfood shops, Greek or Cypriot shops (where there may be both coarse and fine grinds – choose the coarse for this dish) and in a surprising number of supermarkets.

It makes a good alternative to rice, cooked in the same way as below, and can be used to make all kind of stuffings, not only for onions but for chicken, game birds, fish or other vegetables.

Instead of tarragon and chervil or parsley, you could use half coriander and half parsley.

SERVES 4

4 large onions
125 g (4 oz) *burghul*
60 g (2 oz) butter
30 g (1 oz) walnuts, chopped
1 teaspoon fresh tarragon, finely chopped
2 teaspoons fresh chervil or parsley, finely chopped
salt and pepper

Slice the top and the bottom off each onion, without actually peeling. Blanch the onions for 5 minutes in boiling salted water. Remove and drain, reserving the cooking water, then peel.

Measure out 300 ml (½ pt) of the cooking water. Bring to the boil, and pour in the *burghul*. Cover, turn down the heat, and simmer for 5–8 minutes, until all the water is absorbed.

Using a sharp knife, hollow out the onions. Try not to pull out a whole central core, leaving a hole at the bottom – it's not the end of the world if you do, it just means that you have to be careful that the filling doesn't fall out when you serve them.

Roughly chop two thirds of the insides of the onions. Soften in 30g (1 oz) butter, without browning. Add the walnuts and stir for about 1 minute to coat well in the butter. Add the onions, walnuts and butter to the *burghul*, together with the herbs and salt and pepper to taste.

Stand the onions in an oven-proof dish and stuff with *burghul*, pressing down firmly. Dot with the remaining butter, and cover loosely with silver foil. Bake at 200C/400F/Gas 6, for 1 hour.

Onion Tart

As a big treat when I was a child, my parents would sometimes take me to the tiny bistro downstairs at La Sorbonne restaurant in Oxford, where they made the most exquisite creamy onion tartlets. This is the nearest I've got so far to recreating them. It's not quite right yet, but I'm getting hot. Had I not been spoilt by their version, I would now be quite content with this.

In fact, I have suggested that you make one large tart – it makes
life slightly simpler, although you will find that the filling will ooze
out as you cut it. You could, of course, add a couple of eggs to the
filling and bake the filled tart until just setting, but personally I
prefer it oozing.

SERVES 6

250 g (8 oz) shortcrust pastry*

Filling:
½ kg (1 lb) onions, thinly sliced
2 tablespoons olive oil
1 tablespoon flour
150 ml (¼ pt) milk
150 ml (5 fl oz) double cream
salt and pepper
ground nutmeg
60 g (2 oz) grated parmesan

Line a 23 cm (9 in) tart tin with the pastry. Leave in a cool place to
relax for 30 minutes. Bake blind*, returning to the oven for 10–15
minutes until lightly browned and crisp.

In a covered pan, sweat the onions very slowly in half the olive oil
until soft, stirring occasionally. Make a white sauce by gently
heating the remaining oil in a medium saucepan, stirring in the
flour. Cook for 1 minute, remove from the heat and gradually blend
in the milk. Leave to simmer for 5–10 minutes until thick. Season
with salt, pepper and nutmeg. Stir in 45 g (1½ oz) of the parmesan.
Taste and adjust the seasoning.

Reheat the tart case if necessary. Mix the onions with the sauce
and pour into the case. Sprinkle with the remaining parmesan, and
brown quickly under a hot grill.

OKRA

Either you love gelatinous okra or you loathe them. Either you will
consume them with relish, or you should avoid them altogether.
Either you'll think this ridiculously quick and easy recipe is a real
winner, or you should turn the page and look for something that
will suit your tastes better.

If okra (also called ladies' fingers, *bhindi, gumbo, bamia* and
variations thereon) are new to you, buy a small quantity, which will

set you back only a few pence, and try cooking them whole in homemade tomato sauce to see what you think of them.

As you might well suspect, I am a devotee and love their strange mucilagenous quality. Some cook books will describe methods of dealing with okra that reduce this, but that seems a total waste of time to me. This is what marks out okra from other vegetables, and is in fact essential to many of the traditional dishes from India, the Middle East, Africa, the West Indies and Louisiana. If you don't like it, then why spend your money on okra when you could be buying any number of vegetables that you would rather be eating?

Pick out okra that are at most 8–10 cm (3–4 in) long. Throw back any that are turning brown – the best are green and firm and well ridged. Before cooking, trim the stalk from the cone, without cutting into the okra itself.

The simplest way to cook them is to stew them gently in butter and oil, seasoning well with salt and pepper and a dash of lemon juice.

Bamia

In this Middle Eastern recipe the okra are simmered in a mildly sweet sour sauce, then left to cool and soak up some of the juice. You can add 250 g (8 oz) or so of peeled, roughly chopped tomato to vary the recipe.

SERVES 4 as a side-dish

½ kg (1 lb) okra, trimmed
1 small onion, chopped
1½ tablespoons olive oil
1 tablespoon caster sugar
juice of 1 lemon
1 sprig of oregano
salt and pepper
1 tablespoon fresh parsley, chopped

Soften the onion in the oil, without browning, then add the okra. Fry gently for 4 minutes, then add all the remaining ingredients except the parsley, and enough water to fill the pan to a depth of about 1 cm (½ in). Stir, then cover and simmer until the okra are really tender.

Arrange in a serving dish, and serve either warm or at room temperature, scattered with the parsley.

Okra and Bacon With Eggs

This is a good quick supper dish of okra and bacon with tomatoey scrambled eggs.

SERVES 2–3

1½ tablespoons olive oil
1 small onion, finely chopped
1 clove of garlic, chopped
250 g (8 oz) okra, trimmed and cut into 1 cm (½ in) slices
4 rashers of smoked back bacon, rind removed and cut into strips
125 g (4 oz) tomato, skinned* and chopped
4 eggs, beaten
salt and pepper
fresh chives, chopped

Heat the oil in a frying pan. Add the onions, garlic and okra, and cook over a medium heat, stirring until the onions and okra are almost tender. Add the bacon, and raise the heat. Fry until everything begins to brown. Lower the heat, and add the tomato and pepper. Cook for 1 minute more. Season the eggs and pour into the pan. Scramble over a low heat until creamy, but not too solidly set.

Serve quickly on toast, and/or with a salad, for supper, lunch or brunch.

Hot Potato and Pepper Salad

Waxy-textured salad potatoes don't collapse when cooked and, like new potatoes, are good hot, boiled or steamed.

They are perfect, too, for making potato salads. If you cannot find any proper salad potatoes, use new potatoes. This is one of my favourite potato salads, wildly garlicky.

SERVES 4

¾ kg (1½ lb) waxy potatoes*
2 tablespoons dried sweet peppers
2–3 cloves of garlic
1 tablespoon red wine vinegar
1 teaspoon French mustard
¼ teaspoon sugar
4 tablespoons olive oil

Boil the potatoes with the dried peppers. Drain, and slice thickly. Peel them now, if you wish to. Peel and crush the garlic and mix with the potatoes and peppers.

While the potatoes are cooking, place the vinegar in a screw top jar with the mustard, sugar, salt and pepper and olive oil. Close and shake well. Add enough of this vinaigrette to the hot potatoes to moisten well, and serve it hot or cold.

Fricot D'Pais et D'Patates With Cocombre A La Jerriaise

Although this recipe for a *fricot d'pais et d'patates* comes from Jersey, it is the standard floury types of potato that you should use, not the famous Royals. A homely, peasant dish – merely a variation on mashed potatoes and a cucumber salad – but the combination is a real success. The cucumber is cool, crisp and sharp, while the potatoes and beans are hot, soft and mild. It makes an enjoyable supper dish.

SERVES 4

Cucumber salad:
1 cucumber, peeled and thinly sliced
2 teaspoons salt
2 tablespoons wine vinegar

Potatoes and beans:
250 g (8 oz) French beans, topped and tailed
½ kg (1 lb) potatoes, peeled and quartered
1 onion, chopped
30 g (1 oz) lard or dripping

Spread out the cucumber in a colander or sieve, and sprinkle with salt. Leave to drain for 30 minutes, then pat dry with kitchen paper or a clean tea-towel. Pile into a bowl, and add the vinegar. Set aside for 1–2 hours before serving.

Snap the French beans in half. Place in a pan with the potatoes and enough lightly salted water to cover. Bring to the boil, and simmer until both are cooked. Drain well.

While the vegetables are cooking, fry the onion very slowly in the lard or dripping, turning up the heat after about 15 minutes so that the onion is nicely browned. Add the onion and cooking fat to the cooked potatoes and beans, mix well, add plenty of salt and pepper,

and serve the hot mashed potatoes and beans with the cool sharp
cucumber.

Spiced Potatoes

The humble and plain potato is transformed with spices and
coconut. It is good enough to eat as a main course, with nothing
more than a few green vegetables, or serve it as a side-dish with a
Middle Eastern or Indian meal.

SERVES 3–4 as a side-dish

½ kg (1 lb) floury potatoes, peeled and cubed
2 tablespoons oil
1 onion, chopped
4 cloves of garlic, finely chopped
2 green chillis, seeded and finely chopped
2 teaspoons whole cumin seeds
1 tablespoon fresh coriander leaf, chopped
1 × 400 g (14 oz) tin chopped tomatoes
150 ml (¼ pt) coconut milk★
salt
1 teaspoon sugar
dash of lemon juice

Drop the potato cubes into a bowl of cold water, and soak for 10
minutes.

Heat the oil in a frying pan large enough to take all the potatoes.
Cook the onion, garlic and chillis gently in the oil until soft, without
browning. Turn up the heat slightly and add the cumin seeds. Cook
for 1 more minute. Add the remaining ingredients, bring to the boil
then add the potatoes. Simmer for 30 minutes until the potatoes are
tender. Taste and adjust the seasoning.

Four-Coloured Potato Pancakes

This is a pretty twist on an old theme. I adore these thin, grated
potato pancakes, soft and melting at the centre, crisp and whiskery
at the edges. Besides the plain potato and onion version, I've added
grated carrots, courgettes and beetroot, all of them as good as the
original. These pancakes are best eaten crisp and hot from the pan,
or at least warm. They can also be made an hour or 2 in advance,

and reheated in a single layer on a baking sheet at 220C/425F/Gas 7 for 10–15 minutes.

SERVES 6 as a first course or side-dish

½ kg (1 lb) floury potatoes, coarsely grated
60 g (2 oz) carrots, coarsely grated
60 g (2 oz) courgettes, coarsely grated
60 g (2 oz) raw beetroot, coarsely grated
60 g (2 oz) onion, coarsely grated
1 tablespoon flour
1 egg
salt and pepper
olive or tasteless oil

Weigh all the vegetables immediately after grating. Squeeze the potatoes hard to remove as much water as possible, then spread out on a treble layer of kitchen paper. Cover with a treble layer of kitchen paper, and pat until the upper layer is damp. Turn over, and remove the underneath layer of paper, replacing it with a new 3-fold layer. Repeat. Place the potato in a mixing bowl. Dry the other vegetables in the same way, keeping separate.

Add the flour, egg and plenty of salt and pepper to the potatoes. Mix thoroughly – hands are best for this – and divide into 4. To each quarter add one kind of vegetable, and mix thoroughly.

Heat a 1 cm (½ in) layer of oil in a large frying pan until very hot. Take a tablespoon of the courgette mixture, flatten slightly and drop into the oil. Flatten as thinly as you can with the back of the spoon or the fish slice, without actually breaking it up. Make 2 or 3 more fritters in the pan at the same time. Turn each fritter carefully as soon as the underneath is browned, about 1–2 minutes, and brown the other side. Drain on kitchen paper.

Continue until the 4 bowlfuls of vegetables are all used up, progressing first to carrot mixture, then to onion and finally to beetroot.

Sweet Potato Oven Chips

The sweet potato is a native of Central America and was first brought to Europe by Christopher Columbus in the fifteenth century. It's only in the past few years, however, that they have become widely available in England. Now many supermarkets sell them, as well as most ethnic groceries.

Look out for their easily recognisable purpley-pink skins. You do occasionally find some that have white skins, but they are less common. Pick out tubers that are firm and plump.

Sweet potatoes are cooked much like ordinary potatoes. Baked sweet potatoes go well with plainly roast poultry, or game birds, grilled fish, or long-cooked beef stews. Just split them in half and add lots of butter.

They can be peeled and steamed, roast around a Sunday joint, or sliced and used to top a stew, in the same way that we use ordinary potatoes on top of a Lancashire Hot Pot. Mash them, with an egg and again plenty of butter, serve as they are, or use to top a fish pie. The combination of fish and sweet mashed potato completely changes the dish – for the better.

And now my favourite. Sweet potato chips are quite, quite wonderful. You could make them in the same way as ordinary potato chips, but I think this method is better. The longer exposure to heat in the oven gives a crisp outside, the natural sugar of the sweet potato caramelising with the oil, while the centre becomes meltingly soft and creamy.

I like the almost smokey flavour that the olive oil gives, although I wouldn't advise employing your very best, dark green virgin oil. Use a lighter one instead, or just use an ordinary flavourless oil.

SERVES 4

½ kg (1 lb) sweet potatoes
5 tablespoons light olive or sunflower oil
salt and pepper

Peel the sweet potatoes and cut into small chips, roughly 7 cm (3 in) long, by 1 cm (½ in) thick and wide. Length is not that important, but the size of the cross-section is – one wants to get the optimum combination of crisp outside and melting inside. Sometimes I cut them into 1 cm (½ in) cubes.

Parboil the chips in salted water for 3 minutes. Drain well. Pour oil over them in a large bowl, and turn carefully to coat thoroughly without damaging. Spread out in a single layer on a baking sheet, and bake in a hot oven (220–230C/425–450F/Gas 7–8), turning occasionally using metal kitchen tongs, until the outside is lightly browned and caramelised. This may take as long as 40 minutes.

Sweet Potato and Broccoli Knish

'The best knish in Manhattan', it said on the side of the frankfurter cart (it sold both). Two blocks further on, and another street vendor was proclaiming just the same thing. And again, and again. On East Houston Street, on the borders of SoHo, I came across Yonah Schimmel's Knishery, a shabby cramped shop devoted lock, stock and barrel to the art of knish-making.

So what is this knish, then? It's a kind of savoury pastry, filled traditionally with *kasha* (buckwheat) or potato, now common fare on the streets of New York. Fillings have become more varied, though not unreasonably so – mushroom, or vegetable and potato are popular, sweet potato, too, and the broccoli knish has become a minor New York celebrity, according to one friend. Here I've combined sweet potato and broccoli, and chosen the simple crescent shape for ease, rather than the bun-like rotundity of the knishes I sampled *in situ*.

MAKES 10

Pastry:
280 g (9 oz) plain flour, sifted
pinch of salt
125 g (4 oz) butter, melted and tepid

Filling:
1 onion, chopped
30 g (1 oz) butter
500 g (1 lb) cooked sweet potato, chopped
salt and pepper
2 eggs, beaten
½ kg (1 lb) broccoli, cooked until barely *al dente*, chopped

To make the pastry, mix the flour and salt in a bowl. Stir in butter and enough *tepid* water to give a soft, slightly oily dough. Mix very briefly until you have a coherent dough. Roll into a ball, cover and rest for 30 minutes.

Fry the onion in the butter. Mash the sweet potato with the eggs, salt and pepper, and then mix in the onion with its butter, and the broccoli.

Divide the dough into 10 balls. Roll each one out to form a circle about 3 mm (⅛ in) thick, and brush the edges with water. Mound one tenth of the filling in the centre, and flip the pastry over to form a crescent. Press the edges together to seal.

Lay them on a greased baking sheet and brush with the beaten

egg. Bake at 190C/375F/Gas 5 for 35–40 minutes until browned.
Serve hot.

Parsnip and Apple Gratin

As the gratin cooks, the thinly sliced apple melts into the parsnip
purée giving a subtle fruitiness, lovely against the mealiness of the
oatmeal crust.

SERVES 4 as a side-dish

½ kg (1 lb) parsnips, sliced
2 eating apples, quartered and cored
60 g (2 oz) butter
salt and pepper
ground nutmeg
2 tablespoons rolled oats

Steam, boil or microwave the parsnips until very tender. Drain
well, and mash or process with 45 g (1½ oz) butter, plenty of salt
and pepper, and freshly ground nutmeg to taste. Cut each quarter
of apple in half. Slice thinly and mix into the parsnip mixture.

Spread in a baking dish in a layer 4–5 cm (1½–2 in) thick,
depending on the size of the dish. Scatter oats evenly over the
surface and dot with the remaining 15 g (½ oz) butter. Bake at
190C/375F/Gas 5 for 30–40 minutes, until nicely browned – if
necessary finish browning quickly under the grill – and serve
immediately.

Thin Pepper Mayonnaise With a Mélange of Vegetables

The pimiento mayonnaise is a useful sauce – serve it not only with
hot cooked vegetables, but with strips of raw salad vegetables,
grilled meats, or fish. Add a crushed clove of garlic if you wish.

SERVES 6

For the mayonnaise:
1 small tin of pimientos 200 g (6½ oz)
1 egg
75 ml (2½ fl oz) olive oil
75 ml (2½ fl oz) tasteless oil
1 tablespoon wine vinegar
salt and pepper

Plus: a selection of vegetables – carrots, turnips, new potatoes, purple sprouting broccoli, asparagus, cauliflower, for instance.

Drain the pimientos well and liquidise with the egg. Keep the motor running and add the 2 oils in a slow trickle. Stir in the vinegar and season. Keep cool.

Prepare the vegetables. If the carrots are tiny just scrape, otherwise cut into long strips. Peel large turnips and slice, but leave small ones whole. Scrub the new potatoes. Trim the broccoli and the cauliflower and break into small florets. Trim the asparagus, breaking off the woody stems.

Steam or simmer all the vegetables, separately, until *al dente*, except the potatoes which should, of course, be just soft. Arrange the hot vegetables on a serving dish, and pour over a little of the sauce. Serve the rest separately.

Zeytinyagh Biber Dolmasi (Stuffed Peppers)

This recipe was given to me by the chefs of the Divan Hotel in Istanbul, when they arrived in London *en masse* for a week's celebration of Turkish cooking. Stuffed vegetables are a great favourite in Turkey and this filling can also be used to stuff tomatoes, courgettes, or vine leaves.

SERVES 4 as a main course

4 large green peppers
60 ml (2 fl oz) olive oil
150 ml (¼ pt) water

Stuffing:
175 g (6 oz) long-grain rice
2 medium onions, finely chopped
120 ml (4 fl oz) olive oil
2 small tomatoes, skinned* and chopped
30 g (1 oz) currants
30 g (1 oz) pine nuts
2 tablespoons fresh mint, chopped
1 tablespoon fresh dill, chopped
¼ teaspoon ground cinnamon
¼ teaspoon ground allspice
1½ teaspoons sugar
salt and pepper
90 ml (3 fl oz) water

To make the stuffing, rinse the rice well in cold water. Drain. Sauté the onions in the olive oil until golden and tender. Add the rice and cook gently, stirring constantly, for a further 10 minutes. Add all the remaining stuffing ingredients. Simmer gently until the rice is almost but not quite cooked – 10–15 minutes – and most of the liquid is absorbed.

Slice the tops off the peppers and scoop out all the seeds. Stuff with the rice mixture. It will swell a little more as it finishes cooking, so don't fill right up to the top.

To cook on the hob, stand the peppers upright in a snugly fitting saucepan and pour in the olive oil and water, and season. Cover and simmer very gently for 50–60 minutes until the peppers and stuffing are tender. If cooking in the oven, use snugly fitting casserole and bake at 190C/375F/Gas 5 for about 1 hour, basting frequently.

Leave the peppers to cool in their own juices, and serve cold.

Vegetable Spaghetti

The vegetable spaghetti, or spaghetti squash, is a seemingly miraculous vegetable. Once you've cooked it, the flesh does indeed separate out into strands, just like golden spaghetti, and you can serve it with any sauce that would go well with pasta.

To cook one, the best method is to cut it in half, and place the halves cut-side down in a roasting tin filled to a depth of 2–3 cm (1 in) with hot water. Bake for 35–45 minutes at 230C/450F/Gas 8, until the flesh is tender. The only problem with this method is cutting the squash in half – it's tough, so get someone to help. You can always bake it whole which will take a little longer, or steam or boil it. Pierce the skin with a skewer at the stalk end first.

SERVES 4 as a first course or vegetable dish, 2 as a main course

1 vegetable spaghetti squash
1 clove of garlic, finely chopped
90 g (3 oz) butter
1 sprig of marjoram
30–60 g (1–2 oz) grated cheese (parmesan, cheddar, pecorino)
salt and pepper

Cook the spaghetti squash. Halve, scoop out the seeds if they are tough (try one) and drain well. Halve each half if it is to serve 4 people. Melt the butter, and add the garlic and marjoram. Sit over a low heat for 5–10 minutes to allow the flavours to infuse. If you don't like lumps of garlic, strain, otherwise keep warm.

To serve, pour a generous tablespoon of hot butter over each quarter, or more over each half, season, top with grated cheese – quantities will depend on the pungency of the cheese, but it's better to underestimate and provide a bowl of grated cheese on the table for people to help themselves – and whisk to the table as is, or brown quickly under a hot grill. Pour any extra butter into a bowl for those who want more.

Spinach With Chickpeas

A useful recipe, this one – it can either be a fallback storecupboard and freezer recipe, in which case it does wonders for frozen spinach and tinned chickpeas or it can be made with fresh spinach and dried chickpeas. Naturally this is even nicer, though it takes longer to make and demands some forethought.

Serve it as a side-dish, or as a vegetarian main dish with spiced rice.

SERVES 3–4

Either 1 kg (2 lb) fresh leaf spinach or 500 g (1 lb) frozen leaf spinach, thawed
45 g (1½ oz) butter
125 g (4 oz) dried chickpeas or 1 x 400 g (14 oz) tin chickpeas
2 cloves of garlic
1 teaspoon ground coriander seeds
½ teaspoon turmeric
salt and pepper
150 g (5 oz) natural yoghurt

If you are using dried chickpeas, cover with water and leave to soak for 8 hours, or overnight. Drain well, cover with cold water and bring to the boil. Simmer for 1 hour or until the chickpeas are tender. Drain well. If you use tinned chickpeas, pour into a sieve and rinse well with cold water.

Wash the fresh spinach thoroughly to remove the grit. Shake off all excess water, and cut out any thick stems. If using frozen spinach, leave to thaw, then squeeze out as much water as possible (or, if you are pushed for time, cook as briefly as possible and then squeeze). Chop the spinach roughly. Melt 30 g (1 oz) butter in the base of a pan, and add the spinach. Cover, and cook gently, turning occasionally until the spinach is cooked (frozen spinach will need just a couple of minutes to heat up). Add the chickpeas.

In a separate pan, melt the remaining 15 g (½ oz) butter and add the garlic. Fry gently for 2 minutes, then sprinkle the coriander over it. Turn up the heat and cook for 1 more minute until the garlic begins to colour. Tip into the spinach with the turmeric, salt and pepper, stir well and cook for a further 5 minutes.

Remove from the heat, and add the yoghurt. Keep warm, but do not boil, until ready to eat.

TWO COOKED TOMATO RECIPES

The lack of flavour and sweetness in British tomatoes* is a constant complaint, but for the time being any improvement seems unlikely. The vast scarlet-juiced scented tomatoes of the Mediterranean (not to be confused with bland Dutch Beef Tomatoes) are not yet for us.

So, we are left with what we have got, and although they will never be sensational, there are plenty of ways of livening up our little round tomatoes. The first recipe here is immensely successful, and makes either a good first course, with crusty bread to mop up the juices, or a side-dish to a simply cooked main course.

The second recipe is not so rich, but the contrast of crisp topping and soft tomato is delicious. Serve as a side-dish.

Tomatoes Polonnaises

SERVES 4 as a first course or side-dish

8 firm small tomatoes
30 g (1 oz) butter
1 shallot or ½ red onion, chopped
5 tablespoons double cream
salt and pepper

Halve the tomatoes. Melt the butter in a wide frying pan, and sauté the shallot or onion until tender. Add the tomatoes, and cook gently for 4 minutes. Pierce the skins with a sharp knife, and turn over. Cook for another 4 minutes. Spoon the cream around the tomatoes, and add plenty of salt and pepper. Bring to the boil, simmer for 1 minute and serve.

Baked Tomatoes

SERVES 4 as a side-dish

8 firm small tomatoes
60 g (2 oz) brown soft breadcrumbs
45 g (1½ oz) finely grated parmesan, or other hard cheese
2 sprigs of thyme or marjoram
30 g (1 oz) butter
salt and pepper

Halve the tomatoes. Pierce the skins with a sharp knife. Strip thyme or marjoram leaves off stalks and chop. Mix the breadcrumbs with the cheese and herbs.

Nestle the tomato halves, cut side up, in a neatly fitting, lightly buttered oven-proof dish. Season and press the crumb mixture on the upturned tomatoes. Dot with butter and bake at 200C/400F/Gas 6 for 15–20 minutes, until nicely browned.

Poppyseed and Tomato Tart

Food writer Clare Ferguson's dramatic black speckled nutty-tasting poppyseed pastry has become a regular favourite of mine. I've used it here with crumbly pale cheese and thick tomato and onion sauce, to make an irresistible hot or cold tart.

SERVES 6–8

Poppyseed pastry:
45 g (1½ oz) poppyseeds
125 g (4 oz) flour
1 tablespoon dark muscovado sugar
½ teaspoon salt
75 g (2½ oz) chilled butter, cubed
1–1½ tablespoons milk

Filling:
2 large onions, sliced
45 g (1½ oz) butter
1 × 400 g (14 oz) tin chopped tomatoes
½ teaspoon caster sugar
dash of red wine vinegar
4–6 basil leaves, shredded
salt and pepper
125 g (4 oz) wensleydale, caerphilly or feta cheese, crumbled

Put the poppyseeds in a small non-stick frying pan, and shake gently over a high heat until they begin to give off a nutty smell. Cool.

Place the sifted flour in a processor with the poppyseeds, sugar and salt. Add the butter and process in short bursts until it resembles fine breadcrumbs. Pour in the milk a spoonful at a time until you get a crumbly dough. Gather it together into a ball. If you don't have a processor, rub the butter into the dry ingredients by hand, then stir in the milk.

Roll out the pastry on a lightly floured board, and use to line a 23 cm (9 in) tart tin – it is very short and crumbly, but doesn't suffer from being patched and pressed into shape. Prick with a fork, and rest in the fridge for 30 minutes. Line with foil, and weigh down with baking beans. Bake blind at 190C/375F/Gas 5 for 15 minutes. Remove the foil and beans, prick again, and dry out in the oven for a further 5 minutes.

To make the filling, soften the onions in the butter, and add all the remaining ingredients, except the cheese. Let the sauce boil vigorously for 10–15 minutes, until thick. Stir frequently to prevent burning. Scatter the cheese evenly over the base of the tart, and cover with the tomato and onion sauce. Return to the oven for a further 25 minutes. Serve hot, warm or cold.

Les Gâteaux Piments

Les Gâteaux Piments are a Mauritian version of the Middle Eastern *falafel* made not with chickpeas or dried broad beans, but with ground split peas, scented with lemon grass, coriander and chilli.

If you are unable to buy lemon grass, add a pinch of fresh thyme instead. The flavour won't be quite so exotic, but they'll still be very good.

SERVES 4 as a main course

250 g (8 oz) yellow split peas
2 green chillis or ¾ teaspoon chilli powder
4 spring onions, finely chopped
½ tablespoon fresh lemon grass, crushed and finely chopped
1 tablespoon fresh coriander or parsley, finely chopped
generous pinch of bicarbonate of soda
salt
2–3 tablespoons flour

Soak the split peas for 8 hours. If you forget to put them to soak in the morning, you can speed up the process by pouring boiling water over the dried peas and leaving them to soak for at least 2 hours.

Remove the stems and seeds from the chillis and chop finely. Mix with the spring onions, lemon grass and coriander. Drain the peas, and grind thoroughly in a processor. The mixture needs to be fairly finely ground in order for it to stick together. Mix with the herbs, the bicarbonate of soda, plenty of salt and 2 tablespoons flour.

Dampen your hands and take a knob of the mixture, about the size of a small egg, roll into a ball, then flatten – if it seems very crumbly, add a further tablespoon of flour, or return to the processor for a few seconds. Make a depression in the centre with your thumb. Repeat until all the mixture is used up, dipping your hands into cold water frequently to prevent sticking.

Fill a high sided frying pan to a depth of 1 cm (½ in) with oil, heat well, and fry the cakes, turning once, until a deep brown on both sides. Serve quickly, while still piping hot, with a salad if you wish.

Bean and Garlic Purée

Tinned beans, not baked beans, but kidney, haricot (*cannellini*) or butter beans in a plain water, are always a useful storecupboard standby. Whizzed up to a purée, a single can makes a delicious first course, a beany version of houmus. This is enough for 4 people, or even 6 at a pinch if you eke it out with plenty of bread, raw veg, olives, and so on. With larger numbers, double the quantities or make up one batch with *cannellini* beans, one with, say, kidney beans.

SERVES 4–6 as a first course

1 × 400g (14 oz) tin of cooked beans – kidney, haricot, flageolets, or
    butter beans
2 cloves of garlic, chopped
4 tablespoons olive oil, plus a little extra
salt and pepper
lemon juice
paprika
a few fresh herbs, chopped

Drain the beans, rinse under the cold tap and liquidise or process
with the garlic, olive oil, salt, pepper and lemon juice to taste. Pile
into a serving bowl and drizzle a little more olive oil over the top.
Dust with paprika and scatter with fresh herbs. Serve with warm
pitta bread or sticks of raw vegetables, or spooned into hollowed-out
small tomatoes.

Jersey Bean Crock

Jersey is an island full of hidden surprises. On one spring visit, I
was taken to a small farm to buy goats cheese. The cheese-maker
had other goods stashed on the shelves of the outhouse as well –
boxes of goats milk fudge, and bags of dried runner beans.

The beans are used in this hearty traditional Jersey dish, although
other types can be used instead – in fact the list below can be varied
as will and provisions dictate. The shin of beef is optional too – this
recipe was a way of eking out meagre quantities of meat, getting the
maximum flavour and bulk at minimum cost. But don't be tempted
to forego the pig's trotter – it adds a rich gelatinous thickness to the
liquid and, if you are really too squeamish to bring yourself to eat
the thing (though you will be foregoing one of the best bits), it can
be removed before serving.

SERVES 6–8

250 g (8 oz) haricot beans
125 g (4 oz) butter beans
125 g (4 oz) dried runner beans, or red kidney beans
125 g (4 oz) dried black-eyed beans
1 pig's trotter
250 g (8 oz) piece of belly of pork, quartered
375 g (12 oz) piece of shin of beef, quartered
1 onion, sliced
2 carrots, thickly sliced
small bunch of fresh parsley, chopped
4 large sprigs of thyme
salt and pepper

Mix the beans and cover with cold water. Leave to soak for 8 hours
or overnight. Drain, rinse and then drain again. Spread half in a
thick layer in a large casserole. Trim the hairs off the trotters (I find
a disposable razor is best for this, though you can singe them off).
Place in the casserole with all the remaining ingredients, and cover

with the rest of the beans. Pour over enough boiling water to cover.

Cover, and cook for 10 minutes at 230C/450F/Gas 8, then turn down the heat to 140C/275F/Gas 1. Leave it to cook very gently for 5–6 hours. If necessary, add a little extra water, although by the time the meat is tender the liquid should be reduced by at least a third.

When the meat is really tender, fish out as many of the bones as you can. Adjust the seasoning and sprinkle with a little extra chopped parsley. As you serve, make sure that everyone gets a piece of each of the three meats – the velvety trotter, the meaty beef and the belly of pork.

Vegetable Couscous

An all-vegetable couscous (the word couscous applies to both the grain itself and the whole dish of vegetables and grain) is just the thing to knock up when you're providing for a mixed group of vegetarians and non-vegetarians, or when your bank balance is far from healthy. Vary the selection of vegetables according to availability, but try to use at least 7.

SERVES 6–8 as a main course

250 g (½ lb) onions, chopped
375 g (¾ lb) carrots, thickly sliced
375 g (¾ lb) pumpkin, or butternut squash, cubed
250 g (½ lb) turnips, chopped
250 g (8 oz) cooked chickpeas
½ kg (1 lb) courgettes, thickly sliced
1 medium aubergine, cubed
1 or 2 fennel bulbs, chopped
2 green chillis, finely chopped
250–375 g (8–12 oz) tomatoes, peeled* and chopped
125 g (4 oz) dried apricots, cut into strips
1 tablespoon paprika
½ teaspoon ground ginger
salt
1 bunch of fresh parsley, finely chopped
fresh coriander (if available)
salt
500 g (1 lb) couscous
4 tablespoons olive oil

Place the onions, carrots, pumpkin and turnips in a large pan with enough water to cover. Simmer for 15 minutes. Add the remaining ingredients, except the coriander, couscous and oil, and more water to cover. Simmer for 45 minutes. Taste and adjust the seasoning. Before serving, strain the juices from the vegetables into a warmed bowl.

While the stew is cooking, measure the *volume* of the couscous, and pour over an equal volume of water. Stir, and set aside for 15 minutes, until the water has been absorbed. Add salt, and stir in the oil, breaking up any lumps. Pile into a large serving dish, and cover with foil. Heat through in a medium oven (190C/375F/Gas 5) until very hot – 20 minutes or so. Make a well in the centre and fill with the hot vegetables, and sprinkle with coriander or more parsley.

Place the 2 dishes in the centre of the table, and let guests serve themselves with couscous, veg and enough flavoured stock to moisten their grain as they like it.

SALADS

Beetroot, Cucumber and Walnut Salad

I have a passion for beetroot, but only when it has been home-cooked with not a hint of vinegar of any kind. It does have a habit of bleeding its startling pink dye over everything it comes into contact with so, unless you like your cucumber blotchy, only bring the cucumber and beetroot together on one dish just before serving.

SERVES 4

½ cucumber
250 g (8 oz) cooked, peeled beetroot*
about 1 tablespoon fresh dill
30 g (1 oz) walnut pieces

Dressing:
1 tablespoon white wine vinegar
4 tablespoons olive oil
pinch of sugar
salt and pepper

Put the vinegar, oil, sugar, salt and pepper in a screw top jar. Close, and shake well.

Half an hour before you sit down to eat, peel, and shred the cucumber. Use the largest holes on the grater, and hold the cucumber at an angle so that you get the longest possible strips. Spread out in a colander and sprinkle with a little salt. Leave to drain.

Slice the beetroot, and coat with 1–2 tablespoons of the dressing and half the dill. Arrange slices around the edge of a serving dish. Rinse the cucumber and pat dry on kitchen paper or a clean tea-towel. Toss with 1 tablespoon (or more if you prefer) of dressing and the remaining dill, and pile in the centre of the beetroot. Scatter the walnut pieces over the top and serve.

Save any leftover dressing for other salads – it keeps well in a screw top jar in the fridge.

Carrot, Feta and Walnut Salad

There's a lot of very duff so-called feta cheese around, bearing little resemblance to the salty, crumbly cubes of white cheese that are an essential part of a Greek salad in Greece. To be sure of getting the right thing, your best bet is to find your nearest Greek grocer, who will probably sell you cheese cut from big chunks floating in a basin of brine.

Failing that, search the packet for the country of origin – if it says Greece then you should be fine. Once you've sorted out your feta, use it to make the usual Greek salad, with lettuce, tomatoes, onions, cucumber and black olives, dressed with a lemon and olive oil dressing like the one below. Or try this salad with quickly blanched carrots and walnuts.

One more suggestion for that feta – cut it into small sticks, and stuff each stick into the cavity of a fresh date (stone removed first). Eat these stuffed dates for pudding, or with drinks, or whenever you feel peckish.

SERVES 4

½ kg (1 lb) carrots
60 g (2 oz) walnuts, roughly chopped
90 g (3 oz) feta cheese, chopped

Dressing:
2 tablespoons olive oil
1 tablespoon grapeseed or other light oil
1½ tablespoons lemon juice
½ teaspoon oregano
salt and pepper

Scrape the carrots, and cut into julienne strips (matchsticks). Bring a pan of salted water to the boil. Drop the carrots in, bring back to the boil, and simmer for 1 minute. Drain quickly and pat the carrot sticks dry with kitchen paper or a clean tea-towel.

While the carrots are cooking, whisk together the 2 oils, the lemon juice, oregano and salt and pepper. Toss the hot carrots in this dressing, and leave to cool.

Add the walnuts and the feta to the cool carrots, and toss. Serve at room temperature.

Fennel, Apple and Cauliflower Salad

This salad is crisp and delicious, with notes of sweetness and aniseed. The mayonnaise dressing is lightened with yoghurt – less oily that way – and is mildly mustardy.

SERVES 4–6

1 large fennel bulb
375 g (12 oz) cauliflower florets
30 g (1 oz) toasted flaked almonds*
2 crisp eating apples
a few lettuce leaves or a bunch of watercress

Dressing:
4 tablespoons mayonnaise
2 tablespoons Greek strained yoghurt
dash of white wine vinegar
1–2 teaspoons coarse grain mustard
salt and pepper

Mix together the dressing ingredients, taste and adjust the seasoning.

Trim the woody stalks off the fennel, and the base and outer layer, if damaged, saving the feathery green leaves for decoration. Chop the fennel and add to the cauliflower, with the almonds, setting aside a few for decoration. Finally core, and dice the apple and mix with the vegetables and enough of the dressing to coat the chunks, without actually overwhelming them – you'll probably find that about two thirds is quite enough.

Serve the salad in a bowl lined with lettuce leaves, or on a bed of watercress. Scatter with the reserved almonds, and arrange 3 or 4 of the fennel fronds artistically on the top.

Green Bean Salad With Anchovy Dressing

This salad can be served as a first course or a light supper dish (add 2 extra eggs) with plenty of bread. If you cannot find any fresh green beans, use a head of cauliflower, broken into little florets, but steer clear of frozen beans.

SERVES 4

½ kg (1 lb) green beans
2 eggs, hard-boiled
3 tomatoes, skinned* and sliced
fresh parsley, chopped

Dressing:
3 anchovy fillets
1 clove of garlic, roughly chopped
1 tablespoon white wine vinegar
pepper
4 tablespoons olive oil

Top and tail the green beans. Simmer for 5 minutes in salted water, and drain.

While the beans are cooking, make the dressing. In a pestle and mortar, pound the anchovy fillets with the garlic and wine vinegar. Add pepper, and beat in the olive oil spoonful by spoonful. Taste and adjust the seasoning, adding salt if necessary. Toss the hot beans in the dressing, and leave to cool. Shell the eggs.

Drain the beans of the dressing, and arrange on a large plate with the tomatoes and eggs. Dribble the remaining dressing over the egg and tomatoes, and serve at room temperature, sprinkled with the parsley.

Grilled Pepper Salad

Grilled peppers have a unique voluptuousness, and a sweet smokey taste. Emphasise this with fruity olive oil, a hint of lemon juice and simple seasonings, and you have one of the most blissful salads you can imagine.

Throughout the Mediterranean there are countless small variations on the theme, usually served as part of an hors d'œuvre. Here they may add strips of anchovy or a handful of black olives, there a sprinkling of capers, dried flakes of chilli or thinly sliced fresh chilli for heat. Finely chopped garlic, torn leaves of basil, or quartered hard-boiled eggs may make an appearance. Try any of these combinations, and serve as a first course with plenty of bread to mop up the wonderful juices.

SERVES 4 as a first course

4 peppers – green, red, yellow, orange – grilled and skinned*
16 black olives, and/or 4 anchovies, and/or 1 dried chilli, crumbled
fresh parsley

Dressing:
4 tablespoons extra virgin olive oil
1 tablespoon lemon juice
salt and pepper

Cut the peppers into strips, throwing out the seeds and stalks, and spread out in a thick layer on a serving dish. Arrange the olives or anchovies (each fillet cut into thin strips) on top. Whisk the olive oil with the lemon juice, salt and pepper, or crumbled chilli if using. Pour over the peppers. Sprinkle with chopped parsley and, if you have time, leave in a cool place for at least 30 minutes to allow the flavours to mingle. Serve at room temperature.

The dressed peppers will keep, lightly covered in the fridge, for 2–3 days.

Leek and Pepper Salad

Cooked vegetable salads are exceedingly well-tempered. They can be made up to 24 hours in advance and, as long as they are kept cool, won't suffer any detrimental effects. In fact, I would go so far as to say that the wait improves the flavour, allowing time for the ingredients to soak up the dressing. Hanging around does nothing for hard-boiled eggs, however, so add them to this salad only when you are ready to serve it.

The quick bath in boiling water is enough to dampen the raw oniony hiss of the leeks without disposing of it altogether. They stay slightly crisp, a good contrast to the soft grilled peppers.

SERVES 4–6

½ kg (1 lb) leeks
2 red or yellow peppers, grilled and skinned*
8 basil leaves, torn up or chopped
2 hard-boiled eggs

Dressing:
3 tablespoons olive oil
1 dessertspoon red wine vinegar
salt and pepper

Cut the leeks into 8 cm (3 in) lengths then slice lengthways into narrow ribbons. Drop into a pan of boiling salted water, bring back to the boil and drain. Run the leeks under the cold tap, then dry on kitchen paper or a clean tea-towel. Cut the peppers into long thin strips, and mix with the leeks and basil in a shallow dish.

Place the oil, vinegar, salt and pepper in a screw top jar, close tightly and shake. Pour over the leeks and peppers and mix well. Leave to cool. Just before serving, quarter the eggs and arrange on the salad. Serve at room temperature.

WHAT TO DO WITH ROCKET

Smart food lovers have been talking knowledgeably about a plant called rocket for some time now. It has been around for centuries, but is not that well known in England.

I tried it for the first time in Italy, where it is eaten much more widely. Its long dark green leaves are used mainly in salads. It has a strong, aromatic flavour, and so is often used with milder flavoured lettuce in a mixed salad. For myself, I like it so much that I'm happy to eat it neat.

Some of the larger branches of the supermarkets and the grander greengrocers sell rocket, but I usually buy it either from my local wholefood shop, who have a superb range of organic produce, or, and this is where it is most readily available and cheapest, from Greek Cypriot greengrocers.

The Cypriot rocket (usually labelled *rokka*) is more coarsely flavoured than much of the imported French and Italian rocket, but it is still delicious. Look out for bunches of green leaves, rather like curvaceous dandelion leaves. Don't worry if it looks slightly droopy – it will soon perk up if washed, popped into a plastic bag, and left in the fridge for an hour or so. Snip off the roots and discard any yellowing leaves before using. It will keep happily for 3 or 4 days.

Now taste it, and think about how you want to use it. Go gently at first until you get used to, and start craving, the taste.

Salads

Start by making a mixed salad with one third rocket and two thirds lettuce. Dress with a French dressing made with red wine vinegar and olive oil, or a lemon juice and olive oil dressing, in the Italian style. Progress to half or more rocket as soon as you are hooked.

To make a light lunch or supper, add a few thin slices of Parma ham per person and shave some very thin slices off a small chunk of parmesan cheese to scatter over the top – this combination of tastes and textures is sheer delight, but better still in my opinion is a rocket and parmesan sandwich.

Sandwich

Take 2 thin slices of good brown bread – granary or wholemeal – and sprinkle each one with ½ tablespoon French dressing. Pile a dozen or so leaves of rocket on to one slice, top with thin slices of parmesan, and press the second slice of bread on top.

Hot Rocket or Cooked Rocket Salad

Blanch rocket leaves in boiling water for 10 seconds, and immediately drain well. Pat dry with kitchen paper. Toss in melted butter, salt and pepper, and serve quickly with lemon wedges. Alternatively, dress with olive oil, lemon juice, salt, pepper and a pinch of sugar, and leave to cool. Eat as a salad.

Watercress, Kumquat and Chicory Salad

A cool, crisp salad to refresh jaded palates in the winter months, particularly welcome after the constant onslaught of rich food around Christmas and the New Year. If you cannot find any kumquats, substitute 1 or 2 oranges, peeled carefully to remove all the white pith, and cut into chunks.

SERVES 6–8

2 bunches of watercress
3 heads of chicory
125 g (4 oz) kumquats
45 g (1½ oz) walnut pieces

Dressing:
2½ tablespoons olive oil or 2 teaspoons walnut oil and 2 tablespoons
    light salad oil
2 teaspoons sherry vinegar or white wine vinegar
salt and pepper
pinch of sugar

To make the dressing, put all the ingredients into a screw top jar and shake well. Taste and adjust the seasoning. Set aside until needed.

Pick over the watercress, removing any tough stalks and damaged or soggy leaves. Tear into small pieces, and rinse well. Dry and store in a plastic bag in the fridge for up to 4 hours.

No more than 1 hour before serving, slice the chicory across the head. Slice the kumquats. Mix the watercress, chicory, kumquats and walnuts in a large salad bowl. Just before serving, shake the jar of dressing again and pour over the salad. Toss and bring to the table.

Courgette and Crab Salad

Before you tackle this salad, there is one point I'd like to stress. You can ignore it if you wish, but if you do you'll end up with a second rate version of a wonderful summer salad.

Please use freshly caught, cooked and dressed crab, or, if you must, vacuum-packed chilled crab meat, but not frozen, which is utterly tasteless.

SERVES 4

½ kg (1 lb) courgettes
125 g (4 oz) crab meat
1 small tomato, seeded and chopped

Dressing:
4 tablespoons olive oil
juice of ½ lemon
6 large basil leaves
salt and pepper

Cut the courgettes into 1 cm (½ in) thick slices. Spread out in a colander and sprinkle with a little salt. Leave to drain for 30 minutes, then rinse and pat dry. Steam or simmer in salted water until just tender. Drain well. While the courgettes are cooking, put all the dressing ingredients in a screw top jar, shake well and adjust the seasoning. Toss the hot courgette slices in this dressing, and leave to cool.

Drain the excess dressing from the courgettes. Arrange on a large serving plate. Moisten the crab meat with 1–2 tablespoons of the dressing, and pile up in the centre of the courgettes. Sprinkle the tomato over the top. Serve lightly chilled.

Potato and Herring Salad

Scandinavian *matjes* herrings pack a powerful punch, but aren't half as vicious as our own vinegar-sodden rollmops can be.

I sometimes serve them dressed with soured cream, chives, thin slices of raw onion, and lots of crusty bread, as a first course. But to turn them into a more substantial main course, the ideal companions are potatoes and the sweetness of a good firm eating apple, such as Cox's Orange Pippin.

I loathe over-mayonnaised potato-salads, slimey and sickly after a couple of mouthfuls. By dressing the potatoes when hot with a little French dressing, they absorb less oily mayonnaise when cool.

SERVES 4

½ kg (1 lb) salad potatoes or new potatoes‸
1 large eating apple
½ medium onion, chopped
1 tablespoon fresh parsley, chopped
3–4 tablespoons mayonnaise
125 g (4 oz) *matjes* herrings

French dressing★:
4 tablespoons olive oil
1 tablespoon wine vinegar
salt and pepper
½ teaspoon Dijon mustard

Boil the potatoes in their skins until just tender. While the potatoes are cooking make up the French dressing. Peel the potatoes while still hot and cut into rough 2½ cm (1 in) cubes. Toss in 2 tablespoons French dressing and leave to cool. Drain off excess dressing.

Core the apple, but do not peel. Cut into cubes that are about half the size of the cubes of potato. Toss in the remaining French dressing to prevent browning. Add to the potato with the onion and parsley and plenty of pepper. Now toss the whole lot in the mayonnaise – use only 3 tablespoons at first, and add a fourth if it really does look dry.

Arrange the salad on a serving dish (on a bed of lettuce if you like). Cut the herring fillets into long strips and arrange over the salad, to form a criss-cross pattern, or diagonal stripes.

Potato and Coriander Salad

This vigorously flavoured potato salad is based on the one served in my local Greek taverna, the Wild Track (run by Dimitri, a Greek filmstar when he's not looking after the customers). If you cannot find any fresh coriander leaf, then you still get a very good salad if you replace it with plain parsley.

SERVES 4

½ kg (1 lb) salad potatoes or new potatoes*
1½ tablespoons coriander, roughly chopped, plus one whole branch
zest of ½ lemon
4 spring onions, chopped

Dressing:
3 tablespoons olive oil
juice of ½ lemon
salt and pepper

Boil the potatoes in boiling salted water with the branch of coriander until just tender. Drain, discard the coriander, and cut the potatoes into 2½ cm (1 in) cubes.

While the potatoes are cooking, pare the zest from the lemon in strips and shred. Blanch in boiling water for 1 minute, and dry on kitchen paper. Mix the dressing ingredients in a screw top jar, shake well and adjust the seasoning.

Toss the potatoes in this dressing, with the lemon zest. Leave to cool, and add the chopped coriander and spring onions. Taste and add extra oil, lemon juice, salt or pepper if necessary.

Vegetable Salad With Coconut Sambal

Those little blocks of waxy coconut cream have crept quietly from the confines of small Asian cornershops, on to the shelves of many a London supermarket as general interest in cooking Eastern foods has increased. It adds a mild waft of the tropics to any dish – as in this dressing for a salad of crisp vegetables.

SERVES 4

Vegetables:
125 g (4 oz) green beans
2 medium sized carrots
½ cucumber
8 cm (3 in) piece of mooli (white radish) or 6 radishes
1 onion, thinly sliced
1 tablespoon oil

Sauce:
1 tablespoon oil
1 fresh green chilli, seeded and chopped
1 small onion, finely chopped
1 clove of garlic, chopped
1 teaspoon grated ginger
60 g (2 oz) coconut cream*, grated
juice of 1 lime
salt

Fry the chilli, onion, garlic and ginger in the oil, gently at first to soften, then turn up the heat to brown lightly. Add the coconut cream, lime juice, salt and 8 tablespoons water. Simmer for 3 minutes then remove from the heat. Taste and adjust the seasoning. Leave to cool and, if necessary, beat in extra water until you have a dressing the consistency of double cream.

Top and tail the green beans. Cut the carrots into julienne strips (matchsticks). Steam or blanch both until just cooked but still *al dente*. Toss in a little of the coconut dressing and leave to cool. Coarsely grate the cucumber lengthways. Spread out in a colander and sprinkle with a little salt. Leave to drain for 30 minutes, then rinse and pat dry. Slice the mooli or radishes. If using mooli, quarter the slices. Fry the onion in the oil over a high heat until well browned.

Mix all the vegetables, except the onion, together with the remaining dressing. Sprinkle the onion over the top and serve at room temperature.

Repentance Salad

This is a filling main course winter salad, to enjoy when you've over-indulged in stodgy cold weather comfort food.

SERVES 6 as a main course

Salad:
12 quails' eggs, or 6 hens' eggs, hard-boiled
1 tablespoon wine or cider vinegar
1 celeriac
2 red peppers
4 heads of chicory
500 g (1 lb) unpeeled prawns
half a head of frisée lettuce
30 g (1 oz) breadcrumbs
15 g (½ oz) butter

Dressing:
2 x 225 g (8 oz) cartons Greek yoghurt
3 tablespoons fresh mint, finely chopped
3 teaspoons clear honey
salt and pepper

To make the dressing, beat the yoghurt with the mint, honey, salt and pepper. Chill.

Peel the eggs, and quarter the hens' eggs if using. Add the vinegar to a bowl of cold water. Peel the celeriac and cut into small matchstick strips, and drop into acidulated water to prevent discolouration. Deseed the peppers and cut into strips. Slice the base off the chicory and separate the leaves. Peel all except a dozen of the prawns. Wash and dry the lettuce.

On a large plate, lay a bed of lettuce. Drain the celeriac and dry in kitchen paper or a clean tea-towel. Pile in a mound in the centre of the frisée. Arrange the chicory leaves, pepper, prawns and eggs around it. Fry the breadcrumbs in butter until golden and crisp, and scatter over the salad. Decorate with the unpeeled prawns and serve with the yoghurt dressing in a separate bowl.

Smoked Chicken and Melon Salad

Fruit is a natural partner with smoked meats – Parma ham with figs, for instance. Smoked chicken, when it hasn't been ruined by over-smoking, is a natural with melon.

SERVES 8 as a first course, 4 as a main course

1 smoked chicken
1 ripe ogen melon
4 sprigs of fresh mint
pepper

Dressing:
½ tablespoon balsamic or red wine vinegar
1 tablespoon olive oil
1 tablespoon grapeseed oil
salt and pepper

Carve the chicken as you would an unsmoked one, and cut the meat from the thighs and drumsticks as well. Halve the melon and scoop out the seeds. Cut each half into quarters, and cut the flesh from the rind. Slice each quarter into 3 or 4 long crescents.

Arrange the melon slices and chicken slices alternately in a large serving dish. Place all the dressing ingredients in a screw top jar, shake well and adjust the seasoning. Brush the dressing over the chicken and melon. Keep a few mint leaves whole for decoration. Chop the rest and sprinkle over the salad. Finally, grind plenty of black pepper over the top.

Walnut Dressing For a Green Salad

Throughout the summer I like to keep at least 1 or preferably 2 or 3 different lettuces, leaves washed and dried ready to use, in a plastic bag in the fridge. Then I can put together a single-leaf or mixed-lettuce salad at a moment's notice. Either that or I go for the easy option and buy one of the bags of mixed salad leaves that are sold by some of the better supermarkets. Avoid those where the bulk of the selection is made up of cabbage, and if the leaves look remotely limp or elderly steer absolutely clear. Dress with a simple olive oil and wine vinegar dressing, or try this walnut dressing for a change.

4½ tablespoons grapeseed oil
1 tablespoon rice or cider vinegar
30 g (1 oz) walnut pieces, roughly chopped
1 clove of garlic, finely chopped
salt and pepper

Heat 2 tablespoons of the oil in a small frying pan, and sauté the nuts and garlic until golden – stand over the pan and watch carefully, as this only takes a minute or so. Remember, too, that they will continue to cook in the hot oil after you've taken them off the heat.

Let the contents cool slightly, then place approximately one third in the liquidiser with the remaining oil, vinegar and salt and pepper. Blend.

Pour into a bowl, and add the remaining nuts, garlic and oil from the pan. Beat in well, and leave to cool completely.

If you're not all that keen on garlic, or you're keen on garlic but the rest of the meal is heavily laced with the stuff, leave it out – it is still a good dressing.

Alternatively, for a thinner dressing don't liquidise the cooked walnuts with the remaining ingredients, just whisk the whole lot together.

White Radish and Pear Salad

Most larger supermarkets and good greengrocers now stock long tapering roots of white radish. It may be labelled with one of several names, mooli or daikon for instance. The roots should be smooth and firm. If it is not available, use the common or garden radishes, thinly sliced.

SERVES 4

15 cm (6 in) piece white radish (mooli)
2 ripe pears
30 g (1 oz) toasted pine nuts or hazelnuts*

Dressing:
1 tablespoon rice vinegar or white wine vinegar
½ teaspoon Dijon mustard
pinch of sugar
salt and pepper
4 tablespoons light oil
1 tablespoon fresh tarragon, chopped

Make the dressing by beating the vinegar with the mustard, sugar, salt and pepper, and then whisking in the oil a tablespoon at a time. Add the chopped tarragon. Taste and adjust the seasoning.

Peel and thinly slice the mooli and toss in half the dressing. Core the pears, and slice thinly into circles. As you work, turn the pear slices in the remaining dressing. Drain any excess dressing from the mooli and pears, and arrange on a serving dish. Scatter the nuts over the top.

Avocado and Nectarine Salad With Herb Dressing

One of the most felicitous innovations in our greengrocers' shops and supermarkets over recent years has been the gentle introduction of a quantity of fresh herbs* – not only parsley and chives, but half a dozen or more others, tarragon and chervil, rosemary, sage, mint, and my two favourites, basil and sorrel.

They're hardly cheap, I know, in those tiddly plastic wrapped polystyrene trays, but they can turn a simple and average meal, with a few snips of the scissors, into a firework display of taste.

The vivid green dressing for this salad takes advantage of this wealth. It will keep, sealed, in the fridge for up to 3 days.

PER PERSON:

½ avocado
lemon juice
½ nectarine
½ teaspoon chopped toasted hazelnuts or walnuts
1 tablespoon herb dressing (see below)
a few sprigs of relevant herbs

Dressing:
3 tablespoons light olive oil
2 tablespoons lemon juice
a small bunch of fresh basil leaves, parsley or mixed herbs
salt and pepper

Blend all the dressing ingredients in a processor. Taste and add a pinch of sugar if necessary, or a smidgen more vinegar or salt and pepper.

Choose an avocado that is just ripe, but still firm. Remove the skin with a sharp knife. Turn in the lemon juice, then slice the avocado halves lengthways without cutting right through at the stem end. Lay one half on each plate (or use one large plate) and fan out.

Quarter the nectarines, stone, and again cut each quarter lengthways without cutting right through the end. Arrange in a fan beside the avocado. Spoon over the herb dressing, scatter with hazelnuts, and tuck in a few sprigs of herb for a final decoration.

Jicama, Papaya and Chicken or Prawn Salad

It really doesn't look like much. Bulbous and turnip-like, a dull matt tan-brown, from the tip of the root to the start of the stem. A vegetable that you could easily pass by without even noticing, let alone giving it a second glance. What a mistake you would be making.

The jicama, or yam bean, is a real discovery. I buy them whenever I catch sight of them in Chinese supermarkets. Inside that self-effacing fibrous skin is a sphere of crisp, juicy white flesh, with a texture similar to that of a mooli (white radish) though perhaps a mite starchier. You can cook it (stir-fry for preference), but it is better raw, with its taste of young peas in the pod, eaten straight from the plant.

It originates from South America, and in Mexico it is often served with wedges of lime and a spiced chilli and salt mixture.

SERVES 6

1 jicama or mooli
1 ripe papaya
1 pink grapefruit
either 1 smoked or cooked chicken or 250 g (8 oz) (or more) fresh
    prawns, shelled

Dressing:
juice of 1–2 limes, or 1 lemon
1 teaspoon hot chilli powder
1 teaspoon ground cumin
1 teaspoon ground coriander
2 teaspoons salt

Halve, peel and slice the jicama and papaya, discarding the papaya seeds. Peel the grapefruit, separate into segments and peel segments. If you are using chicken, sever the legs and wings. Slice the breast and thigh meat. Arrange the fruits and chicken or prawns elegantly on a serving dish and squeeze lime juice over them.

Mix the spices and salt. Sprinkle over the salad – you won't need it all. Cover, and serve lightly chilled, with the extra spice mixture in a small bowl for those who would like a little more.

Broad Beans, Grilled Courgette and Shrimp Salad

I'd been working all Sunday morning and needed a walk. Trotting around the backstreets of Upper Holloway turned out to be surprisingly interesting. Gaps between net curtains revealed glimpses of the many Greek men's clubs. One had walls covered with faded prints of doe-eyed Greek heroes, Byronesque in tasselled caps. Middle aged and elderly men gathered together inside, talking, smoking, playing cards – the congregation of the picturesque Greek village square, transferred to grey north London.

Beside one of these clubs was a Greek grocers with a grand display of fresh vegetables, mostly imported from Cyprus. Among them were young fresh broad beans. What a treat! When they are new and young make them the focal point of a course, not just a side-dish.

SERVES 4

½ kg (1 lb) courgettes
1 kg (2 lb) broad beans in their pods, or 250–375 g (8–12 oz) frozen
    broad beans
125 g (4 oz) shelled shrimps

Dressing:
4 tablespoons extra virgin olive oil
1 tablespoon balsamic, sherry or red wine vinegar
1 tablespoon chervil, tarragon or parsley, finely chopped
salt and pepper

First the dressing – put all the dressing ingredients into a screw top jar, and shake well. Or just whisk the vinegar with salt and pepper, and gradually whisk in the oil. Taste and adjust the seasoning.

Trim the courgettes, and cut in half lengthways. Turn in 2 tablespoons of the dressing. Leave for at least 20 minutes, while you pod the broad beans, or read the paper or whatever.

Grill the courgettes under a high heat until tender, and streaked with dark brown. Slice. Meanwhile, cook the beans in boiling salted water (save the water to use as a vegetable stock for soups, etc.). Slit the skins of the larger ones (or all of them if you are feeling patient) and squeeze gently to pop out the tender bright green beans. The more you can bear to do the better, because it makes for the most exquisite salad.

Toss the hot shelled beans and courgettes in enough dressing to coat, and leave to cool. Add the shrimps, taste and adjust the seasoning, adding extra dressing if necessary. Serve at room temperature or lightly chilled, as a first course, with crusty bread.

FISH

⟡⟡⟡

Ceviche

Ceviche, South American marinated fish, is a dish I am extremely fond of. It is simplicity itself to make, but there are two things that make all the difference between a classy *ceviche* and a slovenly one. The first is getting the balance of ingredients right. This is largely a personal matter, I know, which is why there are a hundred and one variations on the recipe.

The other is the quality of the ingredients – your fish must be sparkling with freshness. A must too for the vegetables. If you cannot get limes, use the juice of 1½ lemons and cut up an extra lemon to accompany the finished dish. The acidity of the juice coagulates the protein in the fish as if you had applied heat. So it becomes opaque (in a few minutes) and is effectively 'cooked'.

SERVES 4 as a first course

500 g (1 lb) firm-fleshed white fish fillets, such as cod, bass, halibut, sole, skinned
4 limes
1 fresh green or red chilli, seeded and finely chopped
salt
½ small red onion or shallot or 3 spring onions, finely chopped
1 tablespoon fresh coriander leaf, finely chopped
1 green pepper, seeded and finely chopped
250 g (8 oz) firm tomatoes, seeded and finely chopped
2 tablespoons olive oil

Cut the fish into strips 4–5 cm (1½–2 in) long. Pare the zest from 1 lime. Cover and save. Squeeze the juice of 3 of the limes. Mix with the fish, chilli and a pinch of salt in a bowl (not a metal one). Cover and marinate for 1 hour at room temperature, or 2–4 hours in the fridge. The acidity preserves the fish, so it will keep for 24 hours and longer if need be, though it tastes better when newly marinated.

Drain off the marinade, and toss the fish with the onion and coriander. Pile in the centre of the serving dish, and arrange the pepper and tomato around it. Mix 2 tablespoons of the marinade with the olive oil and trickle over the vegetables. Scatter a few shreds of lime zest over the fish. Divide the last lime into 8 wedges, and serve with the *ceviche*.

Fish Salad

The White Tower Restaurant in Percy Street, in central London, is a delightful place, walls laden with prints of Greek heroes, the haunt of many a politician. It's a Greek restaurant, but not of the plate-smashing raucous variety, with shocking pink tarama (that's all colouring, you know) and endless oceans of floppy Greek salad.

No, the White Tower is quite different, with a menu that includes some of the standards and many dishes you might not know. On a hot summer day, their cold *meze*, a collection of small dishes, make an ideal lunch.

This fish salad, dressed with olive oil and lemon, was inspired by one they serve as part of the *meze*. It makes a perfect centrepiece to a light summery lunch, or a simple first course.

SERVES 6 as a first course, 3–4 as a main course

500g (1 lb) fresh halibut or plaice fillets, or other firm white fish
125 g (4 oz) firm sweet tomatoes, seeded and chopped
½ red onion, finely chopped
salt and pepper
1 tablespoon parsley, finely chopped
½ tablespoon chives, finely chopped
½ tablespoon dill or fennel, finely chopped, or 6 torn basil leaves

Dressing:
6 tablespoons light olive oil
3 tablespoons lemon juice
salt and pepper

Steam the fillets briefly – 1 minute will probably be enough to turn thin fillets of plaice opaque, while it may take 2–3 minutes to cook thicker halibut. Check frequently, and don't overcook – they will continue to cook as they cool, so it is better to err towards under-cooking.

Remove immediately from the heat, and break the fish into very large flakes. Arrange in a shallow dish. Beat the lemon juice with salt, pepper and oil and pour over the fish. Leave to cool. Just before serving, scatter with the tomato, onion and herbs. Serve at room temperature.

Trout, Herring or Mackerel en Escabeche

Fish *en escabeche* takes many forms – it has its origins in Spain though it is now more likely to be found in Latin America or the West Indies. The lists of ingredients vary wildly from country to country, from cook to cook. It is a dish that has been adapted to local ingredients, and reflects national and individual tastes.

But wherever you go, the basic premise stays the same: the fish – usually small whole fish, but it could be fillets – is first fried, and then marinated in an aromatic vinegar. This is my version, but feel free to adapt and improvise. It is a quick dish to put together – perfect if you have friends coming round for dinner tomorrow and know that your cooking time will be severely limited.

SERVES 8 as a first course, 4 as a main course

4 trout, herring or mackerel, cleaned and scaled
juice of 1 lemon
salt and pepper
olive oil

Marinade:
½ cucumber, peeled and thinly sliced
1 red or ordinary onion, sliced paper thin
1 red or yellow pepper, seeded and sliced into rings
1 green or red chilli, seeded and sliced
1 bay leaf
1 teaspoon allspice berries, crushed
1 clove of garlic, chopped
150 ml (5 fl oz) white wine vinegar
90 ml (3 fl oz) olive oil

Rub the lemon juice into both the outside and the inside of the fish. Season, and leave for 30 minutes. Pat dry, and fry in very hot olive oil until browned and crisp on both sides. Place in a shallow dish.

Place the marinade ingredients in a pan, and bring to the boil. Simmer for 3 minutes, then pour over the fish. Cool, cover and leave in the fridge overnight.

Serve as a first course with plenty of bread, or a main course with a crisp green salad and new potatoes.

Mackerel With Spinach and Mushroom Stuffing

Frozen spinach is a great standby, but it honestly falls flat on its face beside fresh. The preparation of fresh spinach may require a little more attention, but not a great deal – and the 10 extra minutes are worth every second.

Think about it – with frozen spinach you've got to thaw that great big block, without burning it, and try somehow to end with spinach that is evenly cooked and retains some character. Even with the aid of the microwave, it still means regular prodding, rearranging and checking. Buy the bounciest, squeaky, firm-leaved fresh spinach and your major task is cleaning it. Then you just stuff it in a pan, cover and cook over a moderate heat for 5 minutes, stir and give it a couple of minutes more. Finito.

Anyway, this simple stuffing for mackerel is just sensational made with fresh spinach, and not at all bad with frozen.

SERVES 4

4 mackerel, cleaned
½ kg (1 lb) fresh spinach, or 375 g (12 oz) frozen leaf spinach,
    thawed but not cooked
1 onion, chopped
2–3 tablespoons olive oil
125 g (4 oz) mushrooms, finely chopped
salt and pepper
lemon juice

With a sharp knife, enlarge the stomach cavity of each mackerel. Rinse the insides well with cold water. Wash the fresh spinach, and trim off any large stalks. Cook briefly. If using frozen spinach, just let it thaw. Squeeze out as much water as you can and chop.

Fry the onion gently in 1 tablespoon of oil until tender, without browning. Turn up the heat and add the mushrooms. Stir, and continue frying until the mushrooms are soft and any liquid has evaporated. Add the spinach to the pan and mix well. Season, and stir for another minute or so. Finally, add the lemon juice to taste – use a fair amount to balance the oiliness of the mackerel, up to ½ a lemon's worth.

Stuff the cavity of each mackerel and secure loosely with a cocktail stick. Arrange the mackerel in a lightly oiled oven-proof dish. Tuck any leftover stuffing around them. Drizzle the remaining oil over the fish and cover with foil. Bake at 200C/400F/Gas 6 for 20–25 minutes, until the fish are cooked through.

Skate With Cucumber and Red Peppers

Skate is the ideal fish for anybody who finds coping with whiskery fish bones tiresome. The flesh nestles snugly on either side of a central sheet of cartilage, and pulls off in boneless strips.

It has a fine flavour, and is as good served cold as hot. Here I've cooked it with peppers, tomato and cucumber. If left to cool, the sauce sets to give a delicious tomatoey jelly. To serve as a cold hors d'œuvre, strip the flesh from the bones while still hot.

SERVES 2 as a main course

½ cucumber
1 teaspoon salt
1 small onion, sliced
1 large clove of garlic, chopped
1 red pepper, thinly sliced
2 tablespoons olive oil
2 × 250 g (8 oz) pieces skate wing, preferably middle
1 × 400 g (14 oz) tin chopped tomatoes
½ teaspoon sugar
pepper
½ tablespoon chopped fresh mint
1 small sprig of thyme

Cut the cucumber into 2½ cm (1 in) lengths, then cut into batons approximately 5 mm (¼ in) thick. Spread out in a colander and sprinkle with salt. Leave to drain while you prepare the rest of the ingredients.

Heat the oil in a large frying pan, and add the onion and garlic. Cook for 1 minute then add the red pepper. Cook, stirring occasionally, for a further 2–3 minutes without browning. Clear a space amid the vegetables, and add the skate to the pan. Cover, and cook for 2 minutes. Turn the fish over, cover and cook for a further 2 minutes.

As soon as the skate is in the pan, rinse the cucumber with cold water, and pat dry in a clean tea-towel, or with a paper towel. Once the skate has done its 2 minutes on each side, remove the lid, and add the tomatoes and their juice, the cucumber, sugar, pepper, mint and thyme. Bring to a simmer, stirring. Simmer for 10–15 minutes, stirring occasionally and turning the skate pieces once. Taste and adjust the seasoning, adding salt if required. Serve hot or cold.

Sautéed Squid

Many people are convinced that squid is naturally tough and chewy. This is a fallacy. Fresh squid is as tender as you can imagine, needing only the minimum of cooking. It only becomes rubbery when it has been frozen. Fresh squid may cost more than frozen but once you've tried it you'll never again be satisfied with the frozen stuff. Try barbecuing fresh squid; slit the cleaned sacs open, score the inside with criss cross lines, brush with olive oil and grill for 30 seconds on each side over a high heat, scored side to heat first. Season with coarse salt and pepper as you turn it over.

This dish of sautéed squid is almost as quick to cook, and can be served hot or cold.

SERVES 3–4 as a first course

500 g (1 lb) fresh squid, cleaned*
3 tablespoons olive oil
2 cloves of garlic, finely chopped
1 dried red chilli, crumbled
finely grated zest and juice of ½ lemon
salt
1 tablespoon fresh parsley, finely chopped
lemon wedges

Chop the tentacles roughly, and slice the sacs into 5 mm (¼ in) thick rings. Rinse under the cold tap, and dry on kitchen paper. Heat the olive oil, garlic, chilli and lemon zest gently in a small frying pan over a low heat for 5 minutes. Raise the heat and add the squid. Stir until it turns opaque, a mere 1–2 minutes. Draw off the heat, and season with salt and lemon juice to taste. Serve hot or cold, sprinkled with parsley, with the extra lemon wedges and good bread to mop up the juices.

Whiting and Tomato Gratin

The thing I love about this dish is that, although it is baked long enough to just cook the fish through, the hot tomato and finely chopped shallot or sweet onion retain a fresh uncooked flavour and texture.

It makes a quick suppertime treat, served with steamed new potatoes and green vegetables, or a crisp green salad. Or you could make half quantities, baked in small individual ramekins, and offer it as a first course.

There's absolutely no reason why you shouldn't use other white fish, such as plaice, or cod. It just so happened that the whiting looked very enticing at the fishmonger when I was shopping for the ingredients to test the recipe. Try it too with fresh basil instead of thyme.

The one ingredient I really wouldn't change is the shallot or sweet red onion. The flavour of the common-or-garden onion is much too pushy and would upset the balance of the whole dish.

SERVES 4

500 g (1 lb) whiting fillets
500 g (1 lb) tomatoes, skinned* and roughly chopped
2 shallots or 1 red onion, finely chopped
4 sprigs of thyme
250 ml (8 fl oz) double cream
90 g (3 oz) cheddar, grated
salt and pepper

Set the oven to 220C/425F/Gas 7. Place a baking tray in the oven to heat through.

Lightly grease an oven-proof dish, and lay the whiting in it in a single layer. Season with salt and pepper. Scatter the shallot or onion over the fish. Spread the tomatoes in a thick layer over the shallot. Season and sprinkle with thyme.

Pour the cream over the top and, finally, top with grated cheddar. Place on the hot baking tray in the oven and bake for 25 minutes, until nicely browned.

Steamed Mussels With Orange and Fennel

Steaming is a marvellous way of cooking shellfish, keeping them moist and plump. In this recipe the full flavour of the mussels shines through. The black of the shells and orange of the flesh are startlingly beautiful against the pale green of the fennel.

SERVES 4 as a first course, 2 as a main course

1 kg (2 lb) mussels*
2 fennel bulbs
1 orange
1 teaspoon coriander seed, crushed
salt and pepper

Prepare the mussels*. Remove any damaged outer leaves from the fennel. Cut off tough stalks, saving any feathery fronds. Chop the fennel bulbs. Peel the orange, taking off as much of the bitter white pith as possible. Chop, saving all the juice that runs out.

Mix the orange and fennel, and spread out on 2 heat-proof plates, or foil-lined steamer baskets. Scatter the coriander on the vegetables. Pour over any orange juice, and season with salt and pepper. Steam for 10 minutes. Add the mussels in a single layer, and steam for a further 3–4 minutes until the mussels have opened. Discard any that remain closed. Scatter with the fennel fronds and serve.

Grilled Salmon With Japanese Ginger

My first attempts at rolling Japanese *sushi* led me to explore the inner recesses of several oriental supermarkets in search of this and that ingredient. All the Japanese books I own said firmly that pickled ginger is the thing to eat with *sushi* and so I dutifully purchased a small tub of rose-petal pink *amasu-shoga* – *shoga* is the Japanese for ginger.

What a discovery! Paper thin slices of tender ginger, milder than I imagined with a cool freshness, not too sweet, not too sour. Since then I've used it in all sort of ways. Finely diced, it gives vegetable salads an instant lift. But even better is pickled ginger with fresh salmon. Simplicity itself, and a great joy to eat.

SERVES 2

2 pieces of salmon fillet, weighing 125–175 g (4–6 oz) each
approx 15 slices Japanese pickled ginger
1 teaspoon pickled ginger juice
1 tablespoon oil
salt

Set the grill to high. Lay each piece of salmon flesh-side up, and make deep slashes, almost to the skin, across the width, angling the cuts towards the tail end. Leave a gap of roughly 1 cm (½ in) between each slash.

Slip 1 or 2 slices of pickled ginger into each slash, spreading them out so that they reach from side to side. Carefully lift the salmon on to the grill pan. Beat 1 teaspoon of the liquid from the ginger with the oil, and brush over the salmon. Grill without turning for about 5 minutes, or until just opaque through to the skin. Sprinkle a little salt over each fillet and serve immediately with boiled waxy potatoes, and a simply cooked green vegetable, such as mangetouts, or green beans.

Sweet Potato and Fish Pie

Fish pie, topped with browned mashed potato, is one of those homely dishes that I adore, but tend to forget about completely for months on end. When it is badly made it is an utter disaster, but when you get a good one it's a real cracker.

This is a surprisingly good variation on the original, with the smokey sugariness of sweet potato contrasting with the savouriness of the filling. If there are no sweet potatoes around, try using half parsnips or celeriac and half potato instead.

SERVES 4

¾ kg (1½ lb) sweet potato
4 eggs
300 ml (½ pt) milk, plus a little extra
1 small onion
5 peppercorns
3 branches of dill
750 g (1½ lb) haddock or other white fish fillet
60 g (2 oz) butter
15 g (½ oz) flour
salt and pepper
125 g (4 oz) shelled, cooked, fresh peas or thawed frozen peas

Cut the sweet potatoes into chunks, and steam or boil in salted water until soft. Peel, and mash 500 g (1 lb) of the potatoes with 1 egg, 30 g (1 oz) butter and enough milk to give a soft consistency.

Hard boil the 3 remaining eggs, shell and quarter. Put 300 ml (½ pt) of the milk into a pan with the sliced onion, the peppercorns and the stalks of the dill. Bring gently to the boil. Lay the fillets in an oven-proof dish, and pour over the hot milk and seasonings.

Bake at 180C/350F/Gas 4 for 15–20 minutes, until the fish is cooked. Strain off the milk and set aside, and discard the onions and seasonings. Flake the fish, and lay on the base of a pie dish. Cover with peas, then the quartered hard-boiled eggs. Sprinkle with dill.

Make a white sauce with 15 g (½ oz) butter, flour and the milk from the fish. Simmer for 5 minutes and season well. Pour over the fish, shaking the dish gently to distribute. Spread potato thickly over the top, and make a wavy pattern on the top with a fork. Dot with the remaining 15 g (½ oz) butter. Bake at 230C/450F/Gas 8 for 10–15 minutes until lightly browned.

Smoked Haddock and Mushroom Pie

The mellow tan of a Finnan Haddie is unmistakable among the violent and unnatural hues of dyed smoked fish piled up high on the fish counter. I won't buy coloured fish; I don't care if the dye is 'natural', whatever that means. Regardless of whether it is or is not harmful, it is totally unnecessary.

Finnan Haddie is the king of smoked haddock, ideal for this generous pie. Cajol any reluctant fishmongers into selling it.

SERVES 6

375 g (12 oz) smoked haddock
500 ml (¾ pt) milk
1 onion, chopped
1 carrot, finely chopped
60 g (2 oz) butter
250 g (8 oz) mushrooms, sliced
45 g (1½ oz) flour
1 blade of mace
1 tablespoon fresh parsley, chopped
lemon juice
salt and pepper
250 g (8 oz) cooked green beans
375 g (12 oz) shortcrust pastry*
1 egg, beaten

Place the haddock in a shallow pan and cover with milk. Heat very slowly until almost simmering and the surface of the liquid trembles. Keep at this temperature for a further 5–10 minutes until the haddock is cooked. Strain off and reserve the milk, and flake the haddock, discarding the bones and skin.

Fry the onion and carrot in the butter without browning, until the onion is almost tender. Add the mushrooms, and continue cooking until the mushrooms are done. Sprinkle on the flour, and stir for 1 minute. Gradually stir in the reserved milk, and add the blade of mace. Bring to the boil, stirring, and simmer for 10 minutes until thick. Add the parsley, lemon juice, pepper to taste and salt if necessary.

Place the fish and green beans in the base of a large pie dish – there should be enough to give a loose layer about 4–5 cm (1½–2 in) deep, and pour over the mushroom sauce. Roll out the pastry thinly. Brush the edges of the dish with egg, and cover with the pastry, supporting with a pie funnel or up-turned egg cup. Make a hole in the centre to let steam escape. Decorate with trimmings, and rest for 30 minutes before cooking. Brush with egg and bake at 200C/400F/Gas 6 for 25–30 minutes, until golden brown.

Fillets of Sole With Anchovy Butter

I've twice been lucky enough to be invited to lunch at the Château Mouton Rothschild, just outside Bordeaux. Well, it wasn't so much me they were inviting, but the winners of the Observer/Mouton Rothschild cookery competition. I was just a hanger on.

On one of these occasions, our first course was fillets of baby sole with anchovy butter. Superb, and the meal went from strength to strength. There was tender local lamb, noodles with lashings of truffles, asparagus and, to finish, a perfect almondy strawberry tart.

This is my attempt to reproduce something similar to that first course. Baby soles are hard to find, expensive and time-consuming in preparation, so I use small but grown-up lemon, or better still dover sole when I'm feeling flush, and turn it into a main course.

Save any leftover butter, and use on pasta or vegetables (excellent with potatoes).

Serves 4

Anchovy Butter:
125 g (4 oz) softened unsalted butter
6 anchovy fillets
1½ tablespoons double cream
squeeze of lemon juice

4 small dover or lemon soles, skinned and filleted
seasoned flour
clarified or concentrated butter
lemon wedges

Process all the ingredients for the anchovy butter until smooth and evenly amalgamated. If you don't have a processor, liquidise the anchovies with the cream and then beat into the butter with the lemon juice. Completely gadget-less? Chop the anchovy fillets finely, then mash with an ounce of the butter. Beat with the remaining butter ingredients. Pile into a bowl and chill.

Dust the sole fillets with seasoned flour. Heat a little clarified or concentrated butter in a frying pan, until foaming. Fry the fillets quickly on either side, until golden. You'll probably need to do this in several batches – speed up the process by using 2 large frying pans. Replace the butter with a fresh knob if it darkens too much. Serve quickly with the lemon wedges, handing round cool anchovy butter separately.

American Crabcakes

I've seen these crabcakes labelled as Baltimore crabcakes, Southern crabcakes, Maryland crabcakes and just plain old crabcakes. The recipes differ only in details, but the theory and essential flavourings remain much the same, and you end up with the most delicious, crisp on the outside, melting inside, all-American crab patties.

Crab is expensive and this is one of the best ways I know of stretching a relatively small amount – roughly the weight you will get out of one medium-sized crab – heartily around 4 people. Mind you, one recipe I found started out with an impressive 2½ kg (5 lb) crab meat and was, it suggested, only enough to feed 10! Now, I would be the first to admit that I could, if hungry and with little else on offer, chomp my way cheerily through two of these crabcakes, but more than that would floor me completely.

SERVES 4

250 g (8 oz) fresh crab meat, brown and white*
salt and pepper
1 egg
1 tablespoon mayonnaise
2 teaspoons Dijon mustard
1 tablespoon parsley, finely chopped
4 spring onions, finely chopped
60–90 g (2–3 oz) dried breadcrumbs
oil

Place the crab in a bowl with salt and pepper. Add the remaining ingredients, except the crumbs and oil. Mix, then add enough crumbs to bind. Quarter the mixture, and pat each part into a flat round cake, about 2 cm (¾ in) thick.

Either fry the cakes in a little oil until browned on both sides, or brush the grill rack and crab cakes with oil and grill until well browned on both sides, turning once. Serve with the lemon wedges and a green or tomato salad.

Baked Hake With Mayonnaise and Potatoes

The Spanish adore fish and wherever you travel the fish markets are always stunning to see, with their huge displays of the glistening fresh fish. Even in Madrid which is, after all, several hundred miles from the sea, you'll never see a tired flabby piece of fish for sale.

Hake is highly prized and turns up in all sorts of guises, fried, baked, stewed, and often served curled round in a circle with its tail caught in its mouth. It is a delicate white-fleshed fish, often overlooked in this country, and as a result relatively cheap. Baking it under a coat of mayonnaise may seem an odd thing to do, but it keeps the flesh moist and tender. Incidentally, without the fish this makes a good potato gratin.

SERVES 4

1 × 1 kg (2 lb) hake
¾ kg (1½ lb) waxy salad potatoes*
1 large onion
1 tablespoon olive oil
125 g (4 oz) mayonnaise
1 clove of garlic, crushed
salt and pepper

Ask the fishmonger to clean and scale the hake, leaving the head and tail but removing the fins. Boil the potatoes in their skins until just cooked but still firm. Peel when cool enough to handle, and slice thinly. Fry the onion in the olive oil until golden brown. Beat the garlic into the mayonnaise.

Grease an oven-proof serving dish with a little extra oil and spread the potatoes on the base in a thick layer. Scatter the onions over the top, and season. Lay the hake on top, curving it round and catching the tail between its toothy jaws. Season the fish and bake at 200C/400F/Gas 6 for 15 minutes.

Remove from the oven and spread the mayonnaise over the fish, leaving the head bare (unless you want to disguise it) and also the surface of the potatoes. Return to the oven for a further 15–20 minutes, until the fish is opaque and pulls easily away from the bone.

Hake in Piquante Sauce

Hake and potatoes again, but this saffron-scented stew is not at all like the preceding recipe. The recipe was sent to me by a reader, Maureen Short, who now lives in Palma. I've made it with both hake and halibut, and both work excellently.

The stock you use is immensely important. A good fish stock is preferable, a good chicken stock is pretty good, and a good vegetable stock would be better than a stock cube. If you don't have any homemade stock at all, use 200 ml (⅓ pt) dry white wine, made up to a pint with water, rather than spoiling the whole caboodle with a cube.

SERVES 4

60–90 ml (2–3 fl oz) olive oil
2 large potatoes, peeled and cut into very thin slices
salt and pepper
1 medium hake, cut into 2–3 cm (1 in) thick steaks, or 4 halibut fillets
1 medium onion, very finely sliced
½ red pepper, thinly sliced
4–5 cloves of garlic, chopped
1 tablespoon fresh parsley, chopped
1 dried red chilli, chopped
¼ teaspoon saffron powder
1 level teaspoon sweet paprika
600 ml (1 pt) stock – fish, chicken, vegetable or a mixture*

Cover the base of a 30 cm (12 in) paella pan, or 2 large deep frying pans, with a thin film of oil. Arrange the sliced potatoes in a single layer to cover the base of the pan(s). Season. Arrange the fish on top, and scatter the onion and red pepper on the fish. Then sprinkle on the garlic, parsley and chilli. Dust with saffron and paprika, and a little more salt.

Drizzle the rest of the olive oil over the dish. Bring the stock to the boil, and pour in. Cover the pan with a large lid, leaving a small gap so that some steam can escape. Cook over a low heat, keeping the liquid barely simmering, for 45–60 minutes, until the potato is tender.

Take to the table in the pan, and serve with good bread to mop up the delicious juices.

Parrot Fish With Curry Butter

The fishmonger's stall has become a riot of colour over the past few years. A whole new wave of fishy imports has been turning up at Billingsgate wholesale fish market, twice a week, on Tuesday and Friday, flown in from the Seychelles and other exotic watery homes.

In terms of colour, the incontrovertible star is the startling turquoise blue-splashed parrot fish and, happily, this delightfully gaudy and attention-demanding fish is also one of the stars when it comes to taste. Parrot fish aren't always blue, however. They can also be red or yellow, hence the name.

The flesh is firm, sweet and moist with a well-defined flavour, on a par with many of our grand fish, such as sole or halibut. The wholesale price of parrot fish is less than that of these, so in theory at any rate it should be a cheaper alternative for the consumer.

If your fishmonger hasn't been trying out these fish, ask him to look out for them and to do a bit of proper promotion on them. They are easy to cook and, baked this way, or steamed, they will retain most of that dandy blue.

SERVES 2–3

125 g (4 oz) softened butter
1 tablespoon vindaloo curry paste
2 tablespoons lemon juice
1 parrot fish weighing ¾–1 kg (1½–2 lb)
oil
salt

Either mash or process the butter with the curry paste and the lemon juice, until smooth and a uniform orangey-brown colour. Pile into a bowl and chill. Alternatively, you could form it into a sausage shape, wrapped in greaseproof paper, and chill, then slice into neatish discs to serve.

Rub the parrot fish all over with the oil, paying special attention to the fins and tail – this will prevent the fish sticking to the foil. Sprinkle the fish lightly with salt, and wrap completely in silver foil, sealing the edges well. Bake at 200C/400F/Gas 6 for 30–40 minutes, until the fish is opaque through to the bone. Lift the fish carefully on to a warmed serving dish, pour the juices over and fillet at the table so that everyone can admire the beautiful blue. Serve the curry butter separately.

Red Mullet and Red Pepper Tart

Whenever I see it, I find red mullet hard to resist. For a start, it looks so pretty and inviting, with its shiny red skin, and then I know that it tastes pretty inviting too. It has a strong individual flavour, which has given it the reputation of being the 'game bird' of the sea.

It's good grilled and baked (leave the liver in – a delicacy), and has a natural affinity with tomato and fennel. In this recipe I've made it part of a tomato and red pepper tart, flavoured with a little Pernod to give a hint of the aniseed flavour of fennel.

SERVES 4–6

250 g (8 oz) shortcrust pastry*
2 small or 1 medium red mullet, filleted
8 black olives
extra olive oil

Filling:
1 tablespoon olive oil
1 onion, chopped
1 red pepper, seeded and chopped
½ kg (1 lb) tomatoes, skinned*, seeded and roughly chopped
1½ tablespoons Pernod
½ teaspoon sugar
dash of red wine vinegar
salt and pepper

Cook the onion and red pepper in the olive oil until soft, without browning. Add all the remaining filling ingredients plus 4 table-spoons of water, or fish stock, and simmer until the sauce is thick. Liquidise, and adjust the seasoning.

Line a 23 cm (9 in) flan tin with the pastry and rest it for 30 minutes in the fridge. Bake the pastry blind★.

Cut the mullet fillets into thick strips. Stone the olives and halve. Spread the tomato and pepper purée out on the base of the tart, then arrange the mullet on top like the spokes of a wheel or in a lattice, skin side up, pressing it into the purée. Dot the olives in the gaps. Brush the fish and olives with a little extra olive oil, and bake at 190C/375F/Gas 5 for 10–15 minutes, until the mullet is cooked through and the tart is hot. Serve hot, or warm.

Cod or Monkfish and Radicchio Gratin

Plump, tightly furled, magenta balls of radicchio are easy enough to find these days, now that we're inching towards being a more health conscious nation. Or was it the design notions of yuppies stretching out towards food that brought radicchio into the supermarket?

Either way, with its distinctive bitterness and colour, it is a welcome addition to salads. But it is also robust enough to take heat, as part of a cooked dish. Grilled radicchio salads have been fashionable, and very good they can be. This is another way of using those pleasingly bitter leaves – in a gratin, with a hint of sharpness, against tender fish. If you wish, you could leave out the fish and double the quantities of the remaining ingredients, except the breadcrumbs, to make a side-dish or first course.

SERVES 4

500 g (1 lb) cod or monkfish fillet, sliced 5 mm (¼ in) thick
1 large onion, thinly sliced
3 tablespoons olive oil
1 large clove of garlic, finely chopped
2 tablespoons fresh parsley, chopped
30 g (1 oz) pine nuts
6 radicchio leaves, thickly shredded
1½ tablespoons white wine vinegar
1 tablespoon fish stock★ or water
½ teaspoon of sugar
salt and pepper
60 g (2 oz) dry breadcrumbs

Lightly oil a baking dish and arrange the fish slices in it in a single layer, overlapping slightly. Place a metal baking sheet in the oven and set to 220C/425F/Gas 7.

Sauté the onion in 1 tablespoon oil until half cooked. Add the garlic and parsley, and cook until the onion is tender. Add the pine nuts, sauté until golden, then add the radicchio. Stir briefly until beginning to wilt, then pour in the vinegar, stock or water, and sprinkle over the sugar, salt and pepper. Stir and let it bubble until the liquid has all but evaporated, and the radicchio is completely softened – a few seconds only. Spread evenly over the fish.

Cover with an even layer of breadcrumbs, and drizzle the remaining oil over the top. Place on the hot tray in the oven and bake for 15–20 minutes, until golden brown. Serve immediately.

Cod With Seville Orange, Parsley and Onion Purée

Have you ever tried using Seville oranges for anything but marmalade? If not, make a note to experiment next January, when their short season is under way.

The juice of the Seville orange is sour, though not as acidic as lemon juice, with a spicier taste than ordinary orange juice. It is sensational as a flavouring for a sweet baked custard, or instead of lemon or lime juice in a *ceviche*. The combination of fish and Seville orange is made in heaven. Try deglazing the pan, after frying the fish fillets, with the juice of a Seville, and finish the sauce with a slurp of double cream, salt and pepper. Or for something less rich, and possibly even nicer, try this Seville-scented parsley and onion purée. Out of season, substitute the juice of half a lemon and half an orange.

SERVES 2

2 cod steaks or 2 175–250 g (6–8 oz) pieces of cod fillet
juice of 1 large Seville orange
1 teaspoon grated ginger
handful of fresh parsley, roughly chopped
1 large onion, chopped
1 large clove of garlic, chopped
2 tablespoons olive oil
salt and pepper

Place the cod in a shallow dish. Mix the Seville orange juice and ginger, and pour over the fish. Cover and leave in a cool place for 1–4 hours, turning occasionally.

Roughly chop enough fresh parsley to fill a measuring jug to the 150 ml (¼ pt) mark. About 30 minutes before you wish to eat, heat the olive oil gently in a heavy based pan. Add the onion, garlic and parsley, and stir. Cover, and cook over a very gentle heat for 15–20 minutes, stirring every 5 minutes or so, until the onion is really tender.

While it cooks heat up the grill, line the grill pan with silver foil, and brush the rack with a little oil. Just before the onions are cooked, take the cod out of the marinade. Uncover the onions, and add the marinade. Turn the heat up slightly, and simmer until the liquid is absorbed, leaving a moist mixture of onions and parsley. Purée with salt and pepper to taste.

Meanwhile, brush the cod with a little extra oil, and grill, turning once, until just cooked. Keep warm. Pour the juices into the purée, stir and reheat gently if necessary. Serve with the cod.

Cod With Chorizo

Most charity cookbooks, however worthy, are far from inspiring in the kitchen. But not all. From the 1988 Lambeth Conference, a gathering of bishops from the world over, there emerged a fascinating exception, *The Bishops' Cook Book*, sold in aid of the Church Urban Fund and the Christian Aid Crisis Fund.

This is an adaptation of a recipe given by the Bishop of the Lusitanian Church, Portugal, and his wife, Mrs Soares. The original called for salt-cod, but I've used fresh cod. The pairing of spicy chorizo sausage and fish is a winner. A small word of advice before you try it. Buy the chorizo from a good delicatessen. I once bought something labelled chorizo in a very reputable supermarket and it was revolting, with no resemblance whatsoever to the real thing.

SERVES 4

¾–1 kg (1½–2 lb) thick cod fillet
175 g (6 oz) spicy chorizo sausage, skinned and thinly sliced
olive oil
90 g (3 oz) wholemeal breadcrumbs
2 cloves of garlic, very finely chopped
salt and pepper

Divide the cod into 4 pieces. Halve each one horizontally without cutting completely in half. Open up like a butterfly. Lay a quarter of the chorizo on to one 'wing' of each butterfly, then fold back to its original shape. Arrange the cod in an oiled oven-proof dish – they should fit snugly. Drizzle over 4 tablespoons olive oil. Season with salt.

Mix the garlic with the breadcrumbs, salt and pepper. Sprinkle evenly over the cod, and drizzle over a final 2 tablespoons olive oil. Bake at 200C/400F/Gas 6 for 30 minutes, until browned.

Spiced Fish Curry With Coconut Milk

This isn't your usual Indian-style curry at all. For a start it is very mildly spiced, though naturally you can pep it up a little more with extra chilli powder if you must, but don't overdo it.

But an even more telling difference is that the liquid used is coconut milk. This is an Indonesian curry, fragrant and creamy. It gives normally dull and cheap white fish a whole new lease of life – I've made it with frozen whiting, and it was superb. But for a smart dinner, use a flasher kind of fish, monkfish for instance. The curry will be sensational, the guests suitably impressed.

SERVES 4

750 g (1½ lb) firm white fish fillets (monkfish, haddock, plaice)
juice of 1 lemon
1 onion, chopped
2 cloves of garlic, chopped
2 tablespoons oil
1 tablespoon ginger, grated
1 bay leaf, halved
½ teaspoon ground fenugreek
½ teaspoon chilli powder
½ teaspoon turmeric
½ teaspoon ground cumin
½ pint coconut milk*
salt

Cut the fish into 2½ cm (1 in) cubes, and toss in the lemon juice.

Fry the onion and garlic in the oil until they begin to brown. Add the ginger, bay leaf and remaining spices, and fry for a further minute. Pour in the coconut milk, cover, and simmer gently for 15 minutes. Add the fish with the lemon juice, and simmer gently for a further 5–15 minutes until the fish is cooked.

Serve with saffron or turmeric rice.

Maltese Tomato and Caper Sauce For Fish

The pickled and brined capers that we buy in little jars are the buds of a plant that grows wild around the Mediterranean. On Malta, and its neighbouring island Gozo, it flowers in late June, one of the few notes of greenery against the rocks and stone walls, surviving the fierce heat of the sun. The ethereal flowers, lasting no more than a day, are breathtaking – 4 pure white petals, and against them a vivid cascade of purple stamens – with a heavenly scent, a blend of honeysuckle, jasmine and caper.

Most of the capers that we buy over here tend not to be of the best quality. They are soaked in cheap vinegar, and what flavour they do have is drowned. I find it helps to pour boiling water over them before using, then rinse under the cold tap, though they are still a pale shadow of the salted capers, fresh and green tasting, that are spinkled liberally on salads and in sauces in Malta and Gozo.

This caper sauce is served with grilled fish in most restaurants on the islands, and the addition of lemon zest and mint makes it special. It is particularly appropriate with the more robust fish, such as tuna and swordfish, or oilier mackerel and herring.

SERVES 4–6

1 large onion, chopped
3 cloves of garlic, chopped
1 tablespoon olive oil
½ kg (1 lb) tomatoes, peeled and seeded, or 1 × 400 g (14 oz) tin
    chopped tomatoes
1 tablespoon tomato paste
½ teaspoon sugar
1 tablespoon lemon juice
salt and pepper
3 tablespoons capers
finely grated zest of ½ lemon
2 sprigs of fresh mint

Fry the onion and garlic in the oil until tender and golden brown. Add the tomatoes, tomato paste, sugar, lemon juice, salt and pepper. Bring to the boil, and simmer for 15 minutes. Add the capers, lemon zest and mint, and simmer for a further 10 minutes, or until the sauce is very thick and there is no trace of wateriness. Serve hot with grilled, fried or poached fish.

POULTRY AND GAME

Blanquette of Chicken and Jerusalem Artichokes

A *blanquette*, as you might well infer from the name, should be an elegant white stew, pale, interesting and subtle, rather than hearty and bold. It is one of the great classics of French cooking, usually made with veal, although other white meats are often used.

The first time I ate a *blanquette de veau*, was in a locally well-thought-of restaurant, in a small town in France. Disaster. The veal was stringy and tough, and the sauce still tasted of the flour used to thicken it. I was in my early teens, and for years after avoided it assiduously on restaurant menus, bemused by its obvious popularity. When I eventually came to try it again, it was quite a revelation. A good *blanquette* is a thing of joy.

In this loose adaptation of the traditional recipe, I use Jerusalem artichokes instead of the more usual pearl onions and pale cultivated mushrooms. You could, if you wished, add other vegetables such as carrots or green beans, or brown the chicken first, but that would mar its purity. Try making it this way first, and experiment next time.

SERVES 4

½ kg (1 lb) Jerusalem artichokes
4 chicken breasts
1 small onion, sliced
30 g (1 oz) butter
250 ml (7½ fl oz) dry white wine
1 bay leaf
150 ml (5 fl oz) double cream

123

Peel and quarter the artichokes. Cut the chicken into 2½ cm (1 in) cubes. Soften the onion in the butter, without browning. Add the chicken and artichokes, and stir until nicely coated in butter. Pour in the wine and enough water (or, better still, chicken stock, if you have any around) to cover, together with the bay leaf. Simmer, uncovered, for 10–15 minutes, until the chicken and artichokes are just cooked. Lift out the chicken and vegetables, and keep warm on serving dish.

Strain the cooking liquor and boil it hard, in a wide pan, until syrupy and reduced by two thirds. Remove from the heat and stir in the cream. Bring back to the boil, and simmer for a further 3 or 4 minutes. Taste and add salt if necessary. If you are a purist you will refrain from adding black pepper – the black speckles sully the ivory pallor – though white would be acceptable. Return chicken and artichokes to pan for a minute or so to heat through.

Poached Chicken With Lemon and Lettuce

The sight of a whole pale boiled chicken may take a bit of getting used to after the brownness of a roast one. I like the elegant pallor of bird against the dark green of the lettuce. However, if you are worried that it might look too anaemic or, as one friend of mine suggested, like a prop from the film *Eraserhead* – he's wrong by the way, it doesn't – you could always brown it in oil or butter first.

It seems a bit of a waste of time to me – easier perhaps to fleck it with fresh parsley before serving it, if you must. Whatever your aesthetic views on the matter, I'm sure you will agree that the chicken tastes good and, surprisingly, so too does the cooked lettuce.

SERVES 4

1 × 1¾–2 kg (3½–4 lb) chicken
1 round lettuce, shredded
1 onion, halved
4 cloves
5 peppercorns
zest and juice of 1 lemon
15 g (½ oz) butter
15 g (½ oz) flour
salt and pepper

Nestle the chicken into a relatively close fitting pan. Tuck the lettuce in around the bird. Stick 2 cloves into each half of onion and add to the pan with the peppercorns. Cut 6 wide strips of zest from the lemon and add. Pour in enough water to half fill the pot.

Bring to the boil, cover, and simmer gently for 1–1½ hours, until the bird is cooked. Take the bird out of the pan and keep warm. Strain the juices, saving the greenery. Boil the juices hard to reduce by one third, skimming off any scum that surfaces. Pile the lettuce around the chicken, picking out any cloves you come across.

Mash the butter with the flour. Turn down the heat under the chicken juices, until they are barely simmering. Add the butter and flour in small dollops, stirring to distribute. Cook for a further 5 minutes, without boiling. Add lemon juice to taste, and season well. Pour a little of the sauce over the lettuce, and serve the rest separately.

Poulet Vallée D'Auge

Poulet Vallée d'Auge is one of the great classics of Normandy cooking, bringing together all the best things that the area produces – plump free-range chicken, cream, butter, apples and Calvados.

The Vallée d'Auge itself is in the heart of the Calvados area of Normandy. This is where the Appellation d'Origine Controllée (AOC) Calvados comes from, the very best apple brandy with an intense fruity aroma and smooth flavour. Instead of Calvados, you could use ordinary brandy in this recipe, though you'll lose the full concentrated apple taste.

SERVES 4

1 × 1¼ kg (2½ lb) chicken
125 g (4 oz) butter
salt and pepper
ground nutmeg
½ kg (1 lb) eating apples such as Cox's Orange Pippins
3 tablespoons Calvados, or brandy
300 ml (10 fl oz) double cream
lemon juice

Melt 90g (3 oz) of the butter in a heavy bottomed flame-proof casserole. Brown the chicken all over in the butter. Season, and sprinkle with nutmeg. Cover tightly, and turn the heat down low. Cook for 45–60 minutes, until the chicken is cooked through. Check occasionally to make sure it isn't burning underneath.

When the chicken is almost cooked, peel and core the apples. Cut into eighths. Melt the remaining butter in a casserole, and sauté the apple slices until just cooked through. Keep warm.

When the chicken is cooked, add the Calvados and carefully set a match to it. When the flames die down, baste the bird generously with the juices, then remove it from the casserole and keep warm. Pour the cream into the sauce, stir well, and let it bubble for 5 minutes. Add a squeeze of lemon juice. Taste and adjust the seasoning.

Surround the chicken with the apple slices, and pour a little of the sauce over the dish. Serve the rest separately.

Moroccan Paprika Chicken

This is an aromatic way of cooking chicken, with rich red buttery juices. Serve it with rice, or better still couscous (see the couscous recipe on page 42, or with the vegetable couscous on page 82), to sop them up.

SERVES 4

4 chicken joints
90 g (3 oz) butter
1 medium onion, chopped
1 teaspoon black peppercorns, crushed
2 teaspoons paprika
1 teaspoon cumin seeds
5 cm (2 in) piece of cinnamon stick
1 tablespoon fresh coriander leaves or parsley, finely chopped
juice of ½ a lemon
salt

Brown the chicken joints in 30 g (1 oz) of the butter. Remove the chicken from the pan, and gently fry the onion in the remaining fat.

Replace the chicken in the pan, with the peppercorns, paprika, cumin seeds, cinnamon stick and remaining butter. Add enough water to cover. Simmer covered for 1 hour, until the flesh comes away easily from the bones. Take out the chicken pieces, and keep warm. Boil the liquid hard, until reduced by half. Strain, then stir in the coriander leaves, lemon juice and salt to taste. Pour over the chicken, and serve with rice, or couscous.

Chicken With Soy Sauce

Another recipe for a chicken stew, with a vigorous dark sauce guaranteed to perk up tired taste buds. This one is rich with dark soy sauce, ginger and sesame oil. Serve with rice or thin Chinese thread noodles to soak up all the sauce.

SERVES 4

1 chicken, or 4 chicken joints
7 tablespoons dry sherry
8½ cm (3 in) piece of ginger
1½ tablespoons cornflour
2 tablespoons oil
4 spring onions, chopped
4 tablespoons dark soy sauce
2 tablespoons sugar
1 teaspoon sesame oil
salt and pepper

Cut the chicken into 8 pieces. Place in a bowl with 3 tablespoons of the sherry. Set aside a 1 cm (½ in) piece of ginger, and slice the rest. Using a garlic press, squeeze the juice out of the sliced ginger on to the chicken. Turn to coat well, then sprinkle with the cornflour. Again, turn and mix so that each piece is covered. Leave the marinade for 30 minutes.

Peel and finely chop the remaining ginger. Heat 2 tablespoons of oil, and brown the chicken in this. Remove the chicken from the pan, and add the ginger and spring onions. Cook over a medium heat for about 1 minute. Return the chicken to the pan, with the remaining sherry, dark soy sauce, sugar, sesame oil, salt and pepper and 5 tablespoons of water. Cover the pan, and simmer gently for 15 minutes, or until the chicken is cooked.

Cerkez Tavugu – Circassian Chicken

This cold dish of chicken with a walnut sauce is one of the Turkish classics. The recipe was given to me by the chefs of the Divan Hotel in Istanbul, when they arrived *en masse* in London. For a week they appropriated part of the Sheraton Park Tower's kitchens and treated the diners to some of the best of Turkish cooking. It can also be served hot – reheat the chicken in the walnut sauce.

SERVES 8–10 as a first course, 6 as a main course

1 × 1½–2 kg (3–4 lb) chicken, jointed
1 large carrot, quartered
1 onion, quartered
salt
150 g (5 oz) walnut pieces
125 g (4 oz) white breadcrumbs
pepper
2 tablespoons of walnut or olive oil
paprika
fresh parsley, chopped

Place the chicken in a large pan or casserole with the carrot, onion and a pinch of salt. Add enough water to cover and bring to the boil. Skim off any scum and simmer for 45 minutes. Lift the chicken out of the pan, but leave the stock simmering. Skin and bone the chicken and return the skin and bones to the pan. Pull the chicken flesh apart into bite-sized pieces. Cool and cover until needed.

Turn up the heat under the stock, and boil until reduced by half. Strain, and skim off any fat. While the stock is reducing, grind the walnuts to a powder, and mix with the breadcrumbs. If you have a processor or a liquidiser, blend the walnuts and breadcrumbs with enough of the hot stock to give a creamy sauce, adding it a ladleful at a time. Without a processor, beat the stock vigorously into the walnuts and breadcrumbs, again a ladleful at a time, until creamy. Season with pepper and extra salt if necessary.

Mix the chicken with half the sauce, and pile on to a serving dish. Pour the remaining sauce over the top, and leave to cool. Just before serving, drizzle the oil over the dish, dust with a little paprika and scatter parsley over the top.

Roast Chicken With Cornbread Stuffing

References in American cookery books to chicken with 'cornbread dressing' used to mystify me, until I realised that their 'dressing' was our 'stuffing'. Whatever you call it, this stuffing with the sweet graininess of cornbread and salt of bacon is a joy with a good free-range chicken. Make cornbread one day, and set aside enough to fill the next day's roast chicken.

SERVES 4

45g (1½ oz) butter
1 small onion, chopped
90 g (3 oz) back bacon, chopped
⅓ quantity of cornbread (page 228)
1 small egg
salt and pepper
1 × 1½–2 kg (3–4 lb) chicken

Fry the onion and bacon in 30 g (1 oz) butter. Crumble the cornbread roughly and add the onion, bacon and fat from the pan. Mix in the egg, salt and pepper.

Season the chicken inside, and fill two thirds full with the stuffing. Smear the skin with butter, and season generously with pepper. Weigh. Roast at 220C/425F/Gas 7 for 15 minutes per pound, until the juices run clear when tested with a sharp knife.

Chicken With Carrot and Ginger Sauce

Grilled chicken on a bed of bright orange sauce flecked with green herbs; a pretty dish, with a clean invigorating taste. Keep the whole meal fresh and lively, adding a green salad, or lightly steamed green vegetables, and new or waxy potatoes.

SERVES 4

4 boneless chicken breasts, skinned
finely grated zest and juice of ½ orange
finely grated zest and juice of ½ lemon
3 tablespoons olive oil
2½ cm (1 in) piece of fresh ginger, peeled and grated
600 g (1¼ lb) carrots, thinly sliced
½ teaspoon sugar
salt and pepper
300 ml (½ pt) chicken stock or 1 small glass white wine
fresh coriander leaves, or chives, chopped

Place the chicken breasts in a shallow dish. Mix the orange and lemon zest and juices, olive oil and ginger, and pour over the chicken. Turn to coat well, cover and leave in a cool place for 1–4 hours.

Drain the marinade into a pan and add sugar, carrots and enough stock or wine and water, barely to cover, and salt and pepper. Simmer until the carrots are very tender. Meanwhile, slash the chicken in 3 places on either side, brush with a little oil, season and grill 8 cm (3 in) away from a hot grill for 5–7 minutes on each side, until done. Baste with oil occasionally.

Liquidise the carrots and cooking liquid, adding, if necessary, enough extra stock or water to thin down to a creamy sauce. Adjust the seasoning.

Spoon a pool of carrot sauce on to each plate, and lay a chicken breast on top. Scatter with coriander leaves or chives, and serve.

Chicken and Tarragon Patties

These are wonderful, though I say so myself. Crisp on the outside, and then inside creamy, soft chicken scented with just a hint of lemon and tarragon, and the mild sharpness of fromage frais.

Children will love them – at least the ones I had to hand did – but grown-ups may refuse to let them get anywhere near. Serve for a family supper, or a smarter dinner party – they'll slot perfectly into either.

SERVES 4–6

125 g (4 oz) fresh breadcrumbs
milk
500 g (1 lb) chicken flesh (use breasts or joints, boned)
1 egg yolk
finely grated zest and juice of ½ lemon
½ tablespoon fresh tarragon, finely chopped
salt and pepper
3 tablespoons fromage frais
1 teaspoon cornflour

Coating:
1 egg, beaten
60 g (2 oz) dry breadcrumbs (white or brown)
melted butter or olive oil

Pour enough milk over the breadcrumbs to cover. Mince or process the chicken flesh. If need be, chop it as finely as you can by hand. Place in a bowl. Squeeze as much milk as you can out of the breadcrumbs and add to the chicken with the egg yolk, lemon zest, 1 tablespoon of the lemon juice, tarragon, salt and pepper. Blend the cornflour into the fromage frais, and add this too. Mix well to form a very thick paste.

Chill for 20–30 minutes, or whip into the freeze compartment for 5 minutes, to give the mixture a chance to firm up. Form 8 hamburger-shaped patties, 2–3 cm (1 in) thick, from the mixture (dampen your hands first to prevent sticking). Dip into the beaten egg and then coat well with the breadcrumbs. Leave in the fridge until ready to cook.

Either fry until golden brown in a mixture of butter and oil, or drizzle over a little oil or butter, and grill until nicely browned.

Hot Chicken Liver Mousse

The texture of these rich little morsels is soft and creamy, just firm, but nowhere near solid – and they look very pretty indeed wrapped in a film of green. If you can't get fresh spinach, use the leaves of a round lettuce instead.

They can be prepared several hours in advance, kept cool until needed, and cooked just before serving. They can also be eaten cold, though as they cool they lose some of their lightness. Serve on their own, or with a cool uncooked tomato sauce (page 271).

SERVES 4 as a first course

250 g (8 oz) chicken livers
½ small onion chopped
1 clove of garlic, chopped
45 g (1½ oz) butter, plus a little extra
1 egg white
1 tablespoon sherry
pinch of ground mace
salt and pepper
4 tablespoons double cream
12 large spinach leaves

Pick over the chicken livers and remove any greeny-yellow bits. Quarter and place in the bowl of the blender or liquidiser. Soften the onion and garlic in the butter over a medium heat, without browning. Let them cool slightly and add to the livers with the egg white, sherry, mace, salt and pepper. Blend until smooth, sieve, then chill for 15 minutes. Beat in the cream a spoonful at a time.

Pour boiling water over the spinach leaves, then drain and refresh under the cold tap. Spread out on the work surface and pat dry with kitchen paper. Snip out any tough stalks, and use the leaves to line 4 buttered dariole moulds or ramekins. Spoon the chicken liver mixture into the moulds, pressing lightly to make sure there are no air holes. Flip any trailing leaf over on to the mousse. Cover each loosely with silver foil, and stand in a roasting tray. Pour in warm water to a depth of 2–3 cm (1 in).

Bake at 180C/350F/Gas 4 for 25 minutes, until just firm. Remove from the oven, let them stand for 4 minutes in the *bain marie*, then turn out.

Chicken and Spinach Pâté

Pâté-making is as easy as pie, probably easier, in fact, and takes little time if you have a friendly butcher who'll mince the pork and bacon for you. You could ask him to throw in the chicken breast as well, but I prefer the rougher texture you get from chopping it by hand. Like most pâtés, this one improves on keeping, so make it at least one day in advance, preferably two.

SERVES 6–8

½ kg (1 lb) belly of pork
60 g (2 oz) streaky bacon
2 large chicken breasts, boned
125 g (4 oz) cooked spinach
2 tablespoons fresh parsley, finely chopped
1 tablespoon brandy
1 egg
1 tablespoon flour
salt and pepper
250 g (8 oz) streaky bacon

Ask your butcher to trim and mince the belly of pork with the 60 g (2 oz) streaky bacon. Remove any skin from the chicken breasts and chop. Add to the minced pork.

Squeeze as much water as you can out of the spinach and chop finely. Add to the meats with the parsley, brandy, egg and flour. Season with plenty of pepper and just a touch of salt (the streaky bacon will already have provided some saltiness). Mix the whole lot together well. Fry a small nugget to test the seasoning, and adjust accordingly.

Snip the rinds off the remaining streaky bacon and use to line a 500 g (1 lb) loaf tin, and pile in the pâté. Press down well, and flip the ends of the bacon over on to the top. Cover with silver foil and bake for 1¼ hours at 180C/350F/Gas 4. Remove from the oven, and weigh down the top with heavy tins. Leave weighted in this way, 8–48 hours. Turn out, and serve with good brown bread and butter, or hot toast.

Curried Turkey Turnovers

This first appeared as a Christmas recipe – another way to use up the mounds of leftover turkey. But it's a good year-round recipe for dealing with the remains of a big Sunday lunch. The ratio of meat to vegetables will vary according to what you have to hand. Altogether you need a total of approximately ¾ kg (1½ lb), excluding the celery, pepper and onion.

SERVES 4

1 onion, chopped (see above)
2 tablespoons olive oil
2 sticks celery, chopped
1 red or green pepper, chopped (optional)
250–400 g (8–14 oz) cooked turkey or chicken, chopped
a selection of vegetables, either raw or cooked: carrots, parsnip,
    cooked or thawed frozen peas, potato, chopped
½–1 tablespoon curry paste
2 tablespoons jellied juices from the turkey, or butter
salt
250 g (8 oz) puff pastry*
1 egg, beaten

Half cook the onion in the oil. Add the uncooked vegetables (except the peas). Sauté until they brown and soften. Add the cooked veg, peas and turkey, and mix well. Stir in the curry paste to taste, cook for a further 30 seconds. Add the butter or meat jelly, and salt. Cool. Quarter the pastry, and roll out each piece to a large circle about 3 mm (⅛ in) thick. Divide the mixture between the 4 circles, brush the edges with egg, and fold the pastry over the filling to form a semi-circle, crimping the edges together firmly. If you have time, rest for 30 minutes in the fridge. Brush with the egg, and bake at 220C/425F/Gas 7 for 15 minutes, until nicely puffed and browned.

Chicken and Soured Cream Pie

Instead of making one large pie, you could also make pasties with this mixture. Use either shortcrust* or puff pastry, roll out and cut out 23 cm (9 in) circles, heap up a mound of filling in the centre, brush the edges of the pastry with beaten egg, then bring up around the filling, pinching the edges firmly to seal. Make a small hole either side of the join to let the steam escape, brush the whole with beaten egg, and bake for 20 minutes at 230C/450F/Gas 8.

SERVES 6

500 g (1 lb) chicken meat (dark and light), finely chopped
2 tablespoons brandy
2 sprigs of thyme
1 small onion, chopped
1 clove of garlic, chopped
250 g (8 oz) carrot, finely chopped
2 sticks of celery, finely chopped
30 g (1 oz) butter
5 tablespoons soured cream
2 teaspoons flour
salt and pepper
500 g (1 lb) puff pastry*
1 egg, beaten

Mix the chicken with the brandy and the thyme. Cover and leave in a cool place for ½–2 hours. Sweat the onion, garlic, carrot and celery in the butter in a covered pan until the vegetables are tender. Add the marinaded chicken, and stir over a medium heat until the chicken is opaque. Beat the soured cream with the flour, and then stir into the chicken with salt and pepper. Leave to cool.

Roll out just over half the pastry, and line a 23 cm (9 in) pie dish. Fill with the chicken mixture. Roll out the remaining pastry. Brush the rim of the pie with a little beaten egg, and lay the pastry lid over it. Trim and crimp the edges to seal. Make a hole in the centre for the steam to escape. Score a few decorative patterns on the top without cutting through the pastry. Rest for at least 20 minutes in the fridge. Brush with the beaten egg.

Put a metal baking tray in the oven and set to 250C/475F/Gas 9. When fully heated, place the pie on the tray and cook for 15 minutes, then turn down the heat to 180C/350F/Gas 4 and cook for a further 20 minutes. Serve hot or cold.

Poussins With Chorizo Stuffing

Poussins, charming as they are to look at on the plate, tend not to be highly charged with flavour, so they need to be helped along with other punchier ingredients. To be fair, the flesh is wonderfully tender and juicy, and so it should be. Just as they haven't had time to develop much flavour, so they haven't had time to get tough and stringy. In this recipe they are filled with a spicy stuffing, and the breasts are protected by strips of bacon, you end up with a well-flavoured, pretty-as-a picture supper.

SERVES 4

4 poussins
olive oil
salt and paprika
7 rashers unsmoked streaky bacon

Stuffing:
½ small onion, finely chopped
1 small clove of garlic, finely chopped
½ red pepper, finely chopped
1 tablespoon olive oil
125 g (4 oz) mild or spicy chorizo sausage, skinned and chopped small
1 tablespoon lemon juice
finely grated zest of ½ a lemon
1 tablespoon fresh parsley, finely chopped
60 g (2 oz) fresh breadcrumbs
salt and pepper
1 small egg, beaten

To make the stuffing, cook the onion, garlic and red pepper in the oil until tender, without browning. Mix with all the stuffing ingredients except the egg. Add just enough egg to bind.

Season the insides of the poussins, and fill two thirds full with the stuffing. Close with a wooden cocktail stick. Any leftover stuffing can be rolled into small balls and baked in the same dish. Rub the skins of the birds with olive oil and season generously with salt and paprika. Time permitting, let them sit in the fridge for 30 minutes.

Snip the rinds off the bacon and lay over the breasts of the poussins. Roast at 180C/350F/Gas 4 for 50–60 minutes, until the juices run clear, basting occasionally. Lift off the bacon after 40 minutes to give the breasts time to brown. Serve with crisp bacon on the side.

Pheasant With Chestnuts

I know that peeling fresh chestnuts is a rotten, tedious job. But it is
worth doing just once or twice every autumn, because the taste of
new chestnuts simmered in a gamey stew is something extra special.
Get someone else to help, allow yourself plenty of time and settle
down to it. You could get away with using dried chestnuts, but they
need to be soaked overnight, and half-cooked before using. Some
delicatessens may stock the high-quality cooked chestnuts in
vacuum packs, though they are not cheap. If you do use them, add
half-way through the cooking time.

SERVES 4

½ kg (1 lb) fresh chestnuts
125 g (4 oz) bacon, derinded and cut into strips
oil or butter
1 onion, chopped
1 large carrot, chopped
1 pheasant
2 sprigs of thyme
finely grated zest of 1 orange
juice of 2 large oranges
salt and pepper
300–600 ml (½–1 pt) chicken or game stock
1 tablespoon redcurrant jelly

Slash the hard outer skin of the chestnuts. Place in a pan and bring
to the boil. Simmer for 2 minutes. Remove from the heat and,
taking no more than 2 or 3 chestnuts out of the water at a time,
remove both the outer and inner skins. If necessary, bring the water
back to the boil. Similarly, if the inner skins prove stubborn, return
to the pan and reheat.

Fry the bacon in just enough fat to prevent sticking. As soon as
the fat begins to run, add the onion and carrot and cook until the
onion is tender. Lift the vegetables and bacon out and spread on the
base of a casserole. Brown the pheasant in the fat, and sit on the top
of the veg, breast-side down. Pour off the excess fat and deglaze the
pan with the orange juice and 300 ml (½ pt) stock. Bring to the boil.

Add the thyme, orange zest, chestnuts, salt and pepper to the
casserole. Pour over the boiling liquid – there should be enough to
cover the chestnuts. If necessary, bring extra stock to the boil and
pour over. Cover tightly, and simmer very gently for 45 minutes, or

bake at 170C/325F/Gas 3, until the pheasant is tender and the chestnuts cooked. Drain off as much liquid as possible and skim off the fat. Keep the pheasant warm, while you pour the juices into a wide frying pan and boil hard until reduced by one third. Stir in the redcurrant jelly, taste and adjust the seasoning and pour over the casserole. Serve immediately.

Duck Breasts With Figs (or Grapes), Honey and Wine

The fresh figs that we buy here cannot, I'm sad to say, match up to the ones I've enjoyed in sunnier Mediterranean countries. To be at its best, a fig must be ripened on the tree, and eaten no more tan a matter of hours after it is picked – in which case it would be sacrilege to start cooking with it.

But the less impressive imported figs we get in England benefit enormously from the application of a modicum of heat, and some well-chosen flavourings. This is a simple, but glamorous dish of duck breasts with figs. Either buy ready-prepared duck breasts, or take the breasts off a whole duck and use the remainder to make a second meal next day, perhaps the ragout that follows this recipe.

SERVES 2

2 duck breasts
1 carrot, chopped
½ small onion, finely chopped
1 stick of cinnamon
1 glass red wine
1 oz butter
1½ tablespoons honey
1 tablespoon red wine vinegar
2 figs, or 250 g (8 oz) white muscat grapes, halved
salt and pepper

Marinate the duck with the carrot, onion, cinnamon and red wine – leave covered in the fridge for at least 1 hour, and up to 24 hours, turning occasionally. Take the duck out of the marinade and dry on kitchen paper. Bring the marinade to the boil, simmer for 1 minute, then strain.

Melt the butter in a heavy frying pan and brown the duck breasts quickly on both sides. Remove from the pan, and pour off the excess fat. Pour in the wine vinegar and marinade. Bring to the boil, stirring and scraping in all the residues. Stir in the honey, and return the duck to the pan. Cover and simmer gently for 10–13 minutes (depending on how well you like your duck cooked).

Remove the breasts from the pan, and keep warm. Boil the juices until reduced to a syrupy consistency. Meanwhile, thinly slice the duck breasts and arrange on plates. Pour any juices from the carving back into the sauce.

When the sauce is very thick and unctuous, add the quartered figs, or the grapes, and cook for a further few minutes, until hot and coated in sauce. Add salt and pepper, and spoon over and around the duck.

Ragoût of Duck With Mushrooms and Onions

We tend to assume that duck is frightfully expensive, and only for special, dressy occasions. But this isn't necessarily so. From a single duck you can make two filling meals for two, and duck stock as well.

Cut off the duck breasts and try the preceding recipe with figs and honey, or you could just grill them (brush the skinless side with a little oil) until crisp and brown on the outside, pink inside. Serve with a salad, or on a bed of lentils.

Use the remainder of the duck to make a stew like this one.

SERVES 2

Either 1 duck carcass (see preceding recipe) or 2 duck breasts
250 g (8 oz) pearl onions
175 g (6 oz) mushrooms, quartered
1 carrot, chopped
30 g (1 oz) butter
1 glass red wine
1 glass stock or water
2 sprigs of thyme
salt and pepper
15 g (½) oz) flour

Sever the drumsticks from the carcass if using, and strip as much meat as you can from the body. Leave the drumsticks whole, and cut the rest into strips. If using duck breasts, cut into strips.

Top and tail the onions, but don't bother peeling. Cook in boiling salted water for 5 minutes, and skin. Brown the onions and carrots lightly in 15 g (½ oz) butter in a large frying pan, then add the mushrooms and duck. Cook for 5 minutes, pour off the excess fat, then add the wine, stock or water, thyme, salt and pepper. Cover and simmer gently for 45–60 minutes, stirring and turning the drumsticks occasionally, until the meat is tender.

Mash the remaining butter with the flour to make *beurre manié*. Turn down the heat so that the sauce is barely simmering. Stir in small pieces of *beurre manié* and cook at this temperature for a further 5–10 minutes, stirring occasionally, until the sauce has thickened. Taste and adjust the seasoning.

Mallard With Satsumas and Pomegranate

One mallard, a wild duck, is enough to feed 2 generously. Unlike its domesticated cousin, the mallard is not at all fatty. It can, occasionally, be on the dry side, so keep basting it as it cooks. Otherwise it is easy to cook, and the gamey flavour marries well with satsuma juice and pomegranate seeds.

Serve this with lots of fresh, simple, green vegetables, or a mixed green salad, and boiled or steamed waxy potatoes.

SERVES 2

1 mallard
3 satsumas
1 pomegranate
30 g (1 oz) butter
salt and pepper

Stuff the mallard with one of the satsumas, halved. Squeeze the juice out of the other 2. Sit the duck on an oven-proof serving dish, and smear with butter. Pour the juice and a quarter of a pint of water over it. Season.

Split open the pomegranate and extract all the red seeds, taking great care to get rid of all the bitter white pith. Scatter over and around the duck. Bake at 230C/450F/Gas 8 for 25–35 minutes, depending on how rare you like it, basting frequently with its own juices.

Grilled Quail With Cherry Salad

Fat, juicy black cherries make an unusual salad to set off crisply grilled little quail. It would also be a pretty foil to a roast wild duck, or grilled duck breasts.

SERVES 2

250 g (½ lb) cherries
2 quail
olive oil or hazelnut oil
salt and pepper

Dressing:
finely grated zest and juice of ½ lemon
1 tablespoon olive oil
½ tablespoon fresh mint, chopped
3 tablespoons single cream
salt and pepper

Slit the cherries and remove the stones – work over a bowl so that the juices that fall in are not lost. You should end up with around 1 tablespoon of juice – if necessary crush a couple of the cherries to get a little extra. Set the cherries aside, and beat a roughly equal quantity of light olive oil, or, even better, hazelnut oil into the cherry juice with a good twist of pepper.

With a sharp pair of scissors, cut along the back bones of the quail, keeping as close as possible to the bone. Then snip down the other side to remove the backbone completely. Flatten the quail out with the heel of your hands, and thread a skewer through each one to keep flat. Place in a bowl, and pour the cherry juice over them. Set aside for at least 20 minutes, or until ready to grill. Add any juice that seeps out of the cherries.

Meanwhile, make the dressing for the cherry salad. Beat 1 tablespoon lemon juice with ½ teaspoon lemon zest, olive oil or hazelnut oil, salt, pepper and mint. When it is well mixed, whisk in the cream a tablespoon at a time.

Grill the quail, skin up, for 10 minutes, then turn over, brush with the marinade and grill the other side for a further 5–6 minutes. Test with a sharp knife to see if it is cooked through.

Just before serving, mix the cherries with the cream dressing, and serve with the grilled quail.

MEAT

Brasato al Barolo – Beef Stewed in Red Wine

Barolo at its best is one of Italy's great wines, rich and fruity and heady. It comes from the hills to the south-west of Turin, hard by the slopes of Asti, home of Asti Spumante. It is the proper wine to use in this recipe, but should you prefer to keep your Barolo for drinking, a lesser red wine is perfectly acceptable. *Brasato al Barolo*, with its long slow cooking, transforms a relatively cheap cut of beef into a melting, tender joint.

SERVES 6

1¼ kg (2½ lb) piece of shin of beef or brisket
125 g (4 oz) unsmoked streaky bacon, cut into strips
seasoned flour
3 tablespoons fresh parsley, chopped
2 leaves of sage, chopped
the leaves of 1 sprig of rosemary, chopped
3 cloves of garlic, finely chopped
¼ teaspoon ground nutmeg
salt and pepper
1½ tablespoons olive oil
30 g (1 oz) butter
1 onion, sliced
2 bay leaves
1 large carrot, finely chopped
2 stalks of celery, chopped
1 bottle Barolo, or another full-bodied red wine

Cut deep slits in the beef with a small sharp knife and push in the strips of bacon with the end of a teaspoon. Coat with seasoned flour. Mix the parsley, sage, rosemary and garlic. Add the nutmeg, salt and pepper. Heat the olive oil with the butter in a frying pan and fry the onion gently until almost tender. Turn up the heat and add the meat, the mixed herbs and spices, the bay leaves, carrot and celery. Brown the meat on all sides, turning frequently.

Lift out the meat and place in a casserole large enough to take the meat with only a 3–5 cm (1–2 in) gap all around. Pour off as much fat as you can from the vegetables, and then sprinkle with 2 tablespoons flour. Stir, then pour in a generous glassful of wine and boil hard until reduced by half. Add the remaining wine, and bring to the boil. Pour the wine and vegetables over the meat. Either simmer very gently on top of the stove, or bake at 150C/300F/Gas 2 for at least 3 hours, preferably 4 or best of all 5, turning occasionally, until the meat is extremely tender.

Lift the meat out on to a serving dish and keep warm. If the sauce seems thin, boil hard to reduce. Pour over the beef. Serve, cut into thick slices, with mashed potatoes or polenta*.

Fillet Steak With Stilton

I'm not much of a red meat eater, but every once in a while I long for a really juicy steak. Not one of those awful leathery thin things, which are such a disappointment. No, if I'm going to eat a steak, then I am prepared to splash out on a thick slice of best fillet or sirloin. It's a rare occasion, after all.

Some people may consider adding stilton to a good steak is gilding the lily. Sometimes I'd be inclined to agree with them. Then again, the thought of a mouthful of rare fillet with melting hot stilton is hard to resist.

SERVES 1

1 fillet steak, about 4 cm (1½ in) thick
30 g (1 oz) stilton
melted butter
pepper

Heat the grill thoroughly, until it is as hot as it can possibly be. Trim the steak and, with a sharp knife, cut a slit horizontally through the centre, to form an inner cavity. Stuff with half the stilton. Season with pepper. Line the grill pan with silver foil.

Brush the rack with melted butter, then the steak too. With the meat close to the heat, grill the steak. For a rare steak, cook for approximately 2½ minutes per side, for medium rare 3 minutes per side, medium 3½ minutes per side, and for well done 5 minutes per side.

Pile the remaining stilton on top of the steak and rush back under the grill for 30 seconds or so, until the cheese is hot and melting. Serve quickly, pouring the juices from the pan over the steak.

Steak Teriyaki

It was another one of my rare yearnings for steak that led me to this recipe. The dark sticky *teriyaki* sauce sets off the meatiness of a good steak to a tee. Real Japanese *sake* (rice wine) brings an irreplaceable taste to the sauce, and many off-licences now sell it in small bottles. What you don't use in the recipe you can drink, hot or cold, with the meal. *Mirin*, a sweet rice wine, is harder to find, unless you have a handy oriental food shop. You can substitute sweet sherry or 2 more tablespoons of *sake* and 1 of sugar. It won't be quite the same of course, but *c'est la vie*.

If your steak is on the thin side, reduce the cooking times accordingly.

SERVES 2

2 sirloin steaks, 2–3 cm (1 in) thick
oil
2 tablespoons *sake*, or dry sherry
2 tablespoons dark soy sauce
2 tablespoons *mirin*, or sweet sherry
1 teaspoon sugar

Coat the base of a heavy frying pan, large enough to take both steaks, with a thin film of oil. Place over a high heat. When very hot, add the steaks to the pan, and cook for 6 minutes, turning once.

About a minute after you have turned the steaks, spoon the *sake* over the meat. Don't worry about all the smoke! Cover the pan, and cook for the final 2 minutes.

Lift out the steaks, put them on a plate and keep warm. Add the soy sauce, *mirin* and sugar to the pan, and stir and scrape all the residue into the liquid. Let it boil hard until reduced by half. Return the steaks to the pan with any juices and cook for about 1 minute more, turning once.

Gujerati Beef Cream Kebabs

I'm often asked what my favourite recipes are. It's an impossible question to answer. It depends on my mood, on the time of the year, on the situation I'm in. Still, I count this recipe as one of the best I've ever cooked. It comes from Madhur Jaffrey's *A Taste of India* (published in paperback by Pan). The book itself is a joy to read, with her vivid descriptions of a childhood in Delhi and later travels throughout India.

The deceptively minimal marinade gives the beef an exquisite balance of flavour, which floods out as your teeth sink through the crisp coating. I've tried it too with venison, and I'd be hard put to say which was better.

SERVES 4

750 g (1½ lb) 2–3 cm (1 in) thick sirloin steak
2 teaspoons ginger, very finely grated
1 clove of garlic, crushed
1–2 teaspoons fresh hot green chilli, very finely chopped
4 tablespoons double cream
¾ teaspoon salt
vegetable oil
1 large egg, beaten
90 g (3 oz) dried breadcrumbs

Trim the meat and cut into 2½ cm (1 in) cubes. Put in a bowl and add the ginger, garlic, green chilli, cream and salt. Mix well. Cover and refrigerate for at least 3 hours, and up to 36 hours.

Just before you are ready to eat, pour enough oil into a wok or deep-frying pan to come to a depth of 2–3 cm (1 in). Heat over a medium-low flame. Put the breadcrumbs in a dish. Dip the meat cubes one at a time into the beaten egg and then into the breadcrumbs, rolling them around until they are encrusted.

When the oil is heated, put in as many meat cubes as the pan will hold in a single layer. Fry, turning occasionally, until golden brown. Try one to see if it is done to your taste on the inside. If need be, give them a minute or so longer.

Grilled Rabbit With Sauce Rémoulade

Rabbit is an unfairly neglected meat, looked down upon as the food of the poor, and occasionally revived in a fashionable 'peasant' dish. Well, oysters, too, were once the food of the poor, and look at them now, right up there with caviar and champagne. I cannot honestly say that I would elevate rabbit to the same heady heights, but it is certainly worthy of more than just the occasional stew. It does have to be young tender rabbit if it's to be cooked quickly, and steer well clear of packets of frozen rabbit chunks from China – nothing political about this advice, but in my experience (once only but that was enough) they are utterly devoid of flavour or substance. If you don't have time to make the sauce, serve with wholegrain or Dijon mustard instead.

SERVES 4

4 rabbit joints
4 tablespoons matzo meal, or fine dry breadcrumbs
salt and pepper

Marinade:
150 ml (5 fl oz) sunflower, safflower or grapeseed oil
75 ml (2½ fl oz) extra virgin olive oil
2 tablespoons chives, chopped
1 tablespoon fresh parsley, chopped

Sauce rémoulade:
3 small pickled dill cucumbers, chopped
1 tablespoon capers
150 g (5 oz) mayonnaise
2 tablespoons French mustard
1 tablespoon chives, chopped
½ tablespoon fresh parsley, chopped
1 teaspoon caster sugar
salt and pepper

Halve each rabbit joint and put in a shallow dish with the marinade ingredients. Turn to coat well. Cover and marinade in a cool place for 1 hour, turning occasionally.

Drain the capers and rinse well. Fold into the mayonnaise with the other sauce ingredients. Taste and adjust the seasoning.

Drain the rabbit, and coat each portion in matzo meal. Grill under a hot grill, basting with the marinade, until just cooked through – this should take about 7–10 minutes on each side. If the

coating is threatening to burn, turn the grill down slightly, or move
the rabbit an inch or 2 further away from the heat. Season and serve
quickly, with the *sauce rémoulade*.

Rabbit and Apricot Terrine

A fruity, thyme-scented terrine for a summer supper, or first
course. You'll need to buy about 750 g (1½ lb) rabbit if the bones
are still in it, then strip off the meat when you get home (unless
you've got a friendly butcher).

Some supermarkets are now selling ready-boned rabbit loin and
leg which makes life even easier. Avoid anything labelled 'casserole'
rabbit, which will as like as not be stringy and tough. Don't
overlook the fact that you'll have to start this recipe at least 24 hours
in advance.

SERVES 4–6

500 g (1 lb) boneless rabbit meat
125 g (4 oz) dried apricots
30 g (1 oz) hazelnuts
2 carrots, thickly sliced
1 stick of celery, thickly sliced
150 ml (¼ pt) dry white wine
½ sprig of thyme
salt and pepper
1 envelope powdered gelatine

Cut the rabbit meat into rough chunks. Stuff each dried apricot
with a hazelnut. Put the carrots, celery, white wine and ¼ pt water
into a pan, and bring to the boil. Simmer for 5 minutes. Leave to
cool. Put rabbit and stuffed apricots into a large bowl. Add the
thyme and the carrots, celery and cooking liquid, and mix well.
Leave to marinade, covered, overnight.

Drain, and season. Pack the meat, apricots and vegetables into a
well-buttered terrine. Heat one third of marinade in a small pan,
until hot but not boiling. Sprinkle gelatine on the surface, and stir
until dissolved. Mix in the remaining liquid, a little at a time. Pour
over the terrine – there should be more than enough to cover, so
keep any extra in reserve.

Cover the terrine with foil, and stand in a roasting dish, filled to a
depth of 2–3 cm (1 in) with hot water. Place in the oven, and bake at

150C/300F/Gas 2 for 2½ hours. Check from time to time, and add more of the marinade if the terrine is looking dry.

Remove from the oven, and weigh down the foil with tins of food, or heavy stones. When cool, transfer to fridge to finish setting. Serve with good bread.

Savoy Cabbage and Ham au Gratin

Like many of the best cabbage dishes, this is simple, homely and pleasing. Use the best cooked ham that you can get. If it must come out of a packet, look for one which states clearly 'no added water' – some ham may have as much as 15% or even 20% water pumped into it. Apart from the annoyance of having to pay for something that you could get straight out of the kitchen tap at no extra cost, ponder too on the taste of the ham. If 15% of it is water, then you are getting a diluted version of the real thing.

SERVES 2

½ small savoy cabbage, shredded
salt
125 g (4 oz) cooked ham, cut into thin strips
30 g (1 oz) butter
½ small onion, chopped
30 g (1 oz) flour
300 ml (½ pt) milk
3 tablespoons parmesan, freshly grated
ground nutmeg
salt and pepper

Drop the cabbage into a pan of lightly salted boiling water. Bring back to the boil and simmer for 1 minute. Drain quickly and run under the cold tap.

Melt the butter and add the onion. Cook until soft without browning, then add the flour. Cook for 1 minute, and draw off the heat. Add the milk gradually to make a white sauce. Return to the heat and bring back to the boil. Simmer gently for 10 minutes, stirring occasionally. Add the cabbage, ham, half the parmesan, nutmeg, salt and pepper to taste. Heat through thoroughly. Spread out in a gratin dish and sprinkle with the remaining parmesan. Whip under a very hot grill until the top is nicely speckled with brown.

Pork Chops With Onion and Pear Marmelade

Onion marmelades and confits or, more prosaically, chutneys, have shown their faces on countless restaurant menus in the past few years – many of the culinary *maîtres* have taken great and justifiable pride in their perfect, elegant balancing of sweet and sour, onion and spices. To make my *marmelade*, I've added dried pears, which go well with pork, as do most dried fruit. The chutney can be made 2 or 3 days in advance and kept, covered, in the fridge.

SERVES 4

3 medium onions, sliced
60 g (2 oz) butter
175 g (6 oz) dried pears
1 teaspoon coriander seeds, lightly crushed
2 tablespoons white wine vinegar or sherry vinegar
4 tablespoons orange juice
4 tablespoons water
½ teaspoon salt
1 teaspoon dark muscovado sugar
4 pork chops
pepper

Melt the butter, and add the onions. Cover and stew over a low heat for 15 minutes. Slice the dried pears thinly, and add to the onions with the coriander seeds. Stew for a further 15 minutes, then add the vinegar, orange juice, sugar, water and salt. Uncover and simmer until the liquid has evaporated and the *marmelade* is thick and melting. Set aside until almost ready to eat.

Brush the pork chops with a little oil, and sprinkle with pepper. Grill under a well-heated grill until nicely browned and cooked through. Meanwhile, reheat the onion and pear *marmelade* very gently. Stir in any juices exuded by the chops, and serve a good dollop alongside each grilled pork chop.

Zampone With Lentils

Zampone, a speciality of Modena in northern Italy, is a pig's trotter stuffed with a mixture of minced pork, salt, pepper, garlic and sometimes other spices. Don't panic. I'm not about to suggest that you make your own *zampone*. That's best left to the experts.

Vacuum-packed *zampone* can be bought from Italian delicatessens in the winter months. They start appearing in late November or early December ready for Christmas and the New Year. My local Italian delicatessen stocks two types. Signora Gerra tells me time and again that the better choice are the ones that need a good 2 or 3 hours' simmering. To her chagrin, I usually take the pre-cooked ones that are ready in 20 minutes or so. With their rich, gelatinous texture and meaty stuffing, they are one of the perfect cold-weather convenience foods.

Big green or brown lentils, which hold their shape well when cooked, are the natural partners to *zampone*. Look out in the wholefood shops and delicatessens for Puy lentils, the choicest of them all. The lentils can be cooked in advance and reheated, with a little extra water, as you cook the *zampone*.

SERVES 4 generously

375 g (12 oz) Puy or large brown or green lentils
1 onion, sliced
3 tablespoons olive oil
1 large clove of garlic, finely chopped
1 large carrot, chopped
2 sticks celery, chopped
1 sprig of marjoram, chopped
1 × 400g (14 oz) tin of tomatoes
salt and pepper
1 tablespoon fresh parsley, chopped
1 *zampone*

Wash the lentils well, in at least 2 changes of water, picking out any stray small stones. Place in a pan, and cover generously with water. Place over a low flame and bring very slowly to the boil. Simmer for 10 minutes until half-cooked. Drain, reserving the cooking water.

Soften the onion in 2 tablespoons of the oil over a medium heat. Add the garlic, carrot and celery and cook for a further 2 minutes. Add the chopped marjoram and the tomatoes, with their juice, and stir with a wooden spoon, crushing the tomatoes against the sides of the pan. Simmer for 5 minutes, then add the par-cooked lentils. Simmer for a further 15 minutes, or until the lentils are soft but still firm, adding a little of their cooking water if necessary. The liquid should be almost totally absorbed. Add salt and pepper to taste, and stir in the remaining olive oil and the parsley.

Meanwhile, simmer the *zampone* for 20 minutes in a large pan of water, or according to the instructions on the packet. Slice, and serve on a bed of lentils.

Pork Escalopes With Pear Sauce

Whenever I'm stuck for ideas for recipes I go shopping, meandering from the butcher's to the greengrocer's and on down the high street until something clicks. What goes with pork, I wondered, as I stared at the pile of pink pork escalopes – apple, sage, both very nice, thank you, but hardly inspired. On to the greengrocers, and there's the answer: a big tray of golden pears.

I made two versions of the pear sauce; the first a plain pear purée, the second a richer version with cream. They were both good – the former perhaps more appropriate for an every day supper, the latter for a swisher occasion. If you cannot buy tender thin pork escalopes, then you could use pork chops instead, and lengthen the cooking time appropriately. Whenever I can, I buy free-range pork. It's not only a question of principles, it really does taste appreciably better.

SERVES 4

4 pears, roughly chopped
4 pork escalopes
seasoned flour
45 g (1½ oz) butter
salt and pepper
150 ml (5 fl oz) whipping cream (optional)
1–2 tablespoons lemon juice

Put the pears, core, skin and all, into a pan with 3 tablespoons water. Cover and stew gently until soft. Sieve to remove the core and skin.

Dust each of the escalopes in seasoned flour. Melt the butter in a large frying pan and, when foaming gently, fry the escalopes *slowly* in the butter, until just cooked through, with no trace of pink – about 4–5 minutes on each side. Remove from the pan, and keep warm.

Tip the pear purée into the pan, season lightly and bring to the boil, stirring and scraping the butter and residue from the escalopes. If you wish to enrich the sauce, add the cream at this point. Let it bubble for about 3 minutes, stirring to prevent sticking. Remove from the heat and stir in the lemon juice to taste. Adjust other seasonings, and pour over the base of a warmed serving dish. Lay the escalopes on top, and serve.

Pork Medallions With Mushrooms and Sorrel Sauce

Speedy but smart, this recipe. With its generous slosh of cream in the sauce it isn't an every day sort of a recipe, but it is a treat worth waiting for once in a while. It's a good number to have up your sleeve for last minute dinner parties, as long as you can find the sorrel (occasionally available in smarter greengrocers' shops), or grow it yourself. It gives the dish a sharp green acidity that balances out the richness.

If sorrel is completely unobtainable use soured cream, and make a mental note to grow your own sorrel next year. It's the one plant I've managed to grow with no problems whatsoever in window boxes, containers, and in the garden. It survives my far from green fingers, so I reckon just about anyone can get it to grow.

SERVES 2–3

1 pork fillet
30 g (1 oz) butter
125 g (4 oz) mushrooms, sliced
a handful of sorrel leaves, shredded
6 tablespoons double cream
salt and pepper

Cut the fillet into slices 2–3 cm (1 in) thick. Melt the butter in a frying pan just large enough to take all the fillets. When it is gently foaming, add the meat and fry gently until nicely browned and cooked right through – check one with a sharp knife.

Remove the meat from the pan, and keep warm. Fry the mushrooms in the butter until tender, and arrange around the pork. Add the sorrel to the pan, and stir until it collapses into a purée. Pour in the cream and bring to the boil. Season, and pour over the meat and mushrooms.

Pork With Stilton Sauce

This is a good quick way to use up the scraggy dried ends of stilton, leftover after a dinner party. You know the ones I mean, sitting somewhere in the back of the fridge, abandoned and dispirited after their initial flush of grandeur.

SERVES 2

375 g (12 oz) boneless pork steaks
seasoned flour
30 g (1 oz) butter or oil
1 tablespoon white wine vinegar
90 ml (3 fl oz) red or white grape juice
90 g (3 oz) stilton, crumbled
cayenne pepper

Cut the pork into 1 cm (½ in) cubes and toss in seasoned flour. Heat
the butter in a medium frying pan, and fry the pork gently until
browned and cooked through. Keep warm. Drain the fat from the
pan, and pour in the vinegar and grape juice. Stir, scraping up all
the meat residues, and bring to the boil. Turn the heat down low
and stir in the cheese until it all melts. Add cayenne pepper to taste.

Either pour over the pork and serve with rice or mashed potatoes,
or toss the pork and sauce into hot tagliatelle or spaghetti.

Rillons

If we lived in France there would be no need for this recipe. *Rillons*,
melting, brown cubes of slow-cooked belly of pork, are a basic item
in the repertoire of every charcuterie in the land.

The French buy them to eat cold, with bread and a salad. Or they
may be heated through in a frying pan in their own fat, and served
on a bed of mashed potatoes with fried slices of apple, or a sharp
apple sauce, and lots of French mustard. Instead of mashed
potatoes, you could cook up a pan full of green lentils. Toss some of
the fat from the *rillons* into the lentils to glaze.

SERVES 4

1 kg (2 lb) belly of pork
60 g (2 oz) lard
salt and pepper
1 bay leaf
6 allspice berries
1 sprig of thyme

Cut the belly of pork into pieces about 8 cm (3 in) long by 5 cm
(2 in) wide. Smear the lard over an oven-proof dish large enough to
take all the pork in a single layer. Place the pork in the dish, and
season very lightly with a little salt and pepper. Tuck the bay leaf,

allspice and thyme in among the pork. Add water to a depth of about 5 mm (¼ in) and cover with silver foil.

Bake at 150C/300F/Gas 2 for about 3 hours, basting occasionally, until the meat is tender. Uncover and drain off the fat and liquid. Strain and leave to set, then lift off the fat. (Use it for frying potatoes, or bread – it has an excellent flavour.)

Return the cubes of meat to the oven uncovered, this time set higher, to 200C/400F/Gas 6, to brown. Once they are lightly browned, remove. Serve hot or cold.

Steamed Garlic and Black Bean Spare Ribs

Chinese or American spare ribs are not the same as English spare ribs. Chinese spare ribs are cut from the belly of pork, whereas ours are located at the neck end. It is a distinction worth remembering when you ask the butcher for spare ribs. We've become familiar with grilled spare ribs, but they can also be steamed to keep them moist and tender.

SERVES 4 as a first course, 2 as a main course

500 g (1 lb) Chinese pork spare ribs
2 teaspoons cornflour
1 tablespoon oil

Marinade:
3 cloves of garlic, very finely chopped
2½ cm (1 in) piece of ginger, very finely chopped
1 tablespoon black bean sauce
½ teaspoon sugar
1 teaspoon five-spice powder
1 tablespoon dark soy sauce
1 tablespoon light soy sauce

Ask your butcher to cut the ribs into 8–10 cm (3–4 in) lengths. It is not the end of the world if they are full length, except that you may not be able to fit them into the steamer basket. Trim off any gristle. Mix all the marinade ingredients. Turn the spare ribs in the marinade, cover and set aside for ½–2 hours.

Sprinkle the cornflour over the spare ribs, and mix well. Find a plate that will sit comfortably in your steamer, leaving gaps around the sides for the steam to circulate. Arrange the ribs on the plate in a single layer (you may need to use 2 plates and tiers). Drizzle the oil over the ribs. Steam fast for 35 minutes, until the pork is tender.

Gammon Steaks With Spiced Nectarines

Within reason, meat and fruit go together extremely well. Which is not to say that all fruit goes with all meat. But lamb with apricots, for instance, can be marvellous. So too can duck with cherries. Mind you, it can also be intensely unpleasant if some cheapskate chef insists on using cocktail cherries and not the real thing.

Gammon and pineapple is another terror of tacky catering. The dreaded cocktail cherry or glacé cherry, equally bad under the circumstances, has a tendency to make an appearance here too, but at least it is not an integral part of the dish. It's the slice of tinned pineapple, still sticky with syrup, laid on top of what might once have been a fairly innocuous piece of gammon, that is the real horror.

Personally, I'm not entirely convinced that fresh pineapple with gammon is much of an improvement. A much better duo is gammon with fresh nectarines or peaches.

SERVES 2

1 nectarine or peach
1½ tablespoons white wine or sherry vinegar
1 tablespoon caster sugar
3 allspice berries, lightly crushed
4 peppercorns, lightly crushed
½ vanilla pod*
pinch of ground nutmeg
2 gammon steaks
oil

Pour boiling water over the nectarine, leave for 20 seconds, drain and refresh under the cold tap. Skin and cut in 8 slices. Place the vinegar, sugar and spices in a pan with 5 tablespoons water. Stir over a medium heat until the sugar has dissolved. Bring up to the boil, remove the vanilla pod, and then simmer for 5 minutes. Strain, and return the liquid to the pan.

Line the grill pan with silver foil. Brush the gammon steaks with a little oil, and grill. While they are grilling, add the nectarine slices to the pan, and bring back to the boil. Simmer, turning the fruit in the juices, for about 5 minutes or until tender. Lift them out with a slotted spoon and keep warm on a serving plate with the gammon steaks. Turn up the heat under the saucepan and boil until the juices are syrupy. Add any juices from the gammon caught in the grill pan, and stir. Pour over the gammon and nectarines and serve.

Steamed Chinese Dumplings

I love wandering around Chinese supermarkets, with their crowded shelves of unfamiliar tins and packages. I have to exercise mammoth self-restraint in the kitchen equipment section, piled up with huge pot-bellied earthenware jars, sharp cleavers, and woks. I've already got a stack of bamboo steaming baskets half-filling one kitchen cupboard.

I use them for steaming all sorts of things, but particularly little Chinese dumplings and dim-sums. For large parties I may cheat and buy frozen dim-sums that lurk in the freezers at the Chinese supermarket. For smaller numbers I make these pork and water-chestnut dumplings myself.

SERVES 10 as a first course, 4–6 as a main course

250 g (8 oz) plain flour
pinch of salt
375 g (12 oz) lean pork, finely minced
6 water-chestnuts, finely chopped
2 spring onions, finely chopped
½ tablespoon dark soy sauce
1 tablespoon sesame oil
½ teaspoon Chinese five-spice powder
pinch of cayenne pepper

Sieve the flour and salt. Add enough water to make a soft dough. Knead until smooth and elastic, adding extra flour if necessary. Cover and leave to relax in the fridge.

Mix the water-chestnuts and spring onions thoroughly with all the remaining ingredients.

Break off walnut-sized pieces of dough and roll out on a floured board into very thin circles. Place a heaped teaspoon of the pork mixture on each circle and fold in half, pressing the edges together to form semi-circles. Steam on a lightly greased foil-lined steaming basket for 10–12 minutes, until cooked through. Serve with extra soy sauce.

Ballotine of Lamb With Couscous Stuffing

A boned stuffed shoulder of lamb is just the thing for a dinner party, especially if, like me, carving isn't your forte. The round 'melon' of lamb is cut in wedges like a cake. It can also be served cold, but use oil not butter and trim as much fat as you can off the meat before stuffing.

SERVES 6–8

Stuffing:
60 g (2 oz) couscous
1 small onion, chopped
30 g(1 oz) butter
125 g (4 oz) dried apricots, chopped
60 g (2 oz) toasted hazelnuts*, skins rubbed off, chopped
2 tablespoons fresh coriander leaf, chopped
1 tablespoon lemon juice
salt and pepper
1 egg, beaten

1 shoulder of lamb, boned
salt and pepper
30 g (1 oz) butter
150 ml (¼ pt) oloroso sherry

Pour 150 ml (¼ pt) boiling water on to the couscous, stir and set aside until the water is absorbed, stirring occasionally. Fry the onion in the butter until golden. Stir into the couscous with the apricots, hazelnuts, coriander, lemon juice, salt and pepper. Add enough beaten egg to bind – you'll probably only need about half.

Spread out the lamb on the work surface, skin-side down. Season and pile the filling in the centre. Now draw the meat up and around the filling – you may find you have a little too much so scoop out any excess. The meat should just enclose all the stuffing.

Cut 4 lengths of string, a good 60 cm (2 ft) long. Slide the first under the lamb, bring the ends up, and knot tightly. Take the second string, and repeat at right angles. Now do the same with the remaining 2 pieces of string, securing the meat between the first 2 ties, so that you end up with a melon-shaped ball of lamb completely enclosing the filling. If necessary, tie more string around, or sew up the gaps with a needle and thread.

Sit the lamb, knot-side underneath, on a lightly buttered oven-proof dish, and smear with butter. Season. Cook at 190C/375F/Gas 5 for 25 minutes to the pound, weighed *after* stuffing. Half-way through the cooking time, pour the oloroso sherry over the lamb. Let it rest for 10 minutes when cooked, snip off the string, and carve in wedges, as if it were a melon.

Grilled Butterflied Leg of Lamb

This is an excellent way of cooking lamb – the inside stays moist and tender, while the outside becomes a deep crusty brown. It is also very simple, so don't be put off by the length of the method; I've given it in some detail, so that you get it just right.

Ask your butcher to bone the leg of lamb for you. He doesn't have to fiddle about with fancy tunnel-boning but should cut through the thinnest part of the meat along the bone. Ask him, too, to trim off the skin and as much fat and sinew as possible. The result should be a flattish, vaguely butterfly-shaped piece of lamb. In fact this is easy enough to do at home, but a good butcher will do it in half the time. Why waste yours?

SERVES 6

1 boned leg of lamb

Marinade:
juice of 2 lemons
1 onion, chopped
3 cloves of garlic, sliced
150 ml (5 fl oz) olive oil
2 bay leaves, crumbled
2 tablespoons fresh mint
8 peppercorns, lightly crushed

Mix the marinade ingredients. Pour a third into a shallow dish large enough to take the lamb flat. Make a few deep slashes in the lamb at its thickest parts. Lie flat in the dish and pour the remaining marinade over the top. Cover, and leave in the fridge or a cool place for 8–24 hours, turning occasionally.

Pre-heat the grill to its highest temperature, and arrange the grill rack so that you can get the meat very close to the heat. Brush bits of onion and herbs off the meat. Strain the marinade, reserving the liquid for basting.

Grill the lamb, cut side up first, very close to the heat, for 5–7 minutes on each side, to give a deep brown crust. Re-arrange the grill rack so that the lamb is 10–12 cm (4–5 in) from the heat, and give it a further 12–19 minutes on each side, depending on how well you like it done. Baste with the marinade every time you turn it. Keep an eye on it, and test by plunging a knife into the centre – I turn off the heat the moment the scarlet translucence of raw meat

disappears, to give the most perfect succulent pink lamb. Lift on to
a serving dish, and relax in a warm oven for 15 minutes before
carving. Serve the meat juices with the lamb.

Rack of Lamb With Green Peppercorn Crust

I go through phases of being wildly enthusiastic about particular
flavourings, herbs, spices or whatever. Usually with some justifi-
cation, because they are especially nice, but I do have to watch out
that they don't appear in every single recipe and article I write.

Fresh ginger, coriander leaves or seeds and mint have all featured
prominently, and so too have green peppercorns. Their strange,
almost metallic taste means that they have to be used with discre-
tion, but they give the crisp crust that coats the lamb in this recipe a
pleasing aromatic spiciness.

If you want to increase the quantities, buy 2 racks of lamb, and
make a Guard of Honour out of them: sew them together at the
base, skin-side outside, and lean them in towards each other so that
the bones criss-cross at the top. Secure with string, and cook in the
same way as a single rack.

SERVES 2–3

1 rack of lamb
1 tablespoon green peppercorns
60 g (2 oz) breadcrumbs
30 g (1 oz) butter, melted
small bunch of watercress

Wrap silver foil around the exposed bones to prevent burning. Trim
off the skin and most of the fat. Place on a roasting tin. Crush the
peppercorns roughly, draining first if they are in brine. Mix with
the breadcrumbs and butter.

Press this mixture on to the skinned side of the lamb, coating
well. Roast at 220C/425F/Gas 7 for 15 minutes per pound, plus 15
minutes extra for slightly pink, juicy lamb. Increase the time by 5
minutes per pound if you prefer it well-done. After 20 minutes or
so, check that the breadcrumbs are not burning – cover with foil if
necessary.

Turn off the oven, and open the door slightly. Leave the lamb to
rest for 5 minutes. Remove the foil from the bone tips, and replace
with paper cutlet frills if you have any. Lift on to a serving plate,
and tuck the watercress around it.

Spiced Lamb Sausages With Tzatziki

I do like contrasts of really hot and really cold foods, both temperature- and spice-wise. This combination is hot and cold in both senses, with chillis in one half and cool cucumber and yoghurt in the other.

If you don't have a processor or mincer, buy the lamb and pork fat from a friendly butcher, and ask him to mince them together for you. If you buy lamb on the bone, get a good ¾ kg (1½ lb) meat to allow for waste.

SERVES 4

½ cucumber
1 tablespoon white wine vinegar
salt and pepper
generous 150 g (5 oz) thick Greek yoghurt
1 clove of garlic, crushed
1 tablespoon fresh mint, chopped
500 g (1 lb) boneless lamb (leg or shoulder)
125 g (4 oz) pork fat
1–2 green chillis, seeded and finely chopped
½ tablespoon fresh ginger, grated
½ teaspoon ground cumin
olive oil

Dice the cucumber and spread out in a colander. Sprinkle with the vinegar and a little salt. Leave to drain for 1 hour, then pat dry with kitchen paper or a clean tea-towel. Mix into the yoghurt with the garlic and mint, and season with pepper and more salt if necessary. Chill.

Mince the lamb and pork fat together. Mix well with the chilli, ginger and cumin and a little salt. Break off a small piece and fry to test the seasoning – adjust accordingly. Divide the mixture into 8 and flatten each piece to form an elongated pattie about 1 cm (½ in) thick.

Brush the grill rack with oil to prevent sticking. Brush the surface of the lamb 'sausages' with oil too, and grill under a high heat until nicely browned on both sides. Serve with the chilled yoghurt and cucumber.

Tomato Bredy

Bay leaves, chillies, cinnamon and garlic may sound like a strange mixture, but in fact they combine very well to give a delicious and unusual flavour to this stew. It's a Cape Malay recipe, from South Africa. Malays were brought over to South Africa by the Dutch as slaves and there developed a spicy and unique style of cooking, of necessity using cheap ingredients.

I first tried this Tomato Bredy when I was at university, using scrag end of lamb, which is a good, cheap alternative to oxtail. I made it in large quantities to feed a small army of fellow students and it was a roaring success. Now that I am no longer constricted by the enforced economies of a student grant, it remains a firm favourite.

The bredy is one of those happy dishes that can be cooked in advance and reheated, and benefits from it. It will also make it easier to pick out the bay leaves and pieces of cinnamon stick before serving if you wish to do so. I usually leave them in, and just warn everyone of their existence. A small amount of effort by each diner is a great deal less irksome than half an hour spent poking around for elusive shards of cinnamon. Anyway, I always manage to miss at least one piece.

SERVES 4–6

1 kg (2 lb) oxtail
flour
3–4 tablespoons oil
6 bay leaves
1 kg (2 lb) onions, sliced
2 large cloves of garlic, finely chopped
2 fresh green chillis, sliced
2 whole cinnamon sticks, broken into thirds
1 kg (2 lb) tomatoes, skinned* and chopped
90 g (3 oz) demerara sugar
1 tablespoon salt

Dust the oxtail with flour. Heat 3 tablespoons oil in a large, thick based pan, and add the oxtail and bay leaves. Fry until the meat is browned. Remove with a slotted spoon. Brown the onions in the same fat, adding more oil if necessary.

Add the garlic, chillis and cinnamon to the onions, cover the pan and lower the heat. Cook for 5 minutes, then add the tomatoes, sugar and salt. Return the meat to the pan and stir. Bring to the boil, then cover and cook over a low flame for at least 3 hours, longer if possible. Alternatively, cook in a slow oven – 160C/320F/ Gas 3. Check the pan occasionally to make sure it is not burning on the base. Serve with rice.

Spiced Frikadeller

Danish *frikadeller* are tender little meatballs, more often than not spiced mildly with allspice and nutmeg which is what distinguishes them from a thousand-and-one other kinds of meatball. They may be round but are more likely to be shaped like half-deflated miniature rugby balls. Nestled together as they cook, they look like some abstract flotilla of brown fishing-boats.

Half beef and half pork is the usual basis for the *frikadeller*, but you might prefer to stick with either one or the other. For a more delicate version, use veal and pork, or plain veal. Whichever, the meat should be very finely minced if possible, to give the proper soft texture with no grainy lumps.

Frikadeller can be served hot, with boiled potatoes or a potato salad – add a tomato sauce too, for good measure. They are often served cold, either sliced and arranged on a slice of rye bread with pickled cucumber and lettuce, or as part of a *smörgåsbord*.

SERVES 4

250 g (8 oz) lean minced beef
250g (8 oz) lean minced pork
3 tablespoons soft breadcrumbs
½ teaspoon salt
plenty of pepper
½ teaspoon ground allspice
¼ teaspoon ground nutmeg
1 small onion, grated
1 egg
30–60 ml (1–2 fl oz) milk
15 g (½ oz) butter, melted
1 tablespoon oil

Ask your butcher to mince the beef and pork together twice. If this is out of the question, process it well, so that it is very fine. If that isn't possible either, then just mix the two together – the texture won't be quite right, but they won't collapse.

Mix the meats with all the ingredients except the milk, butter, and oil. Add enough milk to give a soft, but still cohesive mixture. Using a dessert- or tablespoon dipped into the melted butter, shape into small, pointed ovals.

Fry the *frikadeller* in the remaining melted butter mixed with the oil, until well browned and cooked through to the heart. Serve hot or cold.

Sausages With Plums and Yellow Pepper

Quite a homely little dish, this, but none the worse for that, and it won't take long to make, either. The sweet acidity of plums makes them ideal companions to all kinds of meats. For this recipe choose firm plums, better a touch under- than over-ripe. They are cooked briefly, long enough to heat them through but not long enough to drive them to collapse. The yellow pepper adds a third texture and a flash of bright colour – use a red one if you prefer.

SERVES 4

8 meaty sausages
a little olive oil
1 large red or white onion, finely chopped
1 yellow pepper, cut into 5 cm (2 in) strips
4 firm plums, pitted and cut into eighths
½ tablespoon mustard seed
salt and pepper
2 tablespoons red wine vinegar

Prick the sausages. Use a large frying pan, non-stick for preference, fry the sausages until brown, adding barely enough oil to prevent them sticking. Lift the sausages out of the pan, shaking off as much fat as you can, and quarter each one.

Fry the onion in the fat left in the pan, without browning. Turn up the heat and add the pepper. Cook together, stirring until the onion begins to brown and the pepper to wilt. Add the plums, mustard seed and the sausages, and continue to fry for about 1½ minutes. Season generously, then pour in the vinegar. Stir quickly as it bubbles and evaporates, and remove from the heat.

Black Pudding Bourride

A *bourride* is a thick fish soup, but there's nothing fishy about this recipe. It is named after a restaurant called 'La Bourride' in Caen, where we ate these little squares of bread with black pudding and apple, as the preamble to a sumptuous feast of Normandy cooking. The acidity of apples tempers the cloying texture of black pudding, making this a perfect way to present it.

SERVES 6 as a hearty first course or supper dish

½ kg (1 lb) granny smiths or bramleys, chopped
salt and pepper
250 g (8 oz) black pudding
6 slices white bread
45 g (1½ oz) butter
fresh parsley

Put the apples in a pan, peel, core and all, with 1 tablespoon water. Cover and stew over a very low heat, shaking and stirring from time to time, until the apples are soft and collapsing. Sieve, and discard the debris. Season the apple purée with plenty of salt and pepper. Melt the butter, and brush a baking tray generously with it. Cut the crusts off bread, and quarter. Lay on the baking sheet, and brush with lots more melted butter. Bake in a hot oven (220C/425F/Gas 7) for 10–15 minutes, until nicely browned.

Meanwhile, slice the black pudding. Fry the slices in the remaining butter until piping hot. Reheat the apple purée if necessary. Spread each piece of bread with apple purée, and lay a slice of black pudding on top. Finish with a tiny sprig of parsley, and serve quickly.

Grilled Lambs' Kidneys With Herb Butter

Lambs' kidneys are a treat, subtler in flavour than larger pigs' kidneys, with none of that slightly rancid flavour. They are as good plainly grilled like this, or fried and tarted up with a creamy sauce (see the following recipe). Don't use dried herbs for the herb butter. Stick with fresh ones, and use whatever is available. If you use nothing but parsley you will have made a *beurre maître d'hôtel*.

SERVES 4 as a first course, 2 as a main course

8 lambs' kidneys
oil
salt and pepper
60 g (2 oz) softened butter
a good tablespoon fresh herbs★ – parsley, marjoram, chives –
    chopped
1–2 tablespoons lemon juice
1 large bunch of watercress

To make the herb butter, mash the butter with the herbs, the lemon juice and pepper. Chill. Wash and pick over the watercress, removing any unpleasant-looking leaves.

Split the kidneys in half lengthways and snip out the inner core with a pair of scissors or sharp knife. Thread on to skewers, keeping as flat as possible. Brush with oil, season and cook under a hot grill for 6 minutes, turning once. Remove the skewers.

While the kidneys are grilling, arrange a bed of watercress on a warmed serving dish, or individual dishes. Lay the kidneys on the watercress and place a small knob of cold herb butter on top of each. Serve quickly, passing around any remaining butter separately.

Tongue With Plum Sauce

Once you've cooked tongue yourself at home, you'll never again be tempted to buy it pre-sliced and packaged. It's hard to believe they start off as the same thing. Heaven alone knows what they do in the factory to make it quite so bland and tasteless. A whole tongue is enough to serve 10 or so, but since it is lovely cold, don't let that put you off if there are only 4 or 5 of you to feed. Save the left-overs (press under heavy weights in a close fitting tin as it cools) for sandwiches and salads.

The plum sauce can be made in advance and reheated to coincide with the cooking of the tongue. Alternatively, serve the cold plum sauce as a relish with sliced cold tongue.

SERVES 4–6 (with tongue left over)

1 whole cured ox tongue
1 stick of celery, cut into thirds
1 carrot, quartered
1 onion, quartered
1 bouquet garni
4 peppercorns

Plum Sauce:
600 g (1¼ lb) plums
1 glass red wine
3 tablespoons raspberry or red wine vinegar
4 cloves
½ stick of cinnamon
pinch of ground ginger
3 tablespoons caster sugar
salt and pepper

Put the tongue into a large pan and tuck the vegetables around it with the bouquet garni and peppercorns. Add enough water to cover, and simmer for 3½ hours. Trim off the skin, bones and gristle. Slice enough to feed the assembled crowd, and put the remainder away for tomorrow.

To make the sauce, halve the plums and remove the stones. Chop roughly and place in a pan with the remaining ingredients, and enough water to bring the level of liquid to about 1 cm (½ in) below that of the plums. Simmer for 25 minutes until the plums are soft and pulpy. Remove from the heat and sieve, pushing through as many of the plums as possible. Stir well, and taste. Adjust the seasoning.

Reheat the sauce if necessary and pour a little around the hot tongue, passing around the rest separately.

FRUIT PUDDINGS

———— ❧❧❧ ————

Passion Fruit and Apple Jellies

For many people, a jelly is something that comes out of a packet in little cubes, that probably has canned fruit in it, that wobbles, and that is fit only for serving at children's birthday parties. The wobbling is fair enough, but the rest is wrong.

Making your own homemade jelly from scratch is scarcely more complicated than making the packet variety – the principle is exactly the same – but it tastes a great deal better. Far from being a kid's pudding, a proper jelly makes a sophisticated though simple finale to a meal, that can be prepared well in advance, and is popular with adults and children alike.

All you need is a sachet of powdered gelatine and one pint of flavoured liquid, such as unsweetened apple or orange juice. Melt the gelatine, add a tiny amount of sugar to the juice if necessary and combine. If you want to turn the jelly out of its mould, and serve it free-standing, then use 1½ packets of gelatine. Create your own combination of flavours adding maybe a little alcohol. The marvellous taste of passion fruit makes this version particularly good.

SERVES 6

1 sachet (11 g/0.4 oz) powdered gelatine
5 tablespoons very hot (but not boiling) water
6 passion fruit
60 g (2 oz) sugar
approx. ½ litre cloudy apple juice
single cream

166

Sprinkle the gelatine over the hot water, stand for 1 minute, then stir until completely dissolved. Leave to cool until tepid. Halve the passion fruit, and scoop out the seeds and pulp. Place in a small pan, with the sugar and 3 tablespoons water. Heat, stirring, until hot, but do not boil. Remove from the heat and sieve, pressing through as much as possible of the passion fruit pulp. Save the black seeds that remain in the sieve.

Pour the sieved passion fruit juice into a measuring jug, and make up to 600 ml (1 pt) with apple juice. Warm gently and whisk in the gelatine. If there appear to be a few stray lumps of gelatine floating in the juice, put over a low heat, stirring until the gelatine has dissolved. Do not let it get anywhere near boiling point.

Taste, and stir in more sugar if necessary. Pour into 6 glasses, or 1 large glass bowl, and leave in the fridge to set. If you are in a rush, pop into the freezer for 30 minutes – but don't forget about it. Before serving, pour a thin layer of single cream over the surface, and scatter with a few crunchy black passion fruit seeds.

Pineapple With Pineapple Sauce

To pick a ripe pineapple ready for the table, tug gently at the central leaf. If it comes out easily, then buy the fruit and eat it quickly. Peel it, cut the eyes out and chop it, macerate in a few tablespoons of kirsch, brandy or orange juice.

An even nicer way to present it is with its own pineapple sauce, perfumed with the scent of passion fruit. In fact, it makes such a good sauce that I now serve it with all kinds of fruit and puddings. Try it with slices of fresh mango, or with strawberries, or with sticky wintery steamed pudding.

SERVES 4

1 passion fruit or 1–2 tablespoons kirsch, brandy, or Grand
    Marnier
1 large pineapple
60 g (2 oz) caster sugar

Halve the passion fruit if using, and scoop out the flesh and seeds. Place in a small pan with half the sugar, and heat gently, without boiling. Sieve, and reserve some of the black seeds.

Peel and core the pineapple, removing the eyes, and slice. Set aside the 4 choicest slices. Roughly chop the rest and liquidise with the passion fruit juice or alcohol, and sugar to taste.

Spread the liquidised pineapple on the base of a serving dish. Quarter the pineapple slices and arrange nicely on top. Scatter a few black passion fruit seeds over the top.

Compote of Dried Fruit

Sometimes I make this compote with just one kind of fruit, apricots maybe, sometimes with a whole galaxy of different kinds, so that the tartness of one sets off the sweetness of another. Either way, it is still a very sweet, sticky pudding, and a little goes a long way. If there's any left over, serve it with cereal for breakfast.

Moscatel de Valencia is a very reasonably priced raisin-scented dessert wine, available from many supermarkets and wine-merchants. I use it a great deal in cooking, as well as serving it 'on the rocks' as an aperitif, or lightly chilled with puddings.

SERVES 4

250 g (8 oz) mixed dried fruit, apricots, pears, prunes, peaches, raisins
300 ml (½ pt) Moscatel de Valencia, or other dessert wine
pinch of cinnamon
30 g (1 oz) toasted flaked almonds*
Greek strained yoghurt

Cut the larger pieces of fruit into strips, and place in a saucepan with the wine and cinnamon. Bring gently to the boil. Simmer for 20–30 minutes until the fruit is tender and the liquid is thick and syrupy.

Serve the fruit hot or cold, scattered with almonds, and with lashings of thick yoghurt.

Marsala-Baked Raisins With Walnuts

A friend told me to look out for little leaf-wrapped parcels called *passolini* when I visited Amalfi in the south of Italy. Once I had visited the cool cathedral, with its enchanting *chiostro del paradiso*, the cloister of paradise, I set off to look for *passolini*.

There is only one main street, leading off the central square, up towards the Valley of the Papermills. Near the square, food and hardware shops alternate with souvenir shops, which become rarer as the often abandoned mills come into sight.

In front of several of the food shops were piles of dry, green-brown packages tied with a knot of rafia – the *passolini*. The leaves are lemon leaves from the abundant groves that surround Amalfi. Fold back this brittle wrapping, and inside there is a sticky mass of plump moist raisins.

I brought several *passolini* back to England, but they were quickly consumed. To stretch the last packet around 4 people, I added walnuts and we ate them slowly, with cups of strong black coffee at the end of the meal. It was a good combination, a sophisticated bowl of nuts and raisins.

Lemon leaves are a rare commodity in north London, but by slowly baking big fat raisins (look out for Lexia raisins) with marsala, honey and lemon juice, I recaptured something of the taste of those *passolini*. It's worth trying this yourself, not only for the taste but also for the glorious smell that wafts around the house as it cooks.

SERVES 4

125 g (4 oz) large seedless raisins
150 ml (¼ pt) marsala
2 tablespoons honey
1 tablespoon lemon juice
30 g (1 oz) walnuts
Greek yoghurt

Spread out the raisins in an oven-proof dish, pour marsala over them, and trickle the honey evenly across the surface. Bake in a low oven, 170C/325F/Gas 3 for 1½ hours, stirring occasionally, until the raisins have absorbed the marsala and are plump and sticky. Remove from the oven, and sprinkle lemon juice over them. Leave to cool.

Roughly chop the walnuts, and scatter over the raisins. Serve lightly chilled with thick Greek yoghurt to cut the sweetness.

Hunza Apricots With Yoghurt

Most wholefood shops stock hunza apricots, although they are easy to overlook. They look dull and drab but they taste exquisite, chewed raw like a caramel, or poached with no need for any added sugar. Their caramel richness is quite unlike the taste of ordinary apricots.

They are grown in a remote part of Pakistan, dried on tin roofs in the hills, then transported down the Korkoram highway to be distributed to the rest of the world.

SERVES 4–6

250 g (8 oz) hunza apricots
1 tablespoon lemon juice
225 g (8 oz) tub Greek strained yoghurt

Place the apricots and lemon juice in a pan, and add enough water to cover. Bring slowly to the boil, and simmer gently for 5–10 minutes, until the apricots are tender.

Once the apricots are cooked lift them out, leaving behind as much of the liquid as possible. Boil hard until reduced by one third, then pour over the apricots. They can be served hot or cold as they are, with a swirl of Greek yoghurt or, if you have the time and the inclination, slit each apricot and extract the stone. Crack this and inside you will find an almondy kernel. Mix the kernels with the apricots.

Grapefruit Creams

As you cast your eye over the list of ingredients do not let yourself be put off by the penultimate one. Yes, it is semolina, but not a lot of semolina. Just enough to thicken these very rich little puds, and to give an almost imperceptible graininess to the smoothness of what is, after all, mostly cream!

The sharpness of the grapefruit sauce cuts the richness, but even so you'll find that just one of the little creams is enough per person.

SERVES 6

zest and juice of 1 pink or ruby grapefruit
300 ml (10 fl oz) double cream
150 ml (¼ pt) milk
pinch of salt
90 g (3 oz) sugar
1 tablespoon semolina
2 egg yolks

Pare the zest of half the grapefruit into thick strips, taking care not to include any of the white pith underneath. Blanch for 1 minute and drain.

Place the peel in a saucepan with the double cream and milk, salt and 30 g (1 oz) of the sugar. Bring gently to the boil. Add 4 tablespoons of the hot cream to the semolina, and mix to a paste. Tip into the pan, and stir well. Simmer gently for 5 minutes. Fish out the pieces of zest. Off the heat, add the yolks and whisk well to break up any lumps.

Grease 6 small ramekins or dariole moulds with a little butter. Divide the semolina and cream mixture between them. Stand in a roasting tray half filled with water, and place the tray in the oven at 170C/325F/Gas 3. Bake for 20 minutes, until lightly browned and set. Leave to cool. Squeeze the grapefruit, and place the juice in a pan with the remaining sugar. Bring to the boil, stirring. Simmer for 5 minutes. Leave to cool.

Run a thin-bladed knife round the edge of each ramekin to loosen, and turn out. Pour a little of the sauce around each one, and serve.

Clementine Sorbet With Mango Sauce

This sorbet is light, fruity and refreshing, an antidote to heavy cold weather foods, especially around Christmas and the New Year.

I know that the beating of a sorbet or ice-cream as it freezes is a tedious job, but console yourself with the thought that, once it is done, the damn thing can sit there in the freezer until the moment you need it. The mango sauce is not quite so patient, of course. But you could save the sugar syrup for it in a screw top jar in the fridge, where it will keep happily for weeks.

SERVES 4–6

175 g (6 oz) sugar
10 cloves
6 clementines
juice of 1½ lemons
1 large mango

Put the sugar into a pan with ½ litre (¾ pt) water. Stir over a low heat until clear, then bring to the boil. Add the cloves and boil for 5 minutes. Leave to cool, and pick out the cloves.

Squeeze the juice out of the clementines. Mix with the juice of 1 lemon. Pour in enough of the sugar syrup to sweeten to taste. Start off with a third of the amount, and work upwards from there. Remember, the cold will dampen some of the sweetness, so it should taste a touch over sugared. Save the rest of the syrup for the sauce.

Pour the sweetened juice into a freezing container, and place in the freezer. When the sides are beginning to set, fold into the middle. When the sorbet has almost solidified, but not quite, remove from the freezer and beat well to break up any crystals. Return to the freezer and, if you have the time, repeat when it is again almost set, to get a really smooth texture. Otherwise it will simply be slightly grainy.

To make the sauce, peel the mango and cut into chunks. Liquidise with half the remaining lemon juice, and half the remaining syrup. Now add more lemon juice and syrup until you get the right balance of sweet, sharp and mango.

Move the sorbet from the freezer to the fridge about 20 minutes before you serve it. Pile scoops of the mixture up high in a shallow dish, and trickle the mango sauce around it, in a pool.

Lime Syllabub With Hazelnut Praline

A variation on the classic syllabub, laced with sherry and the sharpness of green lime, and dusted with hazelnut praline. If you are short of time you can leave out the praline, then you have a pudding which takes just minutes to make.

Having said that, though, it really is worth finding the time to make the praline. You won't need it all for this recipe, and it keeps perfectly in an airtight jar or box. Fold it into whipped cream to make a filling for a pavlova, or choux pastries, or scatter over cakes and puddings.

SERVES 4–6

Praline:
60 g (2 oz) sugar
60 g (2 oz) hazelnuts, toasted and skinned★

Syllabub:
2 limes
6 tablespoons dry sherry
90 g (3 oz) caster sugar
300 ml (10 fl oz) double cream

To make the praline, put the sugar in a pan with 2 tablespoons water. Stir over a medium heat until the sugar has completely dissolved, without boiling. Stop stirring and raise the heat. Boil the syrup, tilting and swirling the pan, until it turns a rich caramel brown.

Draw off the heat and quickly stir in the nuts. Pour on to an oiled baking sheet and leave to set. When cool, pound to a coarse powder in a mortar or a processor.

Pare thin strips of zest off one of the limes. Blanch for 1 minute, drain well and shred. Squeeze the juice from both limes and mix with the sherry and sugar, stirring until the sugar has dissolved. Trickle in the cream, stirring constantly. Now whisk until the cream holds it shape, but no more or it may curdle. Pile into 4 or 6 glasses, and scatter each one with a teaspoonful of praline, and curls of lime zest.

Citrons Givrés à L'Anglaise

I had built up a startling collection of lemons. I obviously wasn't going to use them all up in the natural course of things, and so I debated between some sort of lemon conserve, or the temptations of *citrons givrés* – lemon shells filled with lemon sorbet. In fact, what I ended up with was a variation on the latter.

For some reason, I think of condensed milk as a peculiarly English indulgence. Actually, it isn't at all. I remember buying little *berlingots* (miniature tetrapaks) of flavoured condensed milk as a child in France from the dark, dingy shop that I and my friends passed *en route* for school every morning.

Even so, these are a far cry from the usual French *citrons givrés*. The bite of lemon juice shatters the childish sweetness of condensed milk, to make a creamy ice-cream that needs no beating as it freezes. *Citrons givrés à l'anglaise* are easy to make, and will keep for up to a month in a freezer.

SERVES 6

6 large, pretty lemons
1 x 400 g (14 oz) tin sweetened condensed milk

Slice a very thin disc off one end of each lemon, so that it will stand upright. Try not to pierce through the white pith into the yellow flesh – not the end of the world if you do, but better avoided.

Slice across the other end to give a lid. Loosen the flesh inside with a small sharp knife, then scrape out as much as possible into a bowl. With your fingers, pull out as many of the flaps of white membrane as you can without damaging the shell. When you get to the sixth lemon, keep the insides and juice separate from that of the other 5.

Sieve the juice of the first 5 pressing through as much as you can. Beat into the condensed milk. Taste – it should be on the sharp side, since the chilling will dampen the flavour. If you think it could take a little more lemon, add some of the juice from the sixth one.

Spoon the mixture back into the lemons. If there is a hole in the base of any of them, just wrap tightly in cling film before filling. Tap the filled lemons gently against the work surface to expel any air bubbles. Replace their lids, and wrap in cling film. Freeze. Freeze the remaining mixture in a small container, and either serve as a second helping, or save for another occasion.

Move the lemons from the freezer to fridge 15 minutes before serving.

Blood Oranges in Rosemary Syrup

Why is it that the big supermarkets have started rechristening blood oranges 'ruby red oranges'? It infuriates me. I imagine that the powers that be have decided that the wimpish British public can no longer cope with the proper name. They've been called blood oranges ever since I can remember, and for a long time before that, and a perfectly apt and descriptive name it is, too.

When you get good blood oranges, their juice is an intense dark red with an astringent taste. A glass of that first thing in the morning gets the day going with a tremendous kick. It's delicious, too, relaxed with sparkling mineral water, or a slug of gin or vodka.

My mother laces sliced blood oranges with a gingery syrup to make a light spring pudding. This is a variation on her theme, born out of the necessity – no ginger in the house, but facing me on the spice shelf were 2 jars, dried rosemary and Szechuan peppercorns (delicatessens and oriental supermarkets). It's a stunning marriage of flavours. The syrup seems strong at first, but is diluted by the juice of the oranges.

Out of season, use ordinary oranges. Black or green peppercorns can be substituted for the Szechuan peppercorns. Serve it on its own, or with a chocolatey pudding, such as a mousse, for grander occasions.

Serves 6

1 teaspoon Szechuan peppercorns, or green or black peppercorns
150 g (5 oz) caster sugar
150 ml (¼ pt) water
1 sprig of rosemary
6 blood oranges or 4 large oranges

If you use Szechuan peppercorns, dry fry in a small heavy frying pan over a high heat, until they begin to scent the air with incense. Put the sugar, water and rosemary in a pan. Coarsely crush the peppercorns of whatever sort and add those too. Stir over a medium heat until the sugar has completely dissolved. Bring to the boil, turn down the heat, and simmer for 5 minutes. Cool until tepid and strain.

Pare the orange zest off 1½ small oranges, or 1 larger one, and shred. Drop into a small pan of boiling water and blanch for 1 minute. Drain, and dry on kitchen paper. Peel all the oranges, removing as much of the bitter white pith as you can, and slice thinly. Place in a bowl, and pour over the syrup. Scatter with shredded zest. Leave in the fridge for at least 1 hour, and serve lightly chilled, with crisp biscuits.

Valentine Mousse Cake

This is the prettiest, triple layered pudding. The base is dark with nutty toasted poppyseeds, in the centre a light, pink mousse and covering that a thin layer of clear burgundy-coloured jelly. It first appeared on St Valentine's Day, hence the name. Once the blood orange season is over, use the juice of ordinary oranges, though naturally that will upset the romantic colour scheme!

Serves 4

Base:
1 tablespoon poppyseeds
1 large egg
45 g (1½ oz) caster sugar
30 g (1 oz) plain flour, sifted
pinch of salt
finely grated zest of ½ blood orange

Mousse:
170 ml (6 fl oz) blood orange juice (3–4 oranges)
45 g (1½ oz) caster sugar
1 rounded teaspoon (⅓ sachet) powdered gelatine
90 ml (3 fl oz) whipping cream

To make the base, dry fry the poppyseeds in a small pan, until they give off a nutty smell. Cool, reserve ¼ teaspoon, and grind the rest in a coffee grinder. Whisk the egg with the sugar until pale and thick. Fold in the flour, salt, poppyseeds and zest. Pour into an 18 cm (7 in) cake tin, lined with non-stick baking parchment, and bake at 190C/375F/Gas 5 for 10–12 minutes, until just firm. Turn out on to a sheet of greaseproof paper to cool. Peel off the lining paper.

To make the mousse, sprinkle gelatine on to 3 tablespoons water in a small pan. Soak for 5–10 minutes, then heat *very gently*, stirring until dissolved. In a separate pan, warm the orange juice gently with the sugar, stirring until dissolved. Draw off heat, and add the gelatine, stirring until dissolved. Set aside 4 tablespoons of the mixture. Chill the rest, until almost set.

Whip the cream and fold into the chilled jelly. Line four 8 cm (3 in) ramekins, or one larger mould (e.g. a 15–18 cm (6–7 in) cake tin) with cling film, smoothing down the folds neatly. Cut the cake to fit and press snugly into the moulds. Cover evenly with mousse. Chill until firm. Warm the reserved jelly until just runny. Pour a thin layer over the surface, and sprinkle with the reserved poppyseeds. Leave to set in the fridge. To serve, ease the sides and lift out. Peel off the cling film carefully.

Crème Normande

This is a wickedly smooth, creamy baked custard layered over apples soaked in Calvados. It's so rich that this quantity should be quite enough for 6 people after an ample meal, but I'm sure you'll find that 4 less replete diners will have no trouble getting through it on their own.

Instead of baking it in this way, you could make it the filling for a fruit tart. Line a tart tin with shortcrust pastry* and bake blind*. At the same time, bake the apples in a single layer in the oven. Spoon into the pastry case and continue as if using an unlined dish.

SERVES 4–6

½ kg (1 lb) eating apples, such as Cox's Orange Pippins
4 tablespoons Calvados, or brandy
6 tablespoons caster sugar
30 g (1 oz) butter
3 egg yolks
300 ml (10 fl oz) whipping cream
2 tablespoons flaked almonds

Peel and core the apples. Chop roughly, and toss in the Calvados. Set aside for 1 hour.

Drain off the Calvados, and reserve. Either divide the apple pieces between several small oven-proof ramekins, or put them all into a single oven-proof dish. Dot with butter, and sprinkle with half the sugar. Bake at 200C/400F/Gas 6 for 20 minutes. Beat the reserved Calvados with the remaining sugar, the egg yolks and the cream. Take the apples out of the oven, and pour this mixture over them. Scatter the flaked almonds over the top. Stand in a roasting tray, filled to a depth of 2–3 cm (1 in) with water, and return to the oven. Bake for a further 20–30 minutes, until the cream is setting, but not yet solid. Serve hot or warm, or cold.

Apple Meringue Shortbread

This little number is a variation on the Baked Alaska theme with the Alaska taken out and replaced with poached apple slices instead. So in the end it actually has little resemblance to the original, although it is put together in the same way – first a layer of shortbread, then a layer of apple, and finally a swirling coat of caramel-edged meringue.

SERVES 6

Apples:
125 g (4 oz) sugar
1 vanilla pod★
2 Golden Delicious apples
juice of ½ lemon

Shortbread:
60 g (2 oz) caster sugar
175 g (6 oz) flour
125 g (4 oz) butter

Meringue:
125 g (4 oz) caster sugar
2 egg whites

Begin by cooking the apple slices. Place the sugar in a pan with 150 ml (¼ pt) water and stir over a medium heat to dissolve. Add the vanilla pod, and bring to the boil. Simmer for 10 minutes. While it bubbles, core the apples and cut into 5 mm (¼ in) thick slices. Turn in the lemon juice as you work. Poach the apples in the syrup for about 5 minutes until tender, but not yet disintegrating. Drain, and leave to cool.

Next the shortbread. Cream the butter with the sugar and work in the flour to give a soft dough. Roll out to a thickness of 1 cm (½ in) on a floured board, and cut out circles roughly the same size as the apple slices. Slide on to a baking sheet, prick with a fork and bake at 190C/375F/Gas 5 for 15–20 minutes, until pale biscuit-coloured. Leave to cool.

To finish, settle the apple slices on the shortbread circles. Whisk the egg whites until stiff and fold in the remaining sugar. Whisk again until stiff and shiny, and cover each apple slice with a swirl of this meringue. Bake at 250C/475F/Gas 9 for 5–8 minutes, until browned.

Fried Apple Sandwiches

Fried Apple Sandwiches is a rather prosaic name for these fritters of thin apple slices sandwiched together with cream cheese and walnuts. They make a filling pudding for 4 after a light main course, but there's enough here to furnish a little sweetener for 6 or even 8 at the end of a more capacious meal.

SERVES 4-8

175 g (6 oz) cream cheese
60 g (2 oz) walnuts, finely chopped
1½ tablespoons sugar
2 eating apples
lemon juice
flour
1 large egg, beaten
90 g (3 oz) fine dry breadcrumbs
olive oil
lemon wedges

Mix the walnuts into the cream cheese with the sugar. Core the apples and slice thinly, about 3 mm (⅛ in) thick. Toss the apple slices quickly in the lemon juice to prevent discolouring. Now sandwich together pairs of apple slices with a thick layer of the walnuts and cream cheese. You should have enough to make 8 'sandwiches', with some apple left over.

Dust each sandwich with flour, then dip into the beaten egg, and finally coat thoroughly in breadcrumbs. If you are preparing these in advance, cover loosely with cling film, and leave in the fridge until ready to finish.

Pour a 1 cm (½ in) deep layer of oil into a frying pan and heat well. Fry the sandwiches on each side, until a deep golden brown. Drain quickly on kitchen paper, and serve with lemon wedges.

Eve's Christmas Pudding

When I was a student I shared a flat with a friend called Eve. I can still remember the day she discovered a recipe for 'Eve's Pudding' and immediately set about making it. We were all very smitten with the resulting pudding, with its base of apple, topped with a light sponge. As far as I know she still makes it from time to time, and so do I.

One Christmas season a couple of years ago, I felt that I had eaten enough mince pies to last me for ever, but I was left with a lone jar of mincemeat. Waste not, want not, so I used it up in a revamped version of that apple pudding. It was delicious, the sharpness of the grated apple dampening the intense sweetness of the mincemeat.

SERVES 6

250g (½ lb) cooking apples, coarsely grated
300 g (10 oz) mincemeat
60 g (2 oz) butter
60 g (2 oz) sugar
1 egg, beaten
90 g (3 oz) self-raising flour
pinch of salt
grated rind of ½ orange
2-3 tablespoons milk

Mix the grated apple with the mincemeat and spread in a 1 litre (2 pt) oven-proof dish. Cream the butter with the sugar until light

and fluffy, then beat in the egg. Sift the flour with the salt, and fold
in with the orange rind. Add enough milk to give a batter with a
dropping consistency. Spread this over the apple and mincemeat.

Bake at 200C/400F/Gas 6 for 25-35 minutes, until the sponge is
firm. Exact timing will vary with the proportions of your dish and
the depth of the sponge mixture. Test with a skewer, to make sure it
is cooked through. Serve with whipped cream or brandy butter.

Quince and Apple Timbales

As autumn sets in, cast your eye over the boxes of produce stacked
high in front of Greek greengrocers' shops. Somewhere among
them is likely to be one filled with downy golden quinces, hard as a
rock when raw, releasing a heavenly perfume when cooked. Slice
and poach in syrup, with or without apples or pears, for the best of
simple desserts, and for a touch more glamour mould into a cake of
melting caramelised fruit. If the worst comes to the worst and there
is a serious shortage of quinces in your vicinity, use extra apples or
pears instead.

SERVES 6-8

3 quinces
6 Cox's Orange Pippins
150 g (5 oz) sugar
juice of ½ lemon
1 vanilla pod*
60 g (2 oz) butter

Place 60 g (2 oz) of the sugar, the lemon juice and 150 ml (¼ pt)
water in a pan. Stir over a medium heat until the sugar has
completely dissolved. Add the vanilla pod and bring to the boil.
Simmer for 5 minutes.

Peel and core the quinces. Slice thinly. Simmer gently in the
syrup until tender. Lift out and set aside. Peel, core and slice the
apples. Poach briefly in the syrup until tender. Take out of the
syrup and add to the quinces. Remove the vanilla pod from the
syrup and reserve.

Place the remaining sugar in a small pan with 2 tablespoons of the
poaching syrup. Stir over a medium heat until the sugar has
dissolved. Bring to the boil, and boil until it caramelises to a rich
brown. Watch over it as this won't take more than a few minutes.
Pour the caramel into a 18 cm (7 in) diameter cake tin or other metal

mould, or 6 individual moulds, and swirl around to coat the sides. Cool for 10 minutes.

Arrange a layer of apple and quince slices decoratively on the base. Dot with butter. Repeat the layers with the remaining apples, quinces and butter until all are used up – subsequent layers need not be so carefully arranged, though they should be tightly packed. Cover with foil, and bake at 170C/350F/Gas 4 for 40 minutes. Arrange a plate on the surface and weigh down with tins or other heavy weights. Cool and chill lightly. Remove weights and plate. Run a knife around the edge and turn out just before serving.

Serve with cream and the reserved syrup.

Torta di Zucca e Mele

Torta di Zucca e Mele is an unusual, but utterly delicious pudding from northern Italy, a sort of chocolatey baked custard filled to bursting with tender slices of poached apple and pumpkin, dried fruits and grainy crumbs of amaretti biscuits. Swallow your disbelief at the bizarre list of ingredients and try it. You won't be disappointed.

SERVES 8-10

2 eating apples
175 g (6 oz) piece of pumpkin, weighed after removing skin and
    seeds
75 g (2½ oz) caster sugar
2 tablespoons milk
60 g (2 oz) plain chocolate, chopped
60 g (2 oz) amaretti biscuits, crushed
60 g (2 oz) dried figs, finely chopped
30 g (1 oz) sultanas
½ tablespoon cocoa
finely grated zest of 1 lemon
¼ teaspoon vanilla essence
2 tablespoons brandy
pinch of salt
2 eggs, beaten

Peel and core the apples, then slice thinly into a saucepan. Add half the sugar and 3 tablespoons water, and simmer gently, covered, for 15 minutes, until tender but not collapsing. Thinly slice the pumpkin into a separate pan, add the remaining sugar and milk, and cook as the apple. Mix the contents of the 2 pans in a large bowl, and add the remaining ingredients in the order given, stirring in each one well before adding the next.

Line a 23 cm (9 in) cake, or deep tart tin with a removable base with non-stick baking parchment. Pour in the mixture and smooth down. Tap the tin on the table a few times to force out any air bubbles. Bake for 60 minutes at 150C/300F/Gas 2 until just firm. Cool until tepid, run a knife around the edge and unmould. Serve cold.

Baked Fruit Salad

Lucca is one of Tuscany's many walled medieval cities. The old town is a maze of cool dark alleys, breaking here and there into wide open squares, pale stones reflecting the brightness and heat of the Italian sun.

The streets are lined with elegant medieval palaces, the skyline pierced by high towers. Climb to the top of the famous Guinigi Tower and you emerge on to a high terrace, shaded by holm oaks growing in the thin soil on the top of the tower. The view across the town and the cypress-studded hillsides is magnificent.

So too is the Luccan food. 'La Buca di San Antonio' is one of the best restaurants in the town, serving traditional dishes with justifiable pride. The food is filling, but it's worth saving a space for a small taste of this baked fruit salad, with its honey-brown slices of fruit, bathed in sticky caramel syrup, edges blackened here and there by the heat of the oven.

It's a simple dish to make, and once you've got the gist of it, you don't really need a recipe at all. It can be endlessly adapted to use whatever fruits are available in the shops or your garden. As long as you fill the dish well, add a thick layer of sugar, and a good dash of alcohol once it is cooked, you can make it in greater or lesser quantity to fit the occasion.

SERVES 8

2 oranges
3 apples
3 pears
1 pineapple
2 bananas
250 g (8 oz) brown sugar
75 ml (2½ fl oz) brandy or Grand Marnier

Line a large oven-proof dish with a double layer of silver foil. Divide the oranges, skin and all, into eighths. Core the apples and pears, and cut into eighths. Peel the pineapple, and dice, discarding the woody core. Peel the bananas and cut into chunks about 4 cm (1½ in) long. Mix all the fruit together well, and pile into the dish.

Dredge with the brown sugar. Bake for 1 hour at 220C/425F/Gas 7, turning the fruit in its juices every 15 minutes. Pour brandy or Grand Marnier over the fruit and leave to cool, basting occasionally with the juices.

Serve with thick double cream, crème fraîche or thick Greek yoghurt.

Banana and Coconut Cream

The exotic fragrance of coconut turns plain old mashed bananas into a chic winter fool in the twinkling of an eye. Well, maybe 5 minutes is a long twinkle, but it won't take much more than that to put together. If you've a little more time to spare, toast some flaked almonds or coconut flakes to scatter over the top.

SERVES 4

45 g (1½ oz) creamed coconut*, grated
1½ tablespoons honey
4½ tablespoons water
3 large bananas
2 tablespoons lemon juice

Dissolve the coconut with the honey and water in a small pan over a medium heat. Bring to the boil, draw off the hob and cool slightly.

Peel, slice and mash the bananas with the lemon juice. Beat in the coconut cream. Pile into 4 glasses or bowls, cover with cling film and keep cool. Serve with crisp biscuits.

Poached Pears With Chocolate and Red Wine Sauce

Somebody once asked me if they could use tinned pears in one of my recipes, instead of poached fresh pears. The answer was an emphatic 'no!' then I added that, of course, if they really wanted to, they could use whatever they liked, but that tinned pears were a very poor and mousey relation to proper poached pears.

Pears poached in the plainest of sugar syrups, or flavoured with cinnamon, vanilla, ginger or whatever, are transformed into one of the most sublime of puddings, and bear small resemblance to the insipidly flavoured tinned pear.

This takes the idea one step further. The pears, suffused with pink from the red wine syrup, are half submerged in a dark chocolate sauce.

SERVES 6

6 firm pears
lemon juice
125 g (4 oz) caster sugar
300 ml (½ pt) red wine
1 vanilla pod*

Sauce:
125 g (4 oz) plain dark chocolate*, grated or finely chopped
30 g (1 oz) butter, chopped

Peel, core and halve the pears, and toss in the lemon juice. Place the sugar, wine and vanilla pod in a pan large enough to take all the pears. Stir over a medium heat until the sugar has completely dissolved. Raise the heat, and boil for 5 minutes. Lay the pears in the pan, cover and simmer gently until tender. Turn the pears occasionally so that they cook evenly. Leave to cool in the syrup, then drain well.

Boil the syrup hard until reduced to 200 ml (7½ fl oz). Place the chocolate and butter in a bowl, and very slowly pour on the wine syrup, stirring as you do. Arrange the pears in a serving dish, and pour the chocolate sauce around them. Serve hot or cold, with or without cream.

Rice and Almond Cream With Cherry Sauce

I've always loved rice puddings. Any kind of rice pudding, from the deeply unsophisticated one we ate at school to the superb slowly oven-baked French and Portuguese ones, laden with cream. And yes, I have been known to down tinned rice pudding with considerable relish.

Given the breadth and scope of my sampling, I think I can say with some assurance that this Scandinavian rice pudding is one of the best. It is traditionally served at Christmas, laced with sherry and cream, topped with a cherry sauce.

Although I give the winter version here, made with tinned or bottled cherries, in summer take advantage of big fat fresh cherries to make the sauce. Poach 375-500 g (12-16 oz) cherries in a syrup made with 125 g (4 oz) sugar and 150 ml (¼ pt) water.

Alternatively, make a raspberry coulis – sieve fresh or frozen raspberries, sweeten with icing sugar and sharpen with a dash of lemon juice.

SERVES 6

Rice:
600 ml (1 pt) milk
6 tablespoons pudding rice
1 vanilla pod*
30 g (1 oz) caster sugar
30 g (1 oz) almonds, chopped
2 tablespoons dry sherry
150 ml (5 fl oz) whipping or double cream

Sauce:
1 x 400 g (14 oz) jar or tin of morello cherries in light syrup
2 tablespoons dry sherry
2 teaspoons arrowroot

Bring the milk to the boil, and add the rice and vanilla pod. Stir, bring back to the boil. Turn the heat down low, and cover tightly. Simmer very gently for 40 minutes, stirring from time to time to make sure it does not stick. Draw off the heat, and stir in the sugar. Cool until tepid. Remove the vanilla pod and stir in the almonds and sherry. Whip the cream and fold in. Spoon into a serving bowl.

Decorate the compote with 6 or 7 cherries. Strain the syrup from the rest into a pan, and add the sherry and 60 ml (2 fl oz) water. Bring to the boil. Mix the arrowroot with 1 tablespoon water. Mix in 1 tablespoon of the hot sauce, and then a second, then pour the whole lot back into the pan, stirring constantly. Add the remaining cherries and boil for 2-3 minutes, until clear and thick. Serve warm or cold with the rice.

Fresh Apricot and Gin Sauce

Apricots are a frequent source of disappointment to me. Woolly and tasteless. Why do I ever buy them? Because every now and then I find a batch of apricots that are sweet, scented, tender-fleshed without being flabby, as heavenly as any of the grander exotic fruits.

On these rare occasions I wouldn't dream of doing anything but eating them as they are. However, the usual disappointing apricots can be dramatically improved by brief cooking. This sauce, and the 2 recipes that follow, bring out the best in them.

The gin adds a quiet juniper scent to the sauce, subtle enough to be barely detectable, but definitely in attendance. The sauce is simmered after the gin has been added, so the alcohol is burned off and it won't get toddlers tiddly. No gin? Use brandy or Cointreau or Grand Marnier, or add a vanilla pod* instead, but remember to fish it out before puréeing the sauce.

Serve hot or cold with vanilla or chocolate ice-cream, a sweet soufflé, or a selection of artfully arranged fruits, baked bananas, fromage frais, or Greek strained yoghurt.

MAKES APPROX. ½ LITRE (¾ PT)

125 g (4 oz) caster sugar
zest and juice of ½ lemon
4 tablespoons gin
250 g (8 oz) apricots, halved and pitted

Place the sugar in a pan with 150 ml (¼ pt) water. Stir over a medium heat until the sugar has dissolved and the syrup is clear. Bring to the boil and simmer for 2 minutes. Add the remaining ingredients and simmer gently until the apricots are very tender, 10-15 minutes.

Remove from the heat and pass through a *mouli-légumes*, or a fine sieve. Taste and add a dash more lemon juice if necessary.

Summer Fruit With Fruit Cream

Use apricots, peaches and nectarines, or a mixture of all 3 for this recipe.

SERVES 4

8-12 apricots or 4 peaches or 4 nectarines (or a mixture of fruit),
    halved and pitted
juice of ½ lemon
juice of ½ orange
90 g (3 oz) caster sugar
150 ml (5 fl oz) double cream
4 amaretti biscuits or 1 macaroon

Mix the lemon juice with the orange juice and make up to 300 ml (½ pt) with water. Pour into a pan large enough to hold the fruit, and add the sugar. Bring gently to the boil, stirring constantly to dissolve the sugar. Boil for 3 minutes.

Add the fruit, and simmer until tender (between 5 and 20 minutes, depending on ripeness) adding extra water if the level of the liquid falls very low. Using a slotted spoon, remove the fruit from the syrup, leaving behind any skins that come loose.

Leave the fruit to cool, cut side up on a serving dish. Boil the syrup hard, until about 5 tablespoons remain. Strain and cool. Add the cool syrup to the cream, and whisk until stiff. Top each fruit half with a swirl of cream. Crumble the biscuits, and sprinkle over the top.

Apricot and Maple Syrup Upside-Down Cake

This cake is wickedly irresistible, moist and sticky, sweet with maple syrup, sharp from the apricots. One word of warning – don't buy 'maple flavour syrup'. It tastes foul, and may seem to be value for money, but it isn't since it will ruin anything you put it in or on. Splash out on the real thing (check the bottle carefully, the word 'flavour' is often printed very small), or use dark muscovado sugar.

SERVES 8-10

Topping:
125 g (4 oz) sugar
375 g (12 oz) apricots, halved and pitted
4 tablespoons maple syrup
4 tablespoons softened butter
60 g (2 oz) walnut halves

Cake:
60 g (2 oz) softened butter
125 g (4 oz) caster sugar
2 eggs
150 ml (¼ pt) milk
250 g (8 oz) self-raising flour
pinch of salt
finely grated zest and juice of 1 lemon

For the topping, make a syrup with the sugar, and 150 ml (¼ pt) water. Poach the apricots in this syrup until just tender. Drain, and save the syrup for later. Beat the maple syrup with the softened butter and smear this mixture generously, over the base of a 23 cm (9 in) cake tin. Arrange the apricot halves curved side down on the base, and fill the gaps with the walnuts.

To make the cake, cream the butter with the sugar, then beat in the eggs and lemon zest. Sift the flour with the salt. Add the sifted flour and the milk to the mixture alternately, beating well. Spoon into the cake tin, trying not to disturb the fruit. Bake at 180C/350F/ Gas 4 for 45-55 minutes, until nicely browned and firm to the touch.

While the cake is cooking, place the lemon juice in a pan with the syrup from the apricots, and bring to the boil. Boil hard until reduced by half. Pierce the crust of the cake in half a dozen places, and pour the syrup over the hot cake. To serve hot, run a knife around the edge of the cake, and turn out on to a plate. To serve cold, let the cake settle for 5 more minutes, then turn out.

Butterscotch and Peach Toasts

The butterscotch in this recipe is a superbly childish indulgence – as it cools it sets to a soft buttery toffee surround for the peaches. If the thought of all that butter and sugar gives you the collywobbles, try a plainer version, a cinnamon peach toast: ignore the butterscotch bit altogether, and lay the peaches on the grilled bread. Mix 60 g (2 oz) caster sugar with ½ teaspoon ground cinnamon. Taste and add a little more if you like. Sprinkle this over the peaches as thickly as you can and then whizz them under a hot grill until the sugar melts and begins to brown. Let it cool for a few minutes before eating, or you'll burn your mouth.

SERVES 8

2-3 peaches
4 slices of brioche or good white bread
30 g (1 oz) butter, melted
30 g (1 oz) toasted flaked almonds*

Butterscotch:
125 g (4 oz) dark muscovado sugar
60 g (2 oz) caster sugar
75 ml (2½ fl oz) milk
3 tablespoons butter

To make the butterscotch, place both sugars, the milk and butter in a saucepan and stir over a medium heat until the sugars and butter have dissolved. Bring to the boil, and simmer for 12 minutes. Leave to cool until tepid, stirring occasionally to prevent too much of a skin forming.

Pour boiling water over the peaches, leave for 20 seconds and drain. Run under the cold tap, and skin. Slice each peach thinly. Cut the crusts off the bread, and halve each slice. Brush the upper side with melted butter, and grill buttered side up until golden brown. Turn over, brush with butter, and grill the other side.

Spread each slice of bread with a little of the butterscotch, and arrange on a serving plate. Lay the peach slices on the butterscotched bread, and then trickle the remaining sauce over the peach slices. Sprinkle the flaked almonds over the top. Chill lightly in the fridge and serve with whipped cream, or Greek strained yoghurt.

Three Melon and Carambola Fruit Salad

It's about 15 cm (6 in) long, waxy and yellow with 5 ridges around a central core, giving a star-shaped cross-section. What is it? A *carambola*, also known as star fruit.

You may well have seen these rather strange-looking fruit in supermarkets and greengrocers. Raw, they have a sharp, citrus-like taste, best combined with other ingredients in a fruit salad, say, or with shellfish.

But the true beauty of their flavour comes out when they have been poached in a sugar syrup – the sharpness fades, and the marvellous, unusual perfume of the fruit comes through. They perfume the syrup as well, which can then be used, as in this recipe, to add something extra to a fruit salad, or to flavour whipped cream, or even to make a sorbet. That way, one expensive *carambola* can be stretched across 2 or even 3 dishes.

SERVES 8

150 g (5 oz) caster sugar
1 *carambola*
1 small charantais or canteloupe melon
½ ogen melon
750 g (1½ lb) piece of watermelon

Tip the caster sugar into a pan and add 150 ml (¼ pt) water. Bring to the boil, stirring constantly until the sugar has dissolved and the liquid is clear. Simmer for 5 minutes.

Meanwhile, prepare the *carambola*. Trim off any unsightly brown edges, and cut into 5 mm (¼ in) thick slices, discarding any seeds. Add the *carambola* slices to the boiling syrup and cook for a further 5 minutes, until the fruit is tender. Remove from the heat, and lift out the *carambola* with a slotted spoon. Leave both the fruit and the syrup to cool. Cut the melon into chunks, or small spheres, discarding the seeds and skin. Toss the 3 different kinds together. Pour about a third of the syrup over the fruit, and mix well. Put the remainder in a screw top jar, and keep in the fridge to add to other fruit salads. It will keep for up to 2 weeks. Leave the fruit salad in a cool place for at least 30 minutes, stirring occasionally. Lay the star-shaped *carambola* slices on top, and serve.

Canteloupe Soup

Fruit soups are still a bit of an oddity, regarded with some suspicion and a hint of hilarity. But why, for heaven's sake? If it is okay to whizz up vegetables and stock in a liquidiser and serve it as a starter, what's so odd about doing the same to summer fruit and some sweet liquid, and dishing it up at the other end of the meal?

This soup, quick and easy to make, should convince the doubtful. Use a canteloupe or charantais melon, with that gloriously scented orange flesh. There's no way to guarantee perfection when you are buying a melon, but 3 pointers to ripeness are: a) the smell – sweet and perfumed; b) the stalk end should give very slightly when pressed; c) the weight – it should be heavy for its size, so if you've whittled your choice down to 2 equally sized melons, choose the heavier of the pair. Avoid any that are bruised.

SERVES 2

1 orange
1 lime
60 g (2 oz) sugar
1 medium canteloupe or charantais melon
4 tablespoons single cream
15 g (½ oz) toasted hazelnuts*, chopped
1 sprig of mint

Pare half the zest from the orange and lime. Shred, and blanch in boiling water for 2 minutes. Drain well, cover and set aside. Squeeze the juice from the orange and lime and mix with the sugar. Stir over a medium heat until the sugar dissolves. Cool.

Halve the melon and scoop out the seeds. Scoop the flesh out of each half, taking care not to pierce the skins. Liquidise the flesh with the orange and lime syrup. Stir in the cream. Taste, and thin down with a tablespoon or 2 of water if it seems necessary.

To serve, sit the melon halves snugly in 2 bowls, and ladle in the soup. Scatter the hazelnuts and reserved zest over the surface, and float a sprig of mint in the centre. Serve with crisp sweet biscuits, such as *langues de chat* or *palmiers* or, best of all, with a slice of toasted brioche.

Fruit Salad With Amaretti Cream

This is a good all-year round recipe. Start off by gathering together a collection of fresh fruit, exotic or every day, or a mixture of the two. Choose fruits with contrasting textures, and don't go too wild. It makes life simpler and tastes and looks better if you use just three, four or five different fruit. Cut them into small pieces as appropriate, and mix with a tablespoon or two of Amaretto di Saronno liqueur, and sugar to taste if necessary. Marinate at room temperature for 1-2 hours, turning occasionally. Just before serving, taste the juices and add more Amaretto if you wish. Serve with this mixture of whipped cream and crisp almond-flavoured crumbs.

SERVES 6

150 ml (5 fl oz) whipping cream
90 g (3 oz) amaretti biscuits, crushed

Whip cream until stiff, and fold in the amaretti crumbs.

SWEET TARTS
AND PASTRIES

Angels' Hair and Cream Cheese Tart

Angels' Hair might seem a fanciful romantic name, when you discover that it is actually carrot jam. In fact it describes it well. Angels' Hair has an exotic mysterious taste that quite belies its humble ingredients. It reminds me of the rosewater-scented sweet-meats of the Middle East, too sweet to eat in any quantity, but so delicious that you soon long for more.

The recipe for the Angels' Hair is on page 246. In this recipe, the edge is taken off its sweetness by mixing it with cream cheese and yoghurt, as a filling for two crisp puff pastry cases.

SERVES 8–10

500 g (1 lb) puff pastry★
1 egg, beaten
1 quantity of Angels' Hair
250 g (8 oz) cream cheese
225 g (8 oz) Greek strained yoghurt
20 toasted hazelnuts★, skins rubbed off

Divide the pastry in half, and roll 1 piece out to form a large rectangle about 3 mm (⅛ in) thick. Using a ruler, cut a rectangle 13 x 30 cm (5 x 12 in), and 3 strips 30 x 1 cm (12 x ½ in) of puff pastry. Lift the rectangle on to a dampened baking sheet. Brush the edges with water, and lay 1 long strip down each of the long edges.

Cut two 13 cm (5 in) strips from the remaining strip, and lay across the ends, moistening and overlapping the corners. Repeat with the second half.

Prick the base of each case evenly all over with a fork, and bake blind.* (Be careful not to weigh down with the baking beans the strips at the edges which will rise to form walls.) Remove from the oven and leave to cool.

Beat all except 4 tablespoons of the Angels' Hair with the cream cheese and yoghurt and, just before serving, spread this out in the two tarts. Use the rest of the jam to form a long orange line down the centre of each tart, and dot with hazelnuts.

Apricot and Apple Jalousies

Jalousie is the French for jealousy. It also means a venetian blind, and from that meaning comes a third; a *jalousie* is a type of filled pastry. The connection is that the upper layer is slashed horizontally to resemble the slats of a venetian blind. As the puff pastry cooks and rises, the slashes open to reveal a glimpse of the filling.

Since it is the form of the pastry that gives rise to the name, you can slip all kinds of goodies in between the layers, but this combination of sweet apricot jam, sharp apple and nutmeg is especially good with the crisp, buttery puff pastry. Don't be alarmed if they ooze a little as they cook. It is quite normal, so just ignore it.

They are best hot, straight from the oven and with cream, as a pudding – you can make them up an hour or so in advance and pop them in the oven as you sit down to eat the main course (but don't forget that the temperature will need to be turned down if you don't want to burn them). But they are almost as nice rewarmed gently in the oven for tea.

SERVES 4

375 g (12 oz) puff pastry*
4 tablespoons apricot jam
1 large cooking apple, peeled, cored and thinly sliced
ground nutmeg
sugar
1 egg, beaten

Divide the pastry into 4. Roll out each piece so that you can cut a long oblong, about 20 x 15 cm (8 x 6 in). Divide each oblong into 2 equal rectangles 10 x 15 cm (4 x 6 in). Lay 4 of the rectangles on a lightly buttered baking tray. Spread a tablespoon of jam over each one, leaving a 1 cm (½ in) border all the way round. Arrange the apple slices on the jam, and sprinkle each rectangle with a pinch of nutmeg, and ½ tablespoon sugar.

One by one, fold the other rectangles in half loosely down the length, and slash parallel lines at 2 cm (1 in) intervals from the fold to within 1 cm (½ in) of the edge. Unfold. Brush the edges of the apple-laden pastry with water, and lay a slashed rectangle on top, pressing the edges together. Let the pastries rest for 30 minutes in the fridge, covered.

Brush with the beaten egg, and sprinkle with a little more sugar. Bake at 230C/450F/Gas 8 for 10–15 minutes, until browned, then turn down the heat to 180C/350F/Gas 4 and cook for a further 10 minutes.

Greengage Tart

The French for greengage is *reine-claude*. Queen Claude, the wife of François I, adored them and who can blame her? They are, I think, the best of all plums, with the exception perhaps of the little yellow mirabelle. Eat them as the opaque greenness turns to translucent green-gold, or bake them in a pastry shell to make the French patissier's classic *Tarte aux Reine-Claudes*.

SERVES 6–8

Pastry*:
250 g (8 oz) flour
finely grated zest and juice of 1 orange
1 teaspoon salt
125 g (4 oz) butter
1 egg, beaten
1 tablespoon oil

Filling:
¾ kg (1½ lb) greengages
2 generous tablespoons vanilla sugar*, or caster sugar
2 tablespoons apricot jam

Mix the flour with orange zest and salt. Rub in the butter until it resembles fine breadcrumbs. Make a well in the centre and add the egg and the oil. Mix to form a soft dough, adding 1–2 tablespoons of the orange juice if necessary. Roll out and line a 25 cm (10 in) tart tin with the pastry. Rest in the fridge for 30 minutes, and bake blind*.

Set the oven to 220C/375F/Gas 5. Halve and stone the green-gages. Sprinkle the base of the tart evenly with half the sugar, and arrange the greengage halves on it in concentric circles. Pack them in as tightly as possible but do not overlap. Sprinkle with the rest of the sugar and bake for 15 minutes, then reduce the heat to 190C/375F/Gas 5 and cook for a further 10–15 minutes, until the pastry is nicely browned.

While the tart is cooking, put the apricot jam into a small pan with ½ tablespoon of the orange juice. Melt over a medium heat, and sieve. If this glaze seems a little runny, simmer until thickened. Let the tart cool slightly, then brush with the glaze. Serve warm or cold.

Queen Charlotte's Tart

Another queen, Charlotte of Mecklenburg-Strelitz, the wife of King George III. Memories of her are scattered around London. In Queen Square, WC1 there is a statue supposedly of Her Majesty. Her portrait graces a medallion on the façade of Somerset House in the Strand and another, made of coade stone, is on the façade of Trinity House, Trinity Square, EC3. The Queen Charlotte's Maternity Hospital on Goldhawk Road is a more noticeable memorial – the earliest lying-in hospital in the British Isles, founded in 1739 in Jermyn Street, though it had to wait 60-odd years before Queen Charlotte gave it her royal approval, and tacked her name on to it.

This tart is yet another legacy. I came across it in Elisabeth Ayrton's *The Cookery of England* (Penguin Books, London), and couldn't resist trying it out. It's an orangey version of lemon meringue pie, with that lovely tang of citrus fruit pitched against the soft sweetness of the meringue.

SERVES 6–8

375 g (12 oz) shortcrust pastry*

Filling:
grated zest and juice of 2 oranges
grated zest and juice of 1 lemon
150 g (5 oz) sugar
5 eggs, separated

Line a 25 cm (10 in) tart tin with the pastry. Rest in the fridge for 30 minutes then bake blind*.

Whisk the zest and juices of the oranges and lemon with 125 g (4 oz) of the sugar and all the egg yolks. Pour into the half baked pastry case, and bake for 40 minutes at 150C/300F/Gas 2. Five minutes before the cooking time is up, whisk the egg whites until stiff. Fold in the remaining sugar and whisk again until shiny and smooth. Take the tart out of the oven, and turn up the heat to 200C/400F/Gas 6. Spread the meringue on top of the hot tart, forking up and swirling to give peaks and patterns, then pop back into the oven for a further 10 minutes, until the meringue is biscuit-coloured. Serve hot or cold.

Black-Bellied Streusel Tart

I felt that I had to give this tart a passably intriguing name, one that might disguise the nature of its main ingredient and lure the unsuspecting into trying it before they dismissed it out of hand. This is not, I hasten to add, because there is anything wrong with the main ingredient, just that so many people think that they loathe them. I'm talking about prunes, of course.

I understand that shudder of horror produced by memories of the awful stewed prunes of childhood that 'keep you regular'. This rather sophisticated tart should put paid to all that. If you are a prune-hater, then I would recommend that you ignore your prejudices for once and give it a try. You will be pleasantly surprised.

SERVES 8

250 g (8 oz) shortcrust pastry*

Filling:
375 g (12 oz) prunes, pre-soaked if necessary
300 ml (½ pt) light Earl Grey or Darjeeling tea
2 tablespoons caster sugar
2 tablespoons apricot jam
30 g (1 oz) ground almonds

Topping:
90 g (3 oz) flour
60 g (2 oz) butter, melted
60 g (2 oz) caster sugar

Line a 23 cm (9 in) tart tin with the pastry. Rest for 30 minutes in the fridge then bake blind*.

Simmer the prunes gently with the tea until really tender. Sieve. Add sugar to taste, but with restraint – it should be slightly tart, as the topping and jam layers are very sweet.

Mix the apricot jam with the almonds, and spread on the base of the tart. Cover with the prune purée. To make the topping, mix the flour with the sugar. Add the butter and mix until crumbly. Scatter over the purée. Bake at 190C/375F/Gas 5 for 25–30 minutes, until browned and crisp. Serve warm or cold.

Cranberry Tart

There's more to cranberries than sauce, and turkey, and Thanksgiving or Christmas dinners, nice though all of those are. The cranberry is an odd fruit, when you think about it. That characteristic bitter astringency makes them quite unlike any other, begging for some kind of softening sweetness, even when they are to be transformed into a sauce for meat.

As winter approaches, and punnets of cranberries crowd on to the greengrocers' shelves, I begin to use them in abundance. Two favourite recipes, which exploit their unique flavour well, are this buttery translucent tart and the moist cranberry and ginger cake on page 236.

SERVES 6–8

Pastry:
125 g (4 oz) plain flour
125 g (4 oz) wholemeal flour
125 g (4 oz) butter
1 tablespoon oil
1 egg, beaten
salt

Filling:
250 g (8 oz) cranberries
250 g (8 oz) caster sugar
125 g (4 oz) lightly salted butter
2 eggs
30 g (1 oz) flaked almonds

Sift the flours with the salt. Rub the butter into the flour. Make a well in the middle and pour in the egg and oil. Mix with enough cold water (this may be as little as one tablespoon) to form a dough. Set aside on a cool place for 30 minutes to relax.

Place the cranberries in a pan, with 2 tablespoons water and 60 g (2 oz) sugar. Heat gently, stirring, until the sugar has dissolved and the juices begin to run. Bring to the boil, and boil rapidly until the cranberries have all burst – 5–8 minutes. Off the heat, stir in the remaining sugar and the butter. Leave to cool.

Line a 25 cm (10 in) tart tin with pastry, prick the base with a fork, and rest again in the fridge for 30 minutes. Heat the oven to 190C/375F/Gas 5 and bake blind*. Whisk the eggs into the cranberry mixture, and pour into the pastry case. Scatter with the almonds, and bake for 30 minutes. The filling will puff up slightly as it cooks – but once out of the heat of the oven it will soon settle. This tart can be served hot, but is best just warm with a dollop of whipped cream.

Yorkshire Curd Tart

If you ever find yourself in Harrogate or Ilkley with a spare half hour to fill, head for the famous Betty's Tea Rooms to sample a slice of Yorkshire curd tart in its proper setting. Failing that, try making your own. A Yorkshire curd tart is one of best of British cheese-cakes, moist and granular, as opposed to the creamier folderols of American cheesecakes. If that's what you are after, skip on to the next recipe.

The curds themselves are just milk, separated into curds and whey with lemon juice. Buy a yard of butter muslin from a fabric shop to strain off the whey.

SERVES 6–8

2 litres (3 pt) milk
finely grated zest and juice of ½ a lemon
250 g (8 oz) shortcrust pastry*
60 g (2 oz) currants
a pinch of ground nutmeg
90 g (3 oz) sugar
60 g (2 oz) butter, melted
2 eggs, beaten

First make the curds. Bring the milk to the boil. Remove from the heat, and stir in the lemon juice. Leave for 15 minutes for the curds to form, and then strain through muslin. You should end up with around 250 g (8 oz) curds.

Line a 20 cm (8 in) tart tin with the pastry, prick with a fork, and leave to relax in a cool place for 30 minutes. Bake blind*.

Mix the well-drained curds with the zest of the lemon, the currants, nutmeg and sugar. Add the melted butter and the beaten egg and mix well. Pour into the pastry case.

Bake at 190C/375F/Gas 5 for 25–30 minutes, until golden brown. Serve warm.

New York Cheesecake

The New York cheesecake is the best of them all, I was told firmly when I visited the city. Uncluttered and unfussed, creamy and light with a hint of lemon and a hint of vanilla, and absolutely nothing more.

They have got a point. I take my work seriously, and sampled as many genuine New York cheesecakes as I could while I had the chance. In the end, I had to agree that it would be a shame to sully the purity of a perfect specimen with some over-bearing topping.

So here we are, a recipe for the ultimate baked cheesecake, not cloying and gluey as they are far too often, but a dream of simplicity.

SERVES 8

Base:
250 (8 oz) graham crackers, if you can get them, or digestive biscuits
90 g (3 oz) butter, melted

Filling:
500 g (1 lb) cream cheese
½ teaspoon vanilla essence
juice and finely grated zest of 1 lemon
3 eggs, separated
125 g (4 oz) caster sugar
2 tablespoons cornflour
150 ml (5 fl oz) soured cream

Pound the biscuits to crumbs in a plastic bag, or processor. Mix thoroughly with the butter. Press evenly into the base of a greased 23 cm (9 in) springform cake tin. Chill while you make the filling.

Beat the cream cheese with the vanilla, lemon juice and zest, until smooth. Add the egg yolks, then 60 g (2 oz) of caster sugar, cornflour and soured cream and beat until well mixed. Whisk the egg whites until stiff, add the remaining sugar, and whisk again until smooth and shiny. Fold into the cream cheese mixture.

Spoon on to the biscuit crust, and smooth over the surface. Bake for 55–60 minutes at 170C/325F/Gas 3, until nicely browned. The filling nearest the outside should feel firm to the touch, though the very centre will still be slightly gooey – it will continue to cook as it cools. Leave to cool, then run a thin knife blade around the edge, and ease the cheesecake carefully out of the tin. Chill for 4–12 hours in the fridge before serving.

Shoo Fly Pie

Another American classic that is as dark and dense as the New York cheesecake is pale and light. I knew the name from the song, but a few years ago realised that I didn't have the foggiest idea what a shoo fly pie was. I searched and asked around and came up with a fistful of recipes. Essentially they were all much the same, in this one the filling was deeper, in that one there was no nutmeg or cloves, in a third they used all dark muscovado sugar, and so on. This is a distillation of all those recipes, outrageously sweet and sticky and indulgent.

SERVES 8

175 g (6 oz) shortcrust pastry*

Crumble:
125 g (4 oz) plain flour
generous pinch of ground ginger, nutmeg, cinnamon and cloves
pinch of salt
60 g (2 oz) light muscovado sugar
60 g (2 oz) chilled butter

Filling:
90 g (3 oz) raisins
125 g (4 oz) dark muscovado sugar
2 eggs, beaten
6 tablespoons boiling water
½ teaspoon bicarbonate of soda

Line a 23 cm (9 in) tart tin with the pastry. Leave in the fridge for 30 minutes to rest. Put a baking sheet in the centre of the oven, and set to 190C/375F/Gas 5. To make the topping, mix the flour with the spices, salt and sugar. Rub in the butter until the mixture resembles coarse breadcrumbs.

Prick the base of the tart with a fork and scatter with the raisins. Mix together the brown sugar, eggs, and 2 tablespoons cold water. Mix the bicarbonate of soda with the boiling water, then pour into the eggs and sugar mixture, whisk quickly and pour over the raisins. Sprinkle the crumble mixture evenly over the top. Place on the baking sheet in the hot oven and bake for 30–40 minutes, until lightly browned. Serve warm or cold with thick yoghurt, to cut the sweetness.

Edouard de Pomiane's Cherry Tart

If you ever come across a copy of Dr Edouard de Pomiane's *Cooking with Pomiane*, snap it up without hesitation. Inside its covers you will find, as well as a host of enticing recipes, clear scientific explanations of why, for instance, mayonnaise does or does not curdle, or why you need to fry a chip twice to get a perfect outside and melting interior, all related in the wittiest, conversational prose.

This recipe was given to Dr de Pomiane by his neighbour, whose mother used to make little fruit tarts for friends with leftover bread dough, but beware – 'the edges of the tart are slightly burnt, and the top layer of cherries blackened in places.' Like Elizabeth David in her introduction to the book, I like the rough look of the tart, and I love the taste of the syrupy burning hot cherry juice, as it oozes into the yeasty dough. To my mind this is the best of all cherry tarts.

SERVES 6–8

Bread dough:
15 g (½ oz) easy-bake (or easy-blend) dried yeast*
150 ml (¼ pt) warm milk
½ teaspoon sugar
15 g (½ oz) butter
250 g (8 oz) strong white flour
¼ teaspoon salt

Tart:
60 g (2 oz) chilled butter
175 g (6 oz) sugar
¾ kg (1½ lb) ripe cherries

To make the bread dough, dissolve the butter in the warm milk. Sift the flour and the salt into a mixing bowl, and warm slightly. Stir in the yeast. Make a well in the centre and pour in enough of the warm milk to mix to a firm dough. If it becomes too sticky, add extra flour. Knead on a floured surface for about 10 minutes, until satin smooth and elastic. Cover and leave in a warm place until doubled in size (1–2 hours).

Knead again, for 5 minutes, then work in the chilled butter, cut into small pieces. On a floured board, roll out the dough, and use to line a lightly greased 25 cm (10 in) tart tin, trimming off the edges. Prick the base with a fork, then pile in the cherries (take the stones out first if you wish, but it's not absolutely necessary). Dredge with 150 g (5 oz) of the sugar.

Bake at 240C/475F/Gas 8 for 20–25 minutes, until the edges are well browned and some of the cherries are beginning to blacken. Take out of the oven, sprinkle with the remaining sugar, and serve with double cream.

Chocolate and Satsuma Money Bags

In this recipe, squares of filo pastry are twisted around a filling of chocolate and satsuma. Having been plunged into a fiery oven to crisp the pastry, the chocolate will ooze out as you cut into the bag. After a heavy meal, one per person should be ample, but after a lighter meal your guests may well be clamouring for a second. Serve neat, or with a few slices of fresh citrus fruit, mango or pear (toss in lemon juice to prevent discoloration), marinated perhaps in Grand Marnier or Cointreau. The money bags can be prepared 4–5 hours in advance, or frozen and cooked from frozen – add an extra 5 minutes cooking time.

SERVES 3–6

1 large satsuma
90 g (3 oz) plain chocolate*, chopped
2 sheets filo pastry*
30 g (1 oz) butter, melted

Peel the satsuma. Cut the peel into long thin strips, and blanch for 1 minute in boiling water. Dry on kitchen paper. Set aside 6 long strips (at least 8 cms/3 in) and chop the remainder. Using a small sharp knife, carefully peel 6 whole satsuma segments.

Keep the filo pastry covered with a sheet of greaseproof paper, with a dampened tea-towel laid over the top while you work. Cut the filo in half lengthways, then cut each strip into 3 squares.

Brush 2 squares with melted butter and lay one on top of the other. Pile ⅙ of the chocolate in the centre. Top with ½ teaspoon chopped peel and a satsuma segment. Gently gather the edges of the pastry up and around, trying not to tear it on the edges of the chocolate, twisting the ends together to form a little moneybag. Press a strip of peel around the 'neck' of the bag. Sit on a buttered baking sheet.

Repeat with the remaining ingredients, and brush the bags with the last of the butter. Cover and chill until needed. Bake at 250C/500F/Gas 9 for 7–10 minutes, until browned. Eat immediately.

Blackberries in Filo Pastry

This is a simple way of transforming dull farmed blackberries, bringing out a flavour that's close to that of wild blackberries. Of course, it's even better made with blackberries brought back from a ramble in the countryside. *Crème de mûres* is a blackberry liqueur. Look out for miniatures in well-stocked wine shops, or use the more widely available *crème de cassis*.

SERVES 6

90 g (3 oz) cream cheese
1 tablespoon *crème de mûres* or *cassis*
125–175 g (4–6 oz) blackberries
60 g (2 oz) sugar
2 sheets filo pastry*
30 g (1 oz) butter, melted

Sauce:
250 g (8 oz) blackberries
2 tablespoons *crème de mûres* or *cassis*
extra sugar if necessary

Make the sauce first: pick over the blackberries, removing any that are damaged. Place in a pan with the liqueur. Heat gently until they begin to exude juice, then simmer for 5 minutes. Remove from the heat, and sieve or pass through the fine blade of the *mouli-légumes*. Taste, and add sugar if necessary, though the sauce should be slightly tart.

For the filo parcels, beat the cream cheese with the *cassis*. Mix the blackberries with the sugar. Halve the sheets of filo pastry length-ways, and divide each strip into 3 squares. Take 2 squares, brush with melted butter and lay one on top of the other. Place a heaped teaspoon of the cream cheese in the centre and top with blackberries. Gather the pastry up and around, twisting the ends together to form a money bag. Sit on a buttered baking sheet. Repeat until all the ingredients are used. Brush the bags with any remaining butter, cover and set aside. They can be made up to 3 hours in advance.

Heat the oven to 250C/475F/Gas 9. Bake the filo bags for 7–10 minutes, until browned. Divide the sauce between 6 individual plates (reheat it if you like – I prefer it cold). Sit a hot pastry in the centre of each plate and serve, with single cream if desired.

Filo Flowers With Halva Cream

This is another way of using filo pastry, baked without a filling to make crisp little containers. What you then fill them with is up to you. The halva cream I suggest in the recipe is smooth and nutty, but if you fancy something lighter, pile them high with fresh fruit and cream or *crème patissière*.

You can buy packets of halva from many supermarkets and Middle Eastern food shops, but do make sure you are buying the right kind. I didn't look properly last time, and had to pick out dozens of peanuts. Somehow, I couldn't convince myself that they would improve the pudding. Had I chanced upon a block of pistachio halva, however, I might just have left the nuts in.

SERVES 6

3 sheets of filo pastry*
60 g (2 oz) melted butter
90 g (3 oz) sugar
1–2 teaspoons triple strength rosewater

Filling:
150 g (5 oz) thick crème fraîche, or drained fromage frais
175 g (6 oz) plain halva, crumbled
2 spheres of stem ginger in syrup

Lay the sheets of filo pastry in a pile and, using scissors or a sharp knife, cut into 10 cm (4 in) squares – you should have at least 18. Keeping the remaining pastry covered with a sheet of greaseproof paper, topped with a squeezed-out damp tea-towel, take a batch of 3 squares. Brush each with melted butter, and lay one on another to form a flower-shape, with the 12 corners as the petals.

Lift this formation and press gently into the depression of a well-buttered straight sided tartlet tin, gathering the pastry gently so that it fans out prettily over the edges of the tin. Bake blind*.

While the pastry is cooking, make a syrup with the 90 g (3 oz) sugar, and 150 ml (¼ pt) water – simmer for 5 minutes, remove from the heat and stir in the rosewater. When the cases are cooked, stand on a large plate, and pour the syrup over them making sure they are thoroughly coated. Leave to cool.

To make the filling, beat the crème fraîche with the crumbled halva until smooth. Finely chop the ginger and stir in. Just before serving, fill the pastry cases with the cream.

PUDDINGS

Marmalade Ice-Cream With Walnut Sauce

Being a schoolgirl in Oxford brought many benefits. I'm not sure
that my friends and I really appreciated the heady intellectual
atmosphere of the colleges, but we took full advantage of many of
the extra-curricular pastimes spawned by the University. The
summer months were particularly pleasant – punting and boating,
Shakespeare plays in beautiful college gardens, watching cricket in
the Parks, or the Eights races on the Isis. And, of course, there were
the students themselves.

A curious shop came in to its own in May and June, at least as far
as I was concerned. In a side street off Cornmarket, one of Oxford's
main streets, was a cramped bookshop. As well as books, it sold
wrapping paper and cards, and the most inventive range of
homemade ice-creams. The choice changed weekly. There were
usually all the basics – vanilla, chocolate, strawberry, and so on –
but there was always at least one 'joker'. The two that have stayed
most in my mind are the witty smartie ice-cream and, best of all,
their marmalade ice-cream. The slight bitterness of Seville oranges
on the tongue, rich and creamy. I think the shop has now disappeared, but the memories linger on.

For preference, use homemade marmalade for this ice-cream – if
you make your own, it's a good way to clear the shelves before the
winter's new arrivals. Otherwise, try to buy a jar of 'extra-jam'
marmalade, with a high proportion of fruit to sugar.

SERVES AT LEAST 8

Ice-cream:
375 g (12 oz) marmalade
300 ml (10 fl oz) double cream

Sauce:
4 tablespoons marmalade
150 ml (¼ pt) orange juice
150 ml (¼ pt) water
sugar to taste if necessary
45 g (1½ oz) walnuts

To make the ice-cream, tip the marmalade into a large bowl and beat. Whip the cream until stiff, then fold into the marmalade. Freeze. This is one of those miracle ice-creams that doesn't need beating as it freezes, and can be served straight from the freezer – a marvellous thing, that double cream.

For the sauce, place the marmalade, orange juice and water in a pan, and simmer together for 10 minutes. Taste and add sugar if necessary. If you are feeling very conscientious (and it will improve the taste), remove the clinging papery skin from the walnuts as follows: cover with boiling water and leave for 30 seconds. Drain, and peel. Be patient.

If you aren't feeling so conscientious, just break the walnuts into small pieces and, off the heat, add to the sauce. Serve the sauce hot or cold, with the ice-cream.

Panettone di Natale

Around Christmastime, every Italian foodstore has clusters of boxed *panettone* hanging from their ceilings, or piled up on the counter. Inside the boxes is a large, light, yeast-raised cake, packed with raisins and mixed candied peel. A slice of *panettone*, dipped in a frothy cappuccino, makes a lovely quick breakfast – and it is just as good, lightly buttered, with a cup of afternoon tea. Any leftover, slightly stale cake is excellent toasted. A whole *panettone* is a very useful standby in case of unexpected guests, as it keeps for months in its wrapping.

This recipe was given to me by an Italian friend. Her mother would make this stuffed *panettone* every Christmas Eve. The 'lid' is in fact cut from the base of the cake, not the top. The idea is that no-one should be able to tell that it is not just an ordinary *panettone*.

Every year, my friend and the other children would feign wild surprise as their mother cut into the *panettone*, to reveal the filling, although, of course, they remembered full well numerous past Christmas Eve feasts.

SERVES 10

1 x 1 kg (2 lb) *panettone*
500 g (1 lb) ricotta
125 g (4 oz) mixed candied peel, chopped
125 g (4 oz) plain chocolate*, coarsely chopped
2 tablespoons caster sugar
6 tablespoons brandy

Turn the *panettone* upside down, and slice a circle from the base. Lift off and set aside. Carefully scoop out the insides, leaving sturdy walls a good 3–4 cm (1–1½ in) thick. Sprinkle the inside with 2 tablespoons of the brandy.

Crumble the part that was scooped out. Mix with the ricotta, candied peel, chocolate, sugar and remaining brandy. Pile back into the *panettone*. Replace the base, and carefully turn the right way up. Wrap tightly in foil and keep in the fridge for up to 3 days. Serve lightly chilled, cut into big wedges.

Frozen Chocolate Mocha Mousse

This is the most superb pudding, simultaneously an ice-cream and a mousse, rising majestically above the rim of its bowl in imitation of a hot soufflé.

Use the best plain chocolate you can find, with a high percentage of cocoa solids. Be careful not to overheat the chocolate when melting – it loses its gloss and turns grainy. Remove from the heat the very moment it has melted.

SERVES 8

250 g (8 oz) plain chocolate*, broken into squares
1 tablespoon high quality instant coffee
4 eggs, separated
125 g (4 oz) sugar
300 ml (10 fl oz) whipping cream
icing sugar

First prepare the mould. You will need a 14–15 cm (5½-6 in) soufflé dish. Cut a strip of greaseproof paper or foil 15 cm (6 in) wide and long enough to go round the dish, the ends overlapping by 2 cm (1 in). Wrap around the dish, leaving at least 5 cm (2 in) sticking up above the rim, and secure with sticky tape. For extra security, stretch an elastic band or tie a piece of string around the dish just below the rim. Brush the inside of the paper with a little tasteless oil.

Melt the chocolate* with the coffee and 2 tablespoons water, and cool slightly. Whisk the egg yolks with the sugar, until thick and pale. Mix with the melted chocolate. Whip the cream until soft peaks form. Fold into the chocolate. Whisk the egg whites until stiff, then fold in too. Spoon into the prepared mould, and smooth down gently. Freeze.

Move from the freezer to the fridge 10–15 minutes before serving. Carefully remove the paper collar and dust with icing sugar just before taking to the table.

Chestnut and Chocolate Pudding

A pudding of sheer dastardly indulgence, this, for special occasions only. There is absolutely nothing that can be said for it in health terms – it is fattening, full of cholesterol, and if eaten in quantity will probably aid and abet spots. So don't say I didn't warn you.

SERVES 8

125 g (4 oz) plain chocolate*
90 g (3 oz) butter
120 ml (4 fl oz) single cream
90 g (3 oz) caster sugar
1 x 425 g (15 oz) tin unsweetened chestnut purée
10 Nice biscuits
1 tablespoon brandy

Melt the chocolate* with the butter, cream and sugar.

Tip the chestnut purée into a bowl, and beat in the chocolate mixture. Break the Nice biscuits into pieces, and sprinkle with the brandy. Now line a long 500 g (1 lb) loaf tin with silver foil and brush lightly with a little oil. Spread a third of the chocolate and chestnut mixture in the base. Now arrange half the Nice biscuits in a single layer on top. Cover with another third of the chocolate and chestnut, then add the rest of the biscuits and finish by covering with the remaining chocolate and chestnut mixture.

Smooth over the surface, and leave overnight in the fridge to firm up. Ten minutes before you are ready to serve, put it into the freezer compartment – this isn't absolutely necessary, but will make the transfer from tin to plate easier. Lift out of the tin carefully, invert on to a serving dish and peel off the silver foil. If you like, decorate with toasted almonds* or hazelnuts, halves of *marrons glacées*, or *glacéed* fruits. What is really nice served with this is more thin cold single cream, but you might feel that that is a bit over the top.

Salame del Papa (The Pope's Salami)

'The Pope's Salami' is an Easter speciality of Alessandria, in the Piedmont. Lucky Pope, and lucky Alessandrians. It's got nothing at all to do with salami, apart from a certain *trompe-l'oeil* effect. Now I don't mean that it is a two-dimensional sausage masquerading as a three-dimensional one. What I mean is that this devastatingly rich confection is shaped to resemble its namesake, and sliced in the same way.

The 'meat' is a dark chocolate and liqueur-scented butter, studded with crisp pieces of biscuit – the little cubes of fat, as it were. It is an Easter joke, a light-hearted, frolicsome sweet to enjoy with coffee. It can be served too with something light and fruity – try it with the Blood Oranges in Rosemary Syrup (page 174).

It can be made two or three days in advance, as long as it is kept cool and firm in the fridge. In fact, like a salami, you can cut slices off as and when they are required, just the thing for a long weekend shared with friends and family. The truly artistic among you will really go to town on dressing the wrapping to imitate a real salami.

SERVES 8–10

125 g (4 oz) unsalted butter, softened
125 g (4 oz) caster sugar
3 tablespoons single cream
60 g (2 oz) cocoa
1½ tablespoons rum
2 tablespoons marsala
175 g (6 oz) crisp plain sweet biscuits such as Petit Beurre

Cream the butter with the sugar until light and fluffy. Beat in the cream. Gradually work in the cocoa, then mix in the rum and marsala. Crush the biscuits into small pieces (but not too fine – pieces not powder), and fold into the mixture. Taste, and add a little more alcohol if you wish. Chill the mixture for 20 minutes or so, until firm enough to mould.

On a sheet of greaseproof paper, pat the chocolate mixture into a plump sausage shape. Roll up neatly and tie the ends with string, trimming off the excess paper. Chill for at least 4 hours, until set firm.

To serve, peel the paper off one end of your 'salami', and cut a few slices about 5 mm (¼ in) thick. Arrange on a plate with the whole cylinder so that it looks like a real salami, half sliced, for the hors d'œuvre.

The Peat Inn's Chocolate and Rosemary Cream

Novelist Paul Bailey took over my *Evening Standard* column for a fortnight while I took my first break in two years. I was very pleased to see that he included this chocolate cream – I'd tasted it at one of his magnificent lunches. The recipe was given to him by its inventor, David Wilson, who runs The Peat Inn restaurant in Fife.

Rosemary and chocolate sounds an odd sort of mixture, but I can assure you that it tastes superb. Use the best dark plain chocolate for this pudding – anything less is unworthy.

SERVES 6

250 g (8 oz) granulated sugar
250 ml (8 fl oz) dry white wine
juice of half a lemon
600 ml (1 pt) double cream
1 sprig of rosemary
160 g (5½ oz) plain chocolate*, grated

To serve:
6 small sprigs of rosemary
4 blanched almonds, finely chopped

In a heavy-bottomed pan, mix the sugar, white wine and lemon juice. Stir over a medium heat until the sugar has dissolved completely. Stir in the double cream. Cook over a gentle heat, stirring constantly until the mixture thickens.

Add the rosemary, then the chocolate, stirring until completely
dissolved. Bring to the boil. Simmer very gently for about 20
minutes, until the mixture is dark and thick. Cool until tepid.

Pour through a sieve into 6 little ramekins. Cover with cling film,
and refrigerate until set. Decorate each pot with a sprig of rosemary
and a sprinkling of almonds.

Hot Chocolate and Orange Soufflé

Soufflés are not difficult to make; quite the opposite, they are
actually very easy as long as you follow the instructions, and don't
let anybody tell you otherwise. What is more, you don't even have
to prepare them at the last minute, because they can be frozen in
their dishes and cooked straight from the freezer, needing only an
extra 4–5 minutes on top of the usual cooking time.

If I have friends coming over for supper, and know that I'm not
going to have much time to cook, I often make this superb pudding
a week or so in advance. It can be served with extra cream, or a sieved
raspberry coulis (page 213) or, most sensational of all, with the
orange sabayon sauce that follows. Suggest to your guests that they
make a hole in the centre of the hot soufflé and pour the cool sauce
into it, adding more as they eat and the hole gets bigger.

SERVES 6

250 g (8 oz) plain chocolate*, broken into squares
finely grated zest and juice of ½ orange
4 tablespoons single cream
90 g (3 oz) caster sugar
4 egg yolks
6 egg whites
pinch of salt
icing sugar

To prepare dishes:
unsalted butter
caster sugar

Turn your freezer to its highest setting (i.e. make it as cold as
possible). Butter 6 small oven-proof soufflé dishes or ramekins,
each large enough to take 200–300 ml (⅓–½ pt), and dust with
caster sugar. Melt the chocolate* with the orange zest and cream.
Remove from the heat. Stir in the sugar, then the egg yolks,
followed by the orange juice.

Whisk the egg whites with the salt until stiff. Fold into the chocolate sauce. Pour into the prepared soufflé dishes and rush into the freezer.

To cook, heat the oven to 200C/400F/Gas 6. Bake the soufflés from frozen for 20–25 minutes until well risen. Dust with icing sugar, and serve with orange sabayon sauce (see below), raspberry coulis or plain single cream.

Orange Sabayon Sauce

A foamy orange sauce that is blissful with any chocolatey pudding, as well as with countless others. It can be served hot as soon as it has billowed up in its bowl to a light foamy mass, or cold, in which case it can be made up to 8 hours in advance.

SERVES 6

finely grated zest and juice of 2 oranges
juice of 1 lemon
90 g (3 oz) caster sugar
3 egg yolks

Place all the ingredients in a large bowl. Set over a pan of gently simmering water, making sure that the base does not touch the water. Whisk until the sauce is thick and fluffy right through to the base, and has doubled its bulk.

Stand the bowl in a slightly larger bowl of iced water, and continue whisking until the sauce is cold.

Hot Caramel Soufflé With Raspberry Coulis

Oh, you do have a treat in store for you when you make this soufflé. It is light and airy, caramelly and ridiculously more-ish. If you are well-brought up and restrained people, then it will probably stretch around 6 of you. If, on the other hand, you are rather more like me, and get wildly enthused, then 4 of you will probably find yourself fighting over who scrapes out the dish.

Cooking it in an oval gratin dish means you get more of the nice brown top, and that you can prepare it in advance and freeze it (see Chocolate Soufflé). Cook straight from the freezer, adding an extra 5 minutes to the cooking time. If it is made in an ordinary soufflé dish, increase the cooking time by 8 minutes to compensate for the extra depth. You can still freeze it, although it won't rise so well as it cooks.

SERVES 4–6

175 g (6 oz) sugar
20 g (¾ oz) flour
150 ml (¼ pt) milk
1 vanilla pod*
4 eggs, separated
1 egg white
15 g (½ oz) butter
icing sugar

Raspberry coulis:
300 g (10 oz) fresh or thawed frozen raspberries
icing sugar
lemon juice

First make the caramel – place the sugar and 5 tablespoons water in a pan, and stir over a low heat until clear. Turn up the heat, and let the syrup boil without stirring, until it turns a hazelnut brown. Remove from the heat.

In a separate pan, whisk the flour with enough milk to make a thick paste. Gradually whisk in the remaining milk, and add the vanilla pod. Bring to the boil, stirring. Simmer for 1 minute, then whisk in the caramel. Remove from the heat, and beat it for a minute or so to cool slightly. Fish out the vanilla pod, rinse and dry it so that it can be used again.

Beat the egg yolks into the warm sauce, then add the butter. Whisk the egg whites until stiff. Fold into the caramel sauce. Pour into a buttered 30 cm (12 in) oval gratin dish (should be about 5 cm/2 in deep) and dust with icing sugar. Whip it quickly into an oven pre-heated to 200C/400F/Gas 6. Bake for 25 minutes, until puffed and browned.

While the soufflé is cooking, make the sauce. Sieve the raspberries, and sweeten the purée to taste with icing sugar. Add a dash of lemon juice to sharpen. Warm gently without boiling, and serve with the soufflé.

Brown Sugar Meringues With Coffee Cream

The way to make perfect meringues, crisp and light through to the centre, is to cook them at the lowest possible temperature for the longest possible time. They need drying out, rather than cooking. I leave mine overnight, on the lowest oven setting, with the door slightly ajar.

The brown sugar gives these meringues a caramel taste that is delicious with coffee cream. If they are cooked until dry as a bone, they will keep happily for several days in an airtight container.

SERVES 4

2 egg whites
90 g (3 oz) light muscovado sugar
30 g (1 oz) caster sugar
150 ml (5 fl oz) whipping cream
1–2 tablespoons strong coffee
oil

Line 2 baking trays with greaseproof paper, and brush lightly with oil.

Whisk the egg whites until stiff and add both sugars. Whisk again until stiff and shiny. Place dessertspoonfuls of the mixture, evenly spaced, on the baking trays. Bake at 110C/225F/Gas ½ for 2 hours, or an even lower temperature for even longer. When the meringues peel easily off the paper, they are done.

Whip the cream, fold in the coffee to taste, add extra sugar if wished. When the meringues are cool, sandwich together with coffee cream.

Ricotta With Candied Fruit

Italian ricotta must be fresh if it is to be worth using. Once it has been sitting around for 2 or 3 days it develops a bitter edge which mars its pure cool creaminess. Buy it from a shop with a fast turnover, where a new mound of ricotta arrives daily. Ignore the stuff they sell in plastic pots in supermarkets.

This is a quick pudding, of ricotta mixed with candied fruits and plain chocolate and flavoured with the scent of orange flower water or ginger. The mixture can also be used as a filling for pastries, or fresh figs.

Serves 4

375 g (12 oz) fresh ricotta
30 g (1 oz) glacé cherries, chopped
30 g (1 oz) mixed candied peel
30 g (1 oz) angelica, chopped
30 g (1 oz) plain chocolate*, grated or chopped
1–2 tablespoons orange flower water or 2 spheres of preserved ginger,
    chopped, and 1–2 tablespoons syrup from ginger jar
cocoa

Beat the ricotta with the candied fruit, chocolate, and either orange flower water to taste, or ginger and syrup. Pile into bowls, and dust with cocoa.

Ilona's Nasturtium and Rosewater Ice-cream

My wild Polish friend Ilona runs a busy catering company. Whenever we meet we end up talking endless shop. She's always full of ideas, and this ice-cream was one of them. She based her recipe on one used by the chef George Blancs, adding a hint of rosewater for extra fragrance.

I had to steal a bunch of nasturtiums from a neighbour's window box to try this one out – I was living in a small flat at the time. I did own up later and all was forgiven. The flowers give an elusive peppery greenness to the ice-cream, flecking it with orange and yellow.

I've used an Italian meringue base, which means that the tedious task of beating the ice-cream as it sets is redundant. However, unless you have strong arms you will need an electric beater. The mixture can be piped on to a tray covered in cling film, and frozen in swirls, ready to be dished up elegantly with a tumble of fresh fruit and a crisp biscuit such as a *langue de chat*. Try adding a sharp raspberry or redcurrant coulis (page 213).

Serves 6–8

8 large nasturtium flowers
1 teaspoon rosewater
250 g (8 oz) caster sugar
2 egg whites
3 tablespoons lemon juice
300 ml (10 fl oz) double cream

Place the sugar in a pan with 150 ml (¼ pt) of water. Stir over a medium heat until the sugar dissolves and the syrup is completely clear. Bring to the boil, and boil for 5 minutes. While the syrup boils, whisk the egg whites until stiff. Pour the boiling syrup on to the egg whites, whisking constantly. Continue to whisk until you have a thick, glossy meringue. Leave to cool.

Liquidise the nasturtium flowers with the lemon juice and rosewater. Fold into the meringue. Whip the cream until stiff, and fold that in too. Pour into a freezer-proof container, or pipe onto a cling film-lined tray and freeze. Serve straight from the freezer.

BREADS, BISCUITS
AND CAKES

———— ❧❧❧ ————

Red Onion Bread

I love red onions, with their dark purple skin and sweet mildness. I'm not alone in this. There's a small town in the south of Italy that holds a week-long festival in their honour, with races and games, culminating in a red onion feast.

Down a twisting alley is a pizzeria where they make a superb red onion pizza. The wood-fired ovens have been there for some 200 years, bunches of herbs and skeins of onions and garlic strung from the beams. You can have pizza or pizza, and they'll rustle up a salad of scarlet tomatoes and, naturally, red onions, if you insist. It's one of the best meals you'll ever eat, but not one that can be recreated at home. Nonetheless, this onion bread, inspired by that pizzeria, is irresistible. And, if needs be, it's still good made with ordinary onions.

olive oil
½ kg (1 lb) red onions, thinly sliced
1 sprig of fresh thyme
salt
1–2 tablespoons caster sugar

Bread dough:
500 g (1 lb) strong bread flour
½ tablespoon salt
1 sachet 'easy-blend' dried yeast*
1 tablespoon olive oil

218

To make the bread dough, sift the flour with the salt, into a bowl. Stir in the yeast. Make a well in the centre and add the olive oil and up to 300 ml (½ pt) warm water, to form a firm dough. Knead for 5–10 minutes, until smooth and elastic. Return to the bowl, pop into a plastic bag and leave in a warm place for about 1 hour, or until doubled in volume. Knead again for 2 minutes.

Heat 4 tablespoons olive oil in a heavy pan. Add the onions and thyme, stir, then cover and turn the heat down low. Cook for about 1 hour, stirring occasionally, until meltingly tender. Salt lightly.

Once the onions are cooking, roll the dough into a large ball, and flatten on an oiled baking sheet to form a circle about 23 cm (9 in) in diameter. Cover loosely and leave in a warm place, until doubled in bulk.

Just before baking, spread the onions on the dough. Sprinkle with caster sugar. Bake at 200C/400F/Gas 6 for 30–40 minutes, until crisply browned between the onions. Best eaten warm.

Mr Egan's Soda Bread

Not long after I included a recipe for soda bread in the London *Evening Standard* I received a letter from a reader. I hadn't got it right at all – instead of making my bread with sour milk in the time-honoured way, I'd cheated with a pinch of cream of tartar. But I didn't always have sour milk to hand, I replied . . .

A poor excuse, it seems. Mr Egan sours fresh milk by stirring in a tablespoon of lemon juice or vinegar and letting it stand and separate for 15 minutes. I've now mended my ways, and use Mr Egan's recipe every time. Even if you have to add on the extra 15 minutes for the milk to sour, it is still quick to make. Soda bread, with its close, cakey texture doesn't keep as well as yeasted bread, but unused bread can be frozen until needed.

MAKES 1 large or 2 small loaves

500 g (1 lb) stoneground wholemeal flour
250 g (8 oz) stoneground strong white flour
1 teaspoon salt
1 teaspoon bicarbonate of soda
600 ml (1 pt) sour milk

Mix the dry ingredients. Make a well in the centre, and pour in the milk. Mix to a firm even dough. Shape into a large round loaf shape, or 2 smaller ones. Place on a lightly greased baking sheet, and with a sharp knife make 2 deep slashes from side to side, at right angles to each other, without cutting right through. Cover each loaf with a large metal cake tin. Bake at 230C/450F/Gas 8 for 40 minutes.

La Galette de Pérouges

An old school friend, who now lives near Lyons, sent me this recipe for a local speciality, *La Galette de Pérouges*. A *galette* is a round flat cake, in this case a bread dough, spiked with lemon zest, rolled out thin and spread with butter and sugar, which meld together in the fierce heat of the oven. A sweet French pizza, you might say, crisp, sugary and buttery. This *galette* should be baked in a single huge impressive circle, but my oven isn't big enough for that, so I compromise and make 2 smaller ones.

Although the dough does take time to rise, the preparation and the final cooking are a matter of minutes. You'll find that the dough, is very amenable. You could make it up several hours before you need it, leave it to rise and, once it has got there, punch it down, cover, and put it in the fridge until called for. You could even leave it there overnight and make the *galette* for breakfast, though it is best served as a dramatic, rustic finale to a good meal.

SERVES 10

280–300 g (9–10 oz) strong flour
pinch of salt
1½ teaspoons dried 'easy-blend' yeast★
125 g (4 oz) caster sugar
200 g (7 oz) softened butter
finely grated zest of 1 lemon
1 egg
150 ml (¼ pt) warm water

Sift the flour with the salt and mix with a third of the sugar and the yeast in a large bowl. Make a well in the centre. Cream 150 g (5 oz) of the butter with the lemon zest, then beat in the egg. Pour into the flour, and add enough warm water to mix to a soft dough. Knead until smooth and elastic and the dough no longer sticks to the fingers, dusting with extra flour if necessary. Cover and leave in a warm place for 1½–2 hours, until doubled in size.

Punch down and divide the dough in 2. Roll each piece out into a 5 mm (¼ in) thick circle. Lay each piece on a baking sheet, and crimp the edges of the pastry upwards to prevent the topping overflowing.

Smear with the remaining butter and sprinkle evenly with the remaining sugar. Bake at your oven's highest setting for 8–10 minutes, until browned and crisp. Serve warm.

Spiced Water Biscuits

A really good piece of farmhouse cheese needs really good biscuits to set it off. I always pick Bath Olivers or make my own, spiced or plain. Homemade water biscuits, fresh from the oven, are hard to beat, and quick and easy to bake.

You can leave out the pepper and cumin if you prefer a plainer biscuit, maybe to go with a subtle cheese, or conversely with a highly distinctive one that might clash. Alternatively, add spices to only half the dough, after it has been made up: divide in 2, roll out 1 half thinly, sprinkle with half the quantity of spices, fold in 2 and roll out again. Treat the other half as in the recipe.

You'll find that some will puff up in the oven and some won't, but they will all taste fine. Tiny 2–3 cm (1 in) diameter water biscuits make good canapé bases – spread with potted cheese, chicken liver pâté, and so on.

MAKES about 20

125 g (4 oz) plain flour
¼ teaspoon salt
½ teaspoon bicarbonate of soda
1 level teaspoon dried green or black peppercorns
1 level teaspoon whole cumin seeds
30 g (1 oz) butter

Sift the flour with the salt and soda. With a pestle and mortar, crush the peppercorns and cumin to a coarse powder, or grind very briefly in a coffee grinder, but not long enough to pulverise to a fine dust. Stir into the flour. Rub in the butter until the mixture resembles fine breadcrumbs. Add enough water to give a firm smooth dough.

Roll out on a lightly floured board, as thin as you possibly can. Prick all over with a fork and stamp out 5 cm (2 in) rounds. Bake on a lightly greased baking sheet at 170C/325F/Gas 3 for 12–15

minutes, until golden brown. The biscuits are best eaten warm, but
they keep in an airtight tin for up to a week. Cool on a cake rack,
and pack away as soon as they are cold.

Corn Meal Crisps

These are a homemade version of the now familiar 'tortilla crisps'.
They are best still warm from the oven, but they keep well for
several days. Nibble at them with drinks before a meal, or use as a
base to take a spoonful of *guacamole*, or maybe a swirl of soured
cream topped with smoked salmon.

MAKES 20

125 g (4 oz) cornmeal or polenta*
90 g (3 oz) flour, plus extra for rolling out
pinch of salt
1 green chilli, very finely chopped
2 cloves of garlic, crushed
1 tablespoon olive oil
6–7 tablespoons milk
melted butter, and extra salt

Sift the flour with the salt. Mix with the cornmeal, chilli and garlic.
When evenly mixed, make a well in the centre and add the oil and
the milk. Stir, drawing in the dry ingredients to form a slightly
sticky dough.

Knead on a floured board, dusting lightly with extra flour as you
go, until you have a smooth dry cohesive dough – about 5 minutes.
Divide the dough into 20 pieces, and roll each into a small ball. Roll
out as thinly as you possibly can on a lightly floured board. If you
want smaller crisps, quarter each circle. Bake on ungreased baking
sheets for 15 minutes at 180C/350F/Gas 4.

As each batch comes out of the oven, brush quickly with melted
butter, and sprinkle with salt.

Cashew Nut Thins

Set a plate of these thin, lacy biscuits on the table at the end of a
meal, and I bet you it will soon be empty. I often serve them
alongside the coffee, a final sweetener to round off the meal, or with
a creamy pudding or just a plain vanilla ice-cream.

In the unlikely event that there are some left over, they keep well for a few days in an airtight container. Instead of cashew nuts, you could substitute some other nut – walnuts, or pine nuts, say – or use vanilla sugar, or add a pinch of cinnamon.

MAKES about 30

25 g (1 scant oz) cashew nuts
60 g (2 oz) plain flour
60 g (2 oz) caster sugar
45 g (1½ oz) butter
1 tablespoon single cream

First chop the cashew nuts fairly finely. Sift the flour, and mix with the sugar and chopped nuts. Melt the butter, and stir into the flour mixture with the cream to form a soft dough. On a sheet of greaseproof paper, mould into a small sausage shape, about 6 cm (1½ in) in diameter. Roll up in paper, and chill until firm.

Slice the biscuit dough sausage – each slice should be about 3 mm (⅛ in) wide, or thinner if possible. Leaving 2 cm (1 in) or so between each slice, lay out on a baking sheet, and bake at 180C/350F/Gas 4 for 4–5 minutes, until lightly browned at the edges. Quickly remove from the oven, before they overcook. Don't try to move for a good 5 or more minutes – while hot, they are more than likely to disintegrate, but on cooling they will become crisp.

Walnut Biscuits

These walnut biscuits are crisp at the edges, with a slightly spongy centre, good with creamy fools and poached fruit, or simply for tea. It never bothers me that my biscuits all turn out different shapes. After all, it does prove that I've baked them myself. But if you are aiming for uniformity, your best bet is to cut out a cardboard template and draw round it. Turn the rice paper over so that the markings show through and then fill in the outline with the mixture.

MAKES about 25

60 g (2 oz) walnuts
3 egg whites
125 g (4 oz) sugar
30 g (1 oz) flour
30 g (1 oz) butter, melted and cooled until tepid

Grind the walnuts to a fine moist powder – almost a paste in fact – in a clean coffee grinder or with a pestle and mortar. Mix well with the sugar and flour. Whisk the egg whites until stiff, then fold into the walnut mixture. Finally fold in the melted butter.

Line several baking sheets with rice paper and, using a palette knife, spread thin, elongated ovals of the biscuit mixture on the paper, leaving a good 4 cm (1½ in) gap between. They should be roughly the same shape as *langue de chat* biscuits.

Bake at 240C/475F/Gas 8 for 5–6 minutes, until lightly browned in the centre with a band of darker, richer brown at the edges. Cool on a cake rack.

Pecan Puffs

For as long as I can remember, a family friend has sent us a tin of pecan puffs for Christmas. Although we knew full well what was inside Mimi's parcel, it was never unwrapped until Christmas morning. The first mouthful of biscuit was a sure sign that the festivities had begun. If there were any left by the end of Boxing Day, it was a minor miracle.

Her recipe comes in fact from the classic American cookbook, *The Joy of Cooking*. Since discovering that, I've started making them for my friends, too. Pecan puffs are devastatingly good, with a buttery short texture, coated in a thin layer of icing sugar. Within a few weeks of the recipe appearing in the London *Evening Standard*, I received half a dozen letters from readers singing their praises. For variations, you could replace the pecans with almonds, or toasted hazelnuts.

MAKES about 35

125 g (4 oz) butter
2 tablespoons caster sugar
¼ teaspoon vanilla essence
150 g (5 oz) pecans or walnuts
150 g (5 oz) plain flour, sifted
icing sugar

Cream the butter, then beat in the sugar. Grind the nuts to a powdery paste, and work into the butter with the flour and vanilla. Roll rounded teaspoonfuls of the mixture into balls, and place on greased baking sheets. Bake for 30 minutes at 150C/300F/Gas 2.

Remove from the oven, and roll quickly in icing sugar, handling the puffs very carefully as they will be fairly fragile. Return to the oven and bake for 1 minute, to set the sugar. Cool on a cake rack. Store in an airtight tin, dusting each layer with icing sugar, and separating with greaseproof paper.

Jersey Galettes

Jersey *Galettes* are a perfect plain biscuit, short and crisp, lightly spiced and not too sweet. Like wholemeal digestive biscuits, you can eat them plain, with cheese or buttered.

Barley flour is not the easiest of flours to lay your hands on. Look for it in healthfood shops, though success is by no means guaranteed. My two local hale and healthy provisioners were unable to oblige. Don't exhaust yourself trying to track it down – plain flour does a fine job in its place.

More important is the potato flour, which I'm glad to say is much easier to locate (mine comes from the Italian deli across the road). This gluten-free starch is essential if the biscuit is to have its proper texture.

MAKES 18

90 g (3 oz) barley or plain flour
90 g (3 oz) potato flour
½ teaspoon bicarbonate of soda
pinch of salt
pinch each of ginger, cinnamon and nutmeg
30 g (1 oz) lard
60 g (2 oz) butter
45 g (1½ oz) sugar
1 tablespoon milk

Sieve the 2 flours with the bicarbonate of soda, salt and spices. Rub in the lard and butter until the mixture resembles breadcrumbs. Add the sugar, and mix evenly with a palette knife. Add the milk and gather up the mixture to form a soft dough.

Leave in the fridge for 30 minutes to firm up, then roll out to a thickness of about 3 mm (⅛ in) on a cool, floured surface. Stamp out 8 cm (3 in) rounds, and lay on a lightly greased baking tray. Gather up the remaining dough and repeat, until all has been used. Bake at 200C/400F/Gas 6 for 10–15 minutes, until a light sandy brown. Leave to cool on the baking sheet.

Chocolate Chip Oat Biscuits

The very first chocolate chip cookie was made in 1930 at the Toll House Inn in Whitman, Massachusetts. In a moment of supreme inspiration, the cook-cum-owner decided to chop up a bar of chocolate that just happened to be near at hand and threw it into the bowl filled with Butter Drop Do cookie mixture. To her great delight, the chocolate bits didn't ooze out messily all over the baking tray as they cooked, but stayed *in situ*. Eaten warm from the oven, but not too hot, the cookies proved to be quite sensational.

A few years later, the fame of these biscuits reached the great Nestlé Company. They bought the rights to the Original Toll House Cookie recipe and proudly displayed it on their packets of chocolate chips. And so the chocolate chip cookie suddenly went nationwide. Since then, chains of cookie shops have spun out across the States, and more recently spread their nets across the Atlantic to Europe. And all from one passing whim back in 1930 . . .

Technically speaking, these aren't true chocolate chip cookies. They've got a lot of oats in them and no flour, which is all wrong. On the other hand, they have got the chocolate chips and the wonderful chewy but crisp bite of the original article.

MAKES 20

1 egg
125 g (4 oz) caster sugar
60 g (2 oz) butter, melted
½ teaspoon salt
125 g (4 oz) rolled oats
90 g (3 oz) chocolate chips, or chopped plain chocolate*

Whisk the egg with the sugar until thick and pale. Stir in the butter, then the salt and oats and finally the chocolate.

Line several baking sheets with non-stick baking parchment, or butter generously, and drop teaspoonfuls of the mixture on to them, flattening slightly and leaving a 5 cm (2 in) gap between dollops. Bake for 12–15 minutes at 190C/375F/Gas 5, until lightly browned.

Cool for 5 minutes on the baking sheets, then finish cooling on a cake rack.

Candied Peel and Pecan Muffins

Northern America, Canada and the USA is muffin-land – not our yeast-raised English muffins, though they are popular too, but the versatile, bun-shaped baking powder muffin. There are plain muffins, naturally, blueberry muffins, inevitably, bran muffins for the health-conscious, and countless others.

At the farmer's Greenmarket in New York's Union Square there's a particularly imaginative muffin stall, with peach muffins, raspberry muffins and a dozen or so more. There's plenty of room for experiment and invention. Use the basic recipe and add your own bits and bobs instead of the peel and pecans.

For pear and pecan muffins, substitute 150 g (5 oz) chopped fresh pear for the candied peel.

MAKES 10–15, depending on the tin size

300 g (10 oz) white flour
60 g (2 oz) light muscovado sugar
4 teaspoons baking powder
generous pinch of salt
90 g (3 oz) mixed candied peel
60 g (2 oz) chopped pecans or walnuts
2 eggs
250 ml (8 fl oz) milk
4 tablespoons melted butter, cooled

Set the oven to 200C/400F/Gas 6. Butter a bun sheet, the deeper the better – or, better still, proper muffin tins.

Mix the flour, sugar, baking powder and salt. Stir in the peel and nuts, coating thoroughly in flour. In a separate bowl, beat the eggs and gradually whisk in the milk, then the butter.

Make a well in the centre of the dry ingredients, and pour in the liquids. Stir until all the flour is dampened, but don't worry about any lumps. Spoon into the bun tins. Bake for 20–25 minutes, until firm and nicely browned. Turn out on to a cake rack.

Corn Muffins

The point of muffins is that they can be thrown together in the blink of an eye, zipped into the oven and out again 20 minutes later. The whole operation should take about 30 minutes from beginning to end, so you can have muffins hot from the oven for breakfast, or whenever you feel in need.

These egg yolk-yellow corn muffins have a grainy texture and are only semi-sweet, so they go well with bacon, eggs and sausage, or simply with butter. Marmalade's not bad either. Or you could get more adventurous and dress them up with Parma ham and sour cream. Lovely, too, for mopping up meaty sauces.

MAKES about 24

125 g (4 oz) self-raising flour
1 tablespoon baking powder
1 teaspoon salt
280 g (9 oz) cornmeal or polenta*
60 g (2 oz) sugar
125 g (4 oz) butter, melted
2 eggs, beaten
300 ml (½ pt) milk

Sift the flour with the baking powder and salt into a mixing bowl. Stir in the cornmeal and the sugar. Beat the melted butter with the milk and then the eggs. Make a well in the centre of the dry ingredients and pour in the liquids. Stir into the flour, to form a smooth thick batter.

Lightly grease a bun tin (the deeper the better) or proper deep muffin tins, and fill about two thirds full with the batter. Bake 200C/400F/Gas 6 for 15–20 minutes, until golden brown. Let them cool for a couple of minutes, then turn out of the tins. They are best eaten warm from the oven, but are pretty good cold as well.

Cornbread With Chilli and Coriander

Cornbread is a southern American favourite, solid and satisfying, and just the thing with fried chicken, or hot soup. The batter is very similar to the muffin batter above, but is zipped up with hot chilli and fresh coriander, then baked in a single slab.

It makes a great basis for a chicken stuffing (page 128), so eat cornbread for supper today, and set aside a third to fill the cavity of a roast chicken tomorrow.

SERVES 4

175 g (6 oz) cornmeal or polenta*
1 teaspoon salt
1 teaspoon baking powder
1½ tablespoons caster sugar
2 tablespoons fresh coriander leaf, finely chopped
2 green chillis, finely chopped
60 g (2 oz) butter, roughly chopped
300 ml (½ pt) milk
4 eggs, beaten

Mix the first five ingredients together. Make a well in the centre. Bring the butter and milk to the boil in a small pan, stirring until the butter dissolves. Pour into the dry ingredients, and beat well. Beat in the eggs. Pour into a buttered 25 x 15 cm (10 x 6 in) loaf tin, or other metal dish (the mixture should be about 1½ in deep). Bake at 200C/400F/Gas 6 for 30 minutes, until a skewer inserted in the centre comes out dry. Cool for 5 minutes, then cut into squares.

Parmesan Cake

This is a cheese cake in the literal sense – a light, cheese-flavoured spongy cake, not creamy sweet cheesecake. Cut into small pieces and serve it with drinks. Let it take the place of bread with a simple hors d'œuvre, or make it a side-dish with a meaty or vegetable stew. You could even serve it as a cheese course in its own right, maybe with a swirl of soured cream and chives.

Any leftovers can be toasted and eaten as they are. Alternatively, top the toasted slices of cake with fried mushrooms and thick Greek yoghurt, or quickly sautéed chicken livers.

The semolina give it a pleasingly grainy texture, so don't let memories of gluey semolina pudding tempt you to leave it out. Use freshly grated parmesan rather than the dry tasteless stuff that comes out of little tubs. The difference is remarkable. It's worth buying a hunk of parmesan, more than the amount you'll need here, since it keeps well, tightly wrapped in foil, in the fridge.

You could use some other hard cheese, though it will need to be grated *finely*. Add herbs too, for variation.

SERVES 8 or more

125 g (4 oz) self-raising flour
½ teaspoon baking powder
½ teaspoon salt
60 g (2 oz) parmesan, grated
60 g (2 oz) semolina
pepper
3 eggs, separated
90 g (3 oz) butter, melted and cooled
175 ml (6 fl oz) milk

Sift the flour with the baking powder and salt. Mix in the parmesan, semolina and pepper. Make a well in the centre, and pour in the butter, egg yolks and milk. Mix well to form a loose batter. Whisk the egg whites stiffly, and fold into the mixture.

Line a 18 cm (7 in) cake tin with baking parchment. Pour in the mixture and bake at 190C/375F/Gas 5 for 30–35 minutes, until firm and nicely browned. Cool for a few minutes, and turn out on to a cake rack.

Jersey Wonders

Jersey Wonders are not some kind of potato, racing up to the forefront to unthrone the Jersey Royal as king of the new potatoes. No, not at all.

Jersey Wonders are doughnuts, more or less. I came across them in Jersey's main town, St Helier. I noticed some rather oddly twisted brown cakes in the windows of several bakeries. Always keen on a bit of edible research, I purchased and tried one forthwith.

The Wonder is an eggy, cakey doughnut – crumbly and dry without being overly so. They are never dredged in sugar, I was firmly informed by the lady behind the counter and, when freshly made, they really don't need to be. Keep uneaten Wonders in an airtight tin and they will last for a week, though they will be a smidgen less enticing than ones that are absolutely fresh.

MAKES 35

375 g (12 oz) self-raising flour
125 g (4 oz) plain flour
pinch of salt
125 g (4 oz) sugar
125 g (4 oz) butter
4 eggs
fat

Sieve together the flours and salt. Rub in the butter until it resembles breadcrumbs. Stir in the sugar and the egg to form a firm dough. Break off golf ball-sized knobs of dough and roll into balls. Cover and leave in the fridge for 1–2 hours to firm up.

Roll out each ball into a rectangle about 5 x 10 cm (2 x 4 in). With a sharp knife, make 2 parallel slits, about 2½ cm (1 in) long, in the centre of each rectangle. Fold the corners over loosely to form a point at either end of the rectangle, and pass them through the slits, pulling them gently out the other side. The result, when laid flat, should be a kite-shaped pastry. Don't worry if it all seems a bit floppy and unlikely – the mixture puffs up and stiffens as you fry it.

When you have twisted all the Jersey Wonders into shape, heat a large pan of oil, or lard. Deep fry the Wonders for about 30 seconds on each side, until golden brown and puffed all over. Drain on kitchen paper, and eat hot or cold.

Ruggelach

It doesn't make sense, really. There's almost as much butter as flour and then, to make matters more unlikely, there's another 125 g (4 oz) cream cheese as well! But believe me, it works, and produces a meltingly light pastry that could be used in other contexts, besides these sweet walnutty pastries.

Ruggelach are pastries I stumbled across again and again in New York, piled high in cake shops, coffee shops, grocery shops. The bought ones were good, but can barely compare with a homemade *ruggelach* still fresh and warm from the oven. Be warned: I intended merely to taste one and save the rest for friends, but it's easier said than done. It took every last shred of willpower to call a halt to my gluttony, after the second heavenly *ruggelach* had disappeared.

MAKES 16

Pastry:
125 g (4 oz) cream cheese
125 g (4 oz) softened butter
150 g (5 oz) flour, sifted

Filling:
60 g (2 oz) light muscovado sugar
½ teaspoon cinnamon
45 g (1½ oz) walnuts, finely chopped
30 g (1 oz) raisins, chopped

Glaze:
1 egg, beaten
caster sugar

Beat the cream cheese vigorously with the butter, until well mixed and softened. Gradually beat in the flour. Gather up into a ball, and wrap in foil or cling film. Chill for 30 minutes.

Mix the sugar with the cinnamon, walnuts and raisins. On a lightly floured board, roll the pastry out into a 30 cm (12 in) circle. Brush with the beaten egg, and sprinkle the filling evenly over the pastry. Cover with a sheet of greaseproof paper, and run the rolling pin over it a couple of times to fix the filling firmly into the pastry. Lift off the paper.

Divide the circle up like a cake into 16 triangles. Roll up each one, starting with the wider end, as if you were making a croissant. Arrange on a baking sheet, brush with egg and sprinkle with caster sugar. Bake at 200C/400F/Gas 6 for 12–15 minutes, until golden brown.

Spiced Nut and Fruit Tea Bread

Home baking, especially tea-time baking, from scones to chocolate cakes and back to shortbreads and Chelsea buns, is something the British are particularly good at. I count moist sticky spiced tea breads among our greatest achievements.

My mouth waters at the thought of a thin slice of this one packed to the hilt with fruit and nuts, lightly buttered, perhaps with a wedge of crumbly lancashire or caerphilly cheese. Make it at least 24 hours, preferably 48 hours, before you cut into it. When freshly made it crumbles when sliced and, although it tastes good, it definitely improves on keeping.

MAKES 1 loaf

250 g (8 oz) self-raising flour
pinch each of cinnamon, nutmeg and ginger
90 g (3 oz) light muscovado sugar
300 g (10 oz) dried figs, apricots, and/or dates, chopped
60 g (2 oz) walnuts or hazelnuts, chopped
60 g (2 oz) honey
250 ml (8 fl oz) very hot water
30 g (1 oz) butter
1 level teaspoon bicarbonate of soda
1 large egg

Sift the flour with the spices, and mix with the sugar, fruit and nuts. Stir the honey and butter into the hot water, until melted. Sprinkle the bicarbonate of soda over the top, and stir to mix well.

Make a well in the centre of the dry ingredients, and pour in the warm liquid and the egg. Mix thoroughly, and pour into a 1 kg (2 lb) loaf tin, lined with non-stick baking parchment. Bake for 1–1½ hours at 180C/350F/Gas 4, until browned and springy to the touch. Turn out and cool on a cake rack. Wrap in foil and keep for 1–2 days.

Stuffed Monkey

When I was a child, my godmother and her children would visit us every now and then, bringing with them a Stuffed Monkey. Not a real stuffed monkey, I hasten to add. Their kind of Stuffed Monkey is a spiced cakey pastry stuffed with candied peel and almonds. It's quite unlike any other, with its thick brown spiced crust and moist almondy centre.

Not long after this recipe appeared in the London *Evening Standard*, I received a letter from an elderly lady, thrilled to have the recipe. When she was a child, her father would occasionally come home bearing a Stuffed Monkey, always from the same Jewish bakery in the East End of London.

SERVES 8–10

250 g (8 oz) flour
175 g (6 oz) lightly salted butter
175 g (6 oz) light muscovado sugar
1 egg
½ teaspoon ground cinnamon
pinch of salt

Filling:
125 g (4 oz) candied mixed peel
125 g (4 oz) ground almonds
45 g (1½ oz) butter
1 egg, yolk
1 egg white, lightly beaten

For the crust, sift the flour with the salt and cinnamon. Rub in the butter until the mixture resembles fine breadcrumbs. Add the sugar and mix with a knife. Beat the egg lightly, and add enough to form a soft dough. Knead the dough until smooth. Divide in half. Press the first half into a 25 cm (10 in) tart tin. Chill the second half until needed.

Mix the candied peel with the ground almonds. Melt the butter and pour in, stir and then add the egg yolk. Mix well. Spread this stuffing over the dough. Roll out the remaining half of the dough on a lightly floured board, so that it will fit neatly into the tin. Lay over the stuffing and press the edges firmly together. Brush with the egg white.

Bake at 200C/400F/Gas 6 for 30 minutes, until nicely browned. Serve warm or cold, cut into squares.

Chocolate Hazelnut Torte

This is my all-time favourite chocolate cake, thrillingly dark, moist and wicked. It should be made 1–3 days before it is eaten for it to be at its best. It is ideal for any celebration – anniversary, birthday or Christmas. Use your favourite liqueur to scent the cake – an orangey one is delicious, and so too are Calvados, brandy or whisky.

SERVES 8–10

200 g (7 oz) plain chocolate*, broken into squares
3 tablespoons liqueur or water
150 g (5 oz) caster sugar
125 g (4 oz) unsalted butter, chopped
3 eggs, separated
90 g (3 oz) ground hazelnuts
pinch of salt
60 g (2 oz) self-raising flour

Chocolate glaze:
100 g (3½ oz) plain chocolate*, broken into squares
1 tablespoon liqueur (optional)
60 g (2 oz) butter, chopped
toasted hazelnuts*

Line a 23 cm (9 in) cake tin with non-stick baking parchment, or butter and flour. Place the chocolate and liqueur in a bowl set over a pan of gently simmering water, making sure that the bowl does not touch the water. Stir occasionally, and remove from the heat as soon as it has melted.

Beat in the butter bit by bit. Whisk the egg yolks with the sugar until pale and thick, then stir in the chocolate mixture. Mix the nuts and flour and add that too. Whisk the egg whites with the salt until stiff, and fold into the cake mixture. Pour into the tin and bake at 190C/375F/Gas 5 for 45–50 minutes, until firm to the touch – it will still be moist in the centre, so the skewer test won't work. Cool for 5 minutes, then turn on to a cake rack to finish cooling. Wrap in foil or cling film and keep in a cool place for at least 1 day and up to 3, before glazing and eating.

To make the glaze, melt the chocolate with the liqueur over simmering water. Remove from the heat and beat in the butter bit by bit. Let it cool for a few minutes until it begins to thicken, then spread over the cake and down the sides. Decorate with the hazelnuts before it sets.

Tosca Cake

You have such a treat ahead of you if you decide to make this cake. I mean it. The cakey bit itself is pretty good, but it is the crisp almond toffee layer on top that makes it extra special. Don't worry that it doesn't rise magnificently high – it's not meant to. Serve it for tea, or as a pudding with single or whipped cream.

SERVES 8

Cake:
125 g (4 oz) butter, softened
90 g (3 oz) caster sugar (vanilla sugar* if available)
90 g (3 oz) self-raising flour
½ teaspoon ground cinnamon
pinch of salt
2 eggs, separated
2 tablespoons milk

Topping:
60 g (2 oz) chopped almonds
90 g (3 oz) butter, melted
90 g (3 oz) granulated sugar
1 tablespoon plain flour
2 teaspoons single cream

For the cake, butter a 25 cm (10 in) loose bottomed cake tin (or line with baking parchment), and set the oven to 180C/350F/Gas 4.

Cream the butter with the sugar, until light and fluffy. Beat in the egg yolks and then the milk. Sift the flour with the cinnamon and salt, and fold in. Whisk the egg whites until stiff, and fold into the cake mixture. Pour into the cake tin and bake for 20–30 minutes, until the cake is just firm.

While the cake is cooking, make the almond topping. Mix the almonds with the butter and sugar in a small saucepan, then stir in the flour, and finally the cream. Stir over a gentle heat until well amalgamated. When the cake is firm, remove from the oven and quickly bring the topping to the boil. Pour over the cake, spreading out the almonds in an even layer. Bake for a further 10–15 minutes, until the topping is a tempting toffee-brown. Let it cool in the tin for 10 minutes or until the topping is crisp, and then unmould. Serve warm or cold.

Cranberry and Ginger Cake

November sees the beginning of the annual cranberry migration across the Atlantic, to be piled up high on our greengrocers' shelves. Cranberries, cranberries everywhere, but not for long, so make the most of them while they are around. Their strange, sharp-bitter flavour is a natural with meat and poultry of all kinds. But don't think that all cranberries are good for is the standard cranberry and orange sauce, nice as that is.

Try adding a handful of cranberries to an apple crumble or pie. They will give a pretty pink blush to a slow-baked rice pudding, flavoured with cinnamon. For a whole berry relish, spread cranberries in a single layer in a roasting tin. Sprinkle with half their weight of sugar, adding spices, orange zest and a dash of orange juice, or some chopped stem of ginger if you wish. Cover and bake at 180C/350F/Gas 4 for 45 minutes, stirring twice.

Which leads me neatly on to this cake. Cranberry and ginger is a perfect combination, and here the sour fruitiness of the baked cranberries with their sugary crust is the crowning glory to a soft, gingery cake. Serve warm with cream for pudding, or cold for tea. It tastes even better if kept well wrapped for 1–2 days.

SERVES 10

125 g (4 oz) butter, softened
175 g (6 oz) light muscovado sugar
2 eggs
1 tablespoon syrup from ginger jar
300 g (10 oz) self-raising flour
½ teaspoon salt
150 ml (¼ pt) milk
4 bulbs stem ginger in syrup, chopped

Topping:
250 g (8 oz) cranberries
90 g (3 oz) caster sugar

Cream the butter with the sugar until fluffy. Beat in the eggs and ginger syrup. Sift the flour with the salt. Toss the ginger in 2 tablespoons flour and set aside. Beat the rest of the flour and the milk a little at a time into the butter and egg mixture, until smooth. Fold in the ginger. Pour into a 23 cm (9 in) cake tin, lined with non-stick baking parchment or buttered and floured.

Top the cake mixture with an even layer of cranberries, and sprinkle with caster sugar. Bake at 180C/350F/Gas 4 for 45–55 minutes, until a skewer inserted into the centre of the cake comes out dry, bar a smear of cranberry juice. Serve warm or cold.

Cherry and Coconut Rice Cake

This is a gem of a cake – golden brown, with a hint of a grainy texture, but light too. Rice flour – available from wholefood shops if you can't find it elsewhere – and coconut give a moist cake with body. Look out for uncoloured glacé cherries. The bright pinky-red we normally associate with glacé cherries is not their natural colour. Uncoloured ones are a dark, dark crimson, and taste a little more of fresh cherries.

SERVES 8

175 g (6 oz) glacé cherries
175 g (6 oz) butter, softened
175 g (6 oz) caster sugar
175 g (6 oz) rice flour
1 rounded teaspoon baking powder
60 g (2 oz) desiccated coconut
finely grated zest of 1 lemon
4 eggs, beaten

Line a 20 cm (8 in) cake tin with non-stick baking parchment or butter and flour. Spread the cherries out on the base.

Cream the butter with the sugar until light and fluffy. Sift the rice flour with the baking powder, and mix with the coconut and lemon zest. Beat a quarter of the eggs into the butter, then a quarter of the rice flour. Repeat until all has been used.

Spoon the mixture into the cake tin and cook at 180C/350F/Gas 4 for 20 minutes. Turn down the heat to 170C/325F/Gas 3 and cook for a further 40 minutes, or until firm to the touch. Cool for 10 minutes in the tin, then lift out and finish cooling on a cake rack.

DRINKS

Sweet or Salted Lassi

As I write this, I have at my elbow a tall glass filled with refreshing salted *lassi* – a simple, Indian yoghurt drink, tailor-made to cool and assuage a raging thirst on a tropically hot day, or brought on by a fiery curry.

The scented sweet *lassi* is lovely as an occasional drink, and many people prefer it to the salted version. I'm not one of them. Salted *lassi* is, in my opinion, more of an anywhere and everyday drink. Each to their own – try both versions and make up your own mind.

MAKES 3–4 glasses

Salted:
300 g (10 oz) yoghurt
300 ml (½ pt) mineral water (still or fizzy)
salt to taste
10 mint leaves

Beat the water into the yoghurt, until smooth. Add the salt to taste. Bruise 6 of the mint leaves, and add. Leave to chill for 15 minutes in the fridge.

Fish out the bedraggled mint leaves, and divide the *lassi* between 3 or 4 glasses. Add a couple of ice cubes to each. Float the remaining mint leaves on the top.

Sweet:
300 g (10 oz) yoghurt
300 ml (½ pt) mineral water (still or fizzy)
seeds from 4 green cardamoms, crushed
2 teaspoons orange flower water
2–4 tablespoons caster sugar
a few rose petals or borage flowers (optional)

Beat the water into the yoghurt, until smooth. Add the crushed cardamom, orange flower water, and sugar to taste. Stir and leave to chill for 15 minutes in the fridge.

Stir, and divide between glasses, adding ice cubes. Scatter rose petals or borage flowers on the top.

Lemon and Orangeade

With row upon row of cartons of fruit juice stacked up on every supermarket shelf, it may well never have occurred to you to make your own versions. Why bother, after all, when you can buy not just orange and apple juice, but an endless variety of 'tropical' and 'exotic' concoctions?

Well, why indeed? A straightforward answer – homemade tastes better, fresher, keener, fruitier. And you can control what goes into it, balancing flavours and sweetness to your personal liking, rather than to some mass-produced uniformity.

For instance, taking this recipe as a starting point, you could simplify it by using all lemons, and no oranges (in which case you might need a little extra sugar), or 2 oranges and 1 lemon, or 2 oranges and 2 limes. You don't have to add the passion fruit, although they do give the most exquisite flavour.

Another advantage of making your own – you won't have to battle with those infuriating cartons. No searching for a pair of suitable scissors, then giving up and using a knife or trying to tear along that dotted line. No fountains of sticky fruit juice arching out across the kitchen and down your front in a remarkable double pronged assault. No more desperate attempts to estimate where exactly to hold the glass in relation to the carton so that the ferocious jet of juice can be caught as it spurts out.

MAKES 1 litre (2 pts)

2 lemons
1 orange
60 g (2 oz) sugar lumps
2 passion fruit
mint leave or borage flowers

Rub the lemons and orange with the lumps of sugar, until all the aromatic oils are drawn out of the zest and the sugar is saturated. As each lump is used up, drop into a large bowl.

Thinly slice the lemons and the oranges, peel and all, and add to the bowl. Halve the passion fruit, and scoop out the flesh into a small pan. Heat gently, until hot but nowhere near boiling (this loosens the juices). Sieve, pressing through as much of the pulp as you can. Add to the lemons and oranges. Pour ¾ litre (1½ pt) boiling water over the fruit and sugar. Cover and leave to steep for 12 hours. Strain.

Serve well chilled, with mint leaves or borage flowers floating on the top.

Lemon Barley Water

This is *the* drink for long hot lazy afternoons, for picnics in the countryside, for the cricket match on the village green, for every soft-focused image of idyllic British summers. Homemade lemonade is better than bought cartons of fruit juice, but homemade barley water completely eclipses commercial barley water.

MAKES about ¾ litre (1½ pt)

300 g (10 oz) pearl or pot barley
zest and juice of 1 lemon, grated
60 g (2 oz) sugar

Place the barley in a saucepan with 1½ litres (2½ pt) water. Bring to the boil, skim off any scum that rises, and simmer for 20 minutes.

Place the lemon zest in a large bowl with the sugar. Pour the hot barley water and barley into the bowl, leave to cool, and infuse. When cold, strain and discard the debris. Stir in the lemon juice. Serve chilled.

Mulled Cider

Mulled wine and cider are to winter what lemonade and barley water are to summer. Just the thought of warming hands numbed with cold on a glass of steaming hot mulled cider conjures up pictures of crackling fires, and cosy evenings.

Both are easy to make, and infinitely adaptable. Although I've used cider here, you can replace it with red wine, and sugar instead of honey – you may find that you need less than 3 tablespoons. I love the orangey flavour of coriander seeds, but for a change try a vanilla pod* instead. Taste frequently as it mulls, and remove the pod the moment the vanilla flavour is strong enough.

Before you invite friends and family round for a glass or two of mulled cider, sort out the equipment you're going to need. It's not that anything elaborate or unusual is required, but it is terribly frustrating when you're ready to get going, and discover that you don't have a large enough, heatproof jug, for example.

Three things are essential: a large earthenware or enamelled jug; a deep saucepan, large enough to hold the jug; a metal trivet, or something that will sit firmly on the bottom of the pan and support the jug of cider – I improvise with a small inverted metal ring mould! The base of the jug should never come into contact with the base of the saucepan.

Helpful, but not absolutely necessary, are a large square of muslin and some string. Fold the muslin in half, and place the spices in a small heap in the centre. Gather up the edges, and knot firmly. Attach a piece of string and hang the bag inside the jug. This saves you having to strain the cider when serving. Failing this, a clean tea strainer is better than nothing.

MAKES 6 glasses

1 litre (2 pt) dry cider
3 tablespoons clear honey
6 cloves
1 teaspoon coriander seeds, lightly crushed
4 cm (1½ in) stick of cinnamon
8 allspice berries, lightly crushed
1 orange, thinly sliced

Place the spices (wrapped in a muslin bag – see above) in jug and pour in the cider. Add the honey and stir. Place in a pan of bubbling water (see above). Heat well, until the cider is hot and steaming, but not boiling. Turn down the heat slightly, and let the flavours develop for 5 minutes.

Drop one slice of orange into each glass. Stand a metal spoon in the first glass, and pour in the cider, through a tea strainer, if necessary (see above). Repeat with the remaining glasses, and serve quickly.

Clementine Ratafia

A *ratafia* is a fruit liqueur (or a little almondy macaroon, but that's another story). Fruit, in this case clementines, is steeped in alcohol for a couple of months, to make a deliciously scented sweet liqueur to sip with coffee, or spoon over a scoop of ice-cream.

MAKES about 600 ml (1 pt)

6 clementines, satsumas or tangerines
175–250 g (6–8 oz) caster sugar
one cinnamon stick, broken into thirds
½ teaspoon coriander seeds, lightly crushed
500 ml (¾ pt) brandy

Squeeze the juice from the clementines and pour into a preserving jar. Pull the spent flesh from the peel and discard. Cut the peel into strips and add to the jar with the spices and sugar. Use the full 250 g (8 oz) if you have a sweet tooth, 175 g (6 oz) or 200 g (7 oz) otherwise. Pour over the brandy. Seal the jar tightly, and leave in a dark place for 2 months, turning occasionally so that the sugar dissolves completely. Strain and bottle the liqueur.

PRESERVES AND SWEETS

⚘⚘

NUT BUTTERS

I was a late developer when it came to peanut butter appreciation.
I had never much liked the texture of either the smooth or crunchy
version. But in my early twenties I came to three major conclusions
on this topic: I shall never like really smooth peanut butter; crunchy
peanut butter spread *thinly* on hot toast is delicious; and homemade
peanut butter is better still, but best of all are hazelnut and cashew
nut butters.

The process itself is simple but you can vary the flavour by using
toasted or raw nuts, and by using different oils. The amount of oil
you need will depend on the type of nut, and whether they are raw
or roasted (raw ones will need more oil).

Basic Recipe

> 250 g (8 oz) shelled nuts, raw or toasted★
> 2–6 tablespoons appropriate oil (see below)
> sea salt

Prepare the nuts if necessary (see below). Place in a grinder or
processor with 2 tablespoons oil, and a good pinch of salt. Process
until the preferred texture is reached, adding more oil if necessary.
Taste, and add extra salt if necessary. Pack into a clean jar, and eat
within 2 weeks.

Peanut Butter

Use either raw or roasted peanuts. Process raw ones with their skins on, or toast them yourself (page 259). Ready-roasted and salted peanuts can be used as well – shake well in a sieve to get rid of excess salt before processing, and do not add any more salt. Dry-roasted spiced peanuts make a delicious butter. Use a tasteless oil, or a little Chinese peanut oil which will enhance the peanut taste. Alternatively, slip in a tablespoon of sesame oil.

Hazelnut Butter

Toast the hazelnuts (page 259) first, and rub off the skins. Use a tasteless oil, or part tasteless and part hazelnut oil.

Cashew Nut Butter

Use raw cashew nut pieces and process as they are, for the best delicate sweet flavour. Use a tasteless oil, such as groundnut or grapeseed, or almond oil.

Gooseberry Curd

If you have ever made your own lemon curd, you will know what a second-rate product the commerical variety is. It just doesn't stand any comparison with the buttery, heaven-scented yellow curds cooked long and slow in your kitchen.

As good, however, is this lovely gooseberry curd, made in much the same way. The fragrance of the gooseberries is set off with a hint of mint or elderflower. It's easy to make, but don't try to rush it. Homemade curds will last for a couple of weeks in the fridge, and can be frozen.

MAKES approximately 1 kg (2 lb)

375 g (12 oz) gooseberries
2 sprigs of mint or 1 head of elderflower
125 g (4 oz) butter
200 g (7 oz) caster sugar
3 eggs

Place the gooseberries in a pan with the mint or elderflower (shaken first to dislodge any wildlife), and 30 g (1 oz) of the butter. Cover and cook over a low heat, stirring occasionally, until the gooseberries have collapsed into a rough purée. Sieve to remove the seeds and the bedraggled mint or elderflower.

Pour the gooseberry purée into a bowl. Add the remaining butter, chopped, and the caster sugar. Beat the eggs together well, then rub through a sieve into the remaining ingredients.

Sit the bowl over a pan of gently simmering water, making sure that the base of the bowl is not immersed in the water. Stir continuously, mixing in the melting butter. Do not allow to boil. When the mixture thickens to the consistency of thick custard, remove from the heat. Pour into clean, warm jars and seal. When cool, store in the fridge for up to 2 weeks.

Angels' Hair

If you saw a jar labelled 'carrot jam' on the supermarket shelf, you might well be forgiven for thinking 'how peculiar', and passing on by. But in fact Angels' Hair, a much prettier name for it, is quite delicious and a stunning translucent orange colour. It is also quick, cheap and easy to make at home.

> 300 g (10 oz) carrots
> 250 g (8 oz) caster sugar
> 1 large lemon
> 3 cardamom pods, split

Trim and scrape the carrots. Grate on a medium sized grater, and weigh out 250 g (8 oz). Put into a pan with the sugar, lemon zest cut in strips, and juice, and the cardamom pods. Heat gently until the sugar dissolves, then boil hard until the mixture is very thick. Pack into a warmed, sterilised jar and seal tightly.

Raspberry Vinegar

Raspberry vinegar became one of the clichés of nouvelle cuisine, but it's hardly a new idea. It was very popular in Victorian times. In the heat of the summer, crinolined ladies might sip at a glass of refreshing pink raspberry water, colour and flavour given by raspberry vinegar. This may sound like a strange sort of drink, but for those of us who don't take any great joy in sugary drinks it is a delight. Try mixing one tablespoon raspberry vinegar with one heaped teaspoon caster sugar and 150 ml (¼ pt) fizzy mineral water. Add a few ice cubes and float a sprig of mint on the top.

Of course, it can also be used in more familiar ways – in salad dressings and to sharpen sauces. It has an intense fruity taste, so a little goes a long way. I find that two bouts of steeping produces a good flavour, but you can make it even more pronounced by repeating the steeping a third time. Other fruit vinegars can be made in the same way – try using black cherries (pitted), black-berries or blackcurrants.

> 500 g (1 lb) raspberries
> 500 ml (¾ pt) white wine vinegar

Place half the raspberries in a preserving jar, pressing down gently to bruise and release the juices. Pour over the white wine vinegar. Cover, and leave for 3 days on a warm, sunny windowsill. Strain through a muslin-lined sieve, pressing through as much of the juice as possible, without any of the flesh. Pour the vinegar over the other half of the raspberries. Leave for another 3 days or even a whole week, then strain again through muslin. This time don't press it – just leave to drip. Bottle and seal tightly.

Cranberry Ketchup

I love cranberry sauce, but this Cranberry Ketchup is delicious too. Like homemade tomato ketchup, it needs a couple of weeks in the bottle to mellow out. Then it will be just the ticket with cold meats of all kinds, and even the leftover Christmas turkey. Try stirring a spoonful into gravies and sauces for a quick lift.

> MAKES ½–¾ litre (1–1½ pints)
>
> 250 g (8 oz) onion, finely chopped
> 1 kg (2 lb) cranberries
> 300 ml (½ pt) water
> 4 cloves
> 5 cm (2 in) stick of cinnamon
> 6 allspice berries
> 10 black peppercorns
> 300 g (10 oz) caster sugar
> 150 ml (5 fl oz) white wine vinegar
> 1 teaspoon salt

Place the onions, cranberries and water in a pan, and bring to the boil. Simmer gently until all the cranberries have burst and the onion is tender. Pass through the fine blade of a *mouli-légumes*, or rub through a fine sieve.

Tie the spices in a small muslin bag. Place the cranberry purée, spices, sugar, vinegar and salt in a preserving pan, and bring to the boil. Boil until thick like double cream and all trace of wateriness has gone – about 15 minutes. Remove the spice bag. Pour into hot, sterilised jars or bottles and seal.

Leave to mature in a cool dark place for at least 2 weeks.

Candied Citrus Peel

I've often made my own candied citrus peel. Not only is it cheaper than shop-bought, it also tastes ten times better. And it's more useful – chop for cakes and puddings, or cut into strips and dip into melted chocolate, to make a delicious sweetmeat to go with coffee.

The peel from thick-skinned fruits works best – yellow or pink grapefruit, sweetie, or pomelo. Wash the fruit, then peel carefully, slashing the skin from top to bottom so that you can remove it in petals. If you can't use it immediately, freeze until needed.

Small quantities are easy to do in the microwave. For larger amounts use the conventional method – in which case calculate the quantities as follows: for every 250 g (8 oz) peel, make syrup with 500 g (1 lb) sugar, and 175 ml (6 fl oz) water.

MAKES almost 375 g ¾ lb (750 g/1½ lb)

125g/4 oz (250g/8 oz) grapefruit, pomelo, thick-skinned orange peel

Syrup:
250 g/8 oz (500 g/1 lb) caster sugar
60 ml/2 fl oz (120 ml/4 fl oz) water

For the microwave method, place the peel in a bowl, with enough boiling water to cover. Cover tightly and cook on high for 6 (8) minutes, stirring once, until the peel is tender. Drain and return to the bowl. Cover again with boiling water. Cover tightly, and cook on high for 3 (5) minutes. Drain well.

To make the syrup, stir the sugar and water in a dish large enough to take the peel in one layer, 6–8 cm (2½–3 in) deep, and strong enough to take boiling sugar. Cook on high for 3–7 minutes stirring occasionally, until the sugar has dissolved and the syrup is boiling. Add the peel and cook on high, uncovered, for 13 (21) minutes, turning and rearranging the peel 3 times. Continue cooking on high in bursts of 30 seconds, allowing the bubbles to subside and rearranging between bursts, until almost all the syrup has been absorbed.

Spread peel (cut into smaller strips if you wish) on a tray lined with greaseproof paper and dry in a warm dry place (such as the airing cupboard) for 1–3 days as necessary, turning from time to time. Store in an airtight container until needed.

For the conventional method, simmer the peel in water until tender. Drain, and then simmer again for a further 20 minutes. Drain. Stir the sugar and water over a medium heat until dissolved. Bring to the boil and add peel. Simmer until most of the syrup has been absorbed – 40–50 minutes – and dry as above.

Candied Pecans

Rehov Dizengoff is one of Tel Aviv's main streets. Lined on either side with shops and cafés, it runs from the north of the city right down to the beginnings of the southern half, then curves round to the east. The newcomer to the city inevitably takes his bearings from this street, and the long shoreline.

Like London's Oxford Street, it is busy and lively throughout the day, and between the clothes and shoe shops there are small kiosks selling sweets and nibbles. Most of them sell nuts of several kinds, as well as dried and candied fruits.

Walking along Rehov Dizengoff, one such kiosk caught my eye. Among all the other goodies was a glowing pile of candied kumquats which I couldn't bear to pass by. And next to them was a box of mahogany brown pecans. They were quite delicious, coated almost imperceptibly with caramel, cooked until it was almost, but not quite, burnt.

Later on in the week, we ate at one of Tel Aviv's Chinese restaurants, the Yin Yang, and among the sweetmeats that arrived at the end of the meal were more candied pecans. They gave us the recipe, which seems simplicity itself, but you do have to guard over them carefully as they cook.

> 125 g (4 oz) shelled pecan halves (or walnuts)
> 60 g (2 oz) caster sugar
> olive oil

Tip the pecans into a large sieve and run under the cold tap. Shake off any excess water. Tip into a mixing bowl. Add the sugar, and stir so that each pecan is coated. Leave them to stand for 24 hours, turning occasionally.

Pour oil to a depth of about 1 cm (½ in) into a frying pan, and heat. Fry the nuts in the oil in small batches, turning occasionally, until a dark mahogany brown. This should take about 3–4 minutes, so if they appear to be cooking too fast, turn down the heat slightly.

Watch them carefully since they can burn quite easily. In fact, cook only 3 or 4 at the first go, so that you know how dark they should be – then if they burn you haven't wasted too many. Lift them out with a slotted spoon, and leave to cool on a lightly greased baking tray, separating the nuts as you work.

These nuts will keep for at least a week, if you are strong-minded enough not to eat them all straight away.

Honeycomb Toffee

I do it every year – I forget to lay up a formidable stock of sweets and biscuits to ward off the threats of the 'trick-or-treaters'. Then I either have to go out somewhere I cannot be got, or sit in darkness until I'm sure that the coast is clear. I suppose that the trick probably wouldn't be too horrendous, but I like to play safe.

This may sound rather churlish, I suppose, but I really cannot work up a wild enthusiasm for this imported American habit – aren't 'penny for the guy' and Bonfire night enough? Obviously not.

Anyway, just in case I forget to stock up again, I've decided to search out some toffee recipes. I had a vague memory of a crumbly bubble-filled toffee that I used to eat occasionally as a child. I eventually found this recipe for it in Sonia Allinson's *Sweets Book*, (Piatkus).

Children will probably like this version best, but I like it even better when the golden syrup is replaced with black treacle, or molasses, which makes a closer match to the honeycomb toffee I remember.

MAKES about ½ kg (1 lb)

125 g (4 oz) golden syrup
125 g (4 oz) clear honey
375 g (12 oz) sugar
60 g (2 oz) butter
1 teaspoon vinegar
4 tablespoons water
2 level teaspoons bicarbonate of soda

Put all the ingredients except the bicarbonate of soda into a large pan – they should only half fill the pan at most. Heat slowly, stirring until the sugar has dissolved. Bring to the boil. Cover and cook for 2 minutes.

Uncover and continue to boil, without stirring, for a further 7–10 minutes, until you reach the hard ball stage. That is, when you drop a little of the mixture into a glass of iced water, it forms a hard toffee ball.

Remove the pan from the heat and immediately stir in the bicarbonate of soda. The mixture will froth up (that's why you needed the large pan). Pour it into a 20 cm (8 in) buttered tin and leave to set. When hard, break up into mouth-sized pieces.

Kumquat or Cape Gooseberry Sweetmeats

Kumquats, those miniature oval oranges, and lace-lanterned cape gooseberries or physallis, dipped in chocolate or fondant icing, make excellent after-dinner sweets to serve with coffee. And because they're fruit-based you can even convince yourself that they are better for you than straight chocolates.

MAKES 25–30

250 g (8 oz) kumquats or cape gooseberries
125 g (4 oz) fondant icing
2 tablespoons Cointreau or Grand Marnier
90 g (3 oz) plain chocolate*
30 g (1 oz) butter

If using cape gooseberries, snip along the petals of the papery lantern that surrounds the fruit inside. Twist them up away from the fruit like wings. Break up the fondant icing and place in a bowl with 1 tablespoon of Cointreau, over a pan of simmering water, making sure that the base does not touch the water. When it has melted, give it a quick stir to mix. Dip each half of the fruit into the fondant. The kumquats should be only two-thirds covered, unless you have a very sweet tooth. Hold the cape gooseberries by the 'wings' and dip the entire fruit. Lay on a baking sheet lined with a sheet of greaseproof paper, and leave in the fridge to set.

Break up the chocolate and place in another bowl with the remaining Cointreau and the butter, again over a pan of gently simmering water, making sure that the base of the bowl does not touch the water. Melt, stirring occasionally, then draw off the heat. Dip the remaining fruit as above. Again, leave to set on a baking sheet lined with greaseproof paper.

Eat within 24 hours.

Charozeth

Charozeth, or *haroset*, is one of the traditional ritualistic foods served at the Jewish 'Seder', part of the Jewish Passover, celebrating the Israelites' deliverance from Egyptian bondage. It is a mixture of finely chopped dried fruits and nuts mixed to a paste, often with raw apple and sweet red kosher wine.

I like this simple version, serving little spheres of it as *petit fours* with coffee.

MAKES 20

30 g (1 oz) walnuts
30 g (1 oz) blanched almonds
60 g (2 oz) pitted dried dates (not the sticky Christmas variety) or
   fresh dates
60 g (2 oz) dried apricots
¼ teaspoon ground ginger
¼ teaspoon ground cinnamon
1 tablespoon honey

Whizz all the ingredients together in a processor, or chop the nuts and fruit very finely then mix in the spices and honey. Roll teaspoonfuls of the mixture into firm little spheres.

A FEW NOTES ON INGREDIENTS AND BASIC TECHNIQUES

ASPARAGUS

Asparagus arrives in our shops most of the year round now, winging its way from all over the world. All that globe-trotting inevitably keeps prices high, making it viable only as an occasional indulgence. The time really to get to grips with asparagus is when the English season rises to full swing in May and June. Prices drop and the flavour improves. Hurray, make the most of it while you can.

In this country we prefer the thin green spears of asparagus. The very tender thin spindly stems are called sprue. From the Continent comes sturdy fat white asparagus, with purplish tips, that has been blanched before cutting.

There are several ways of cooking asparagus, and which one you choose will depend on the quantity and your cooking equipment. First of all, cut off the tougher, woody parts of the stems. With sprue you may find that the whole length is quite edible (nibble the cut end of the raw asparagus to see how the land lies). Some books advise you to peel part of the stems. I rarely do this unless I am convinced that the outer layer is going to be very stringy (possible if the asparagus is on the mature side).

The ideal way to cook asparagus is with the stems submerged in simmering water, the delicate and fragile tips waving above the water line, cooked only by the steam. Dedicated asparagus fans will own a proper asparagus pan, which is tall and thin with a fitted metal basket to lodge the asparagus in. The rest of us will have to stick with more makeshift methods.

If you are cooking asparagus of whatever sort in any quantity, the only way to make a good job of it is by rigging up an impromptu version of the asparagus pan. With string, tie the trimmed asparagus firmly into one large bundle or, if more convenient, two smaller ones. Put 5 cm (2 in) water into a pan tall enough to take the asparagus standing upright. Bring the water to the boil, and stand the asparagus in it, tips upward. Cover with a lid or a dome of silver foil, and simmer for 10–20 minutes, until the asparagus is just tender. Don't wander off and get involved in something else – it takes just a couple of minutes for the tips to go from perfectly cooked to a collapsing mush. Drain well. Rinse immediately under the cold tap to set the colour. Serve warm or cold with a vinaigrette, melted butter, or olive oil and a shave of parmesan.

To cook smaller amounts, enough for 1 or 2 people, or enough to be used as a garnish or part of a dish, use a frying pan or shallow pan, wide enough to take the asparagus lying down horizontally with room to manoeuvre. Fill with 5 cm (2 in) lightly salted water, and bring to the boil. Add the trimmed asparagus and simmer gently. Very tender sprue may need little more than 5 minutes. Thicker stems, and Continental asparagus, may take anywhere between 10 and 20 minutes. Keep checking. Again, rinse under the cold tap once cooked and drained.

I have yet to be convinced that it is worth microwaving asparagus. I've followed the instructions in several different books (usually very reliable) and I still think that they end up losing a great deal of their flavour, deriving a passing resemblance to tinned asparagus.

BEETROOT

Beetroot is one of my favourite vegetables. Throughout my school years I loathed it, blenching at the sight of every oozing vinegary beetroot salad that crossed my path. I cannot understand why anybody should imagine that cooking beetroot in malt-vinegar-saturated water is an idea with any merit. How can any vegetable, even one with the most robust of flavours, survive such treatment?

To enjoy beetroot at its most delicious, sweet and subtly flavoured, you must cook it yourself at home, and eat it up swiftly thereafter. If you own a microwave oven, cooking is a matter of minutes and the taste is glorious. Baking comes a close second for flavour, boiling third, and both require an hour or more depending on the size of the roots.

To prepare, rinse off the dirt. If you are microwaving, trim off the roots and stem and pierce the skins with the tines of a fork. When they are to be boiled or baked, take great care not to break the skins, and leave the roots and about 2 cm (1 in) of stalk in place, so that the juices cannot escape.

To microwave 2 large or 4 medium beetroot, place in a dish with 4 tablespoons water and cover tightly. Cook on high for 8–10 minutes (650–700W oven), turning three times, until they give slightly when squeezed and the skins scrape off easily.

To bake, wrap tightly in foil and roast in a gentle oven (150C/300F/Gas 2) for 3–4 hours, until the skin scrapes away easily.

To boil, simmer in lightly salted water for 1–2 hours, until the skin scrapes away easily.

NB. Beetroot tops, the crisp green leaves, are excellent in salads. Don't let them go to waste.

CHOCOLATE

If you decide to make a wickedly dark gooey chocolatey pudding, don't be half-hearted about it. Go for broke and use the best, darkest chocolate you can lay your hands on. Somewhere on every wrapper will be printed the percentage of cocoa solids in the chocolate. This acts as a rough guide to quality – the higher the percentage, the better the pud will be. It's no indication of sweetness, however. I prefer my chocolate to have as little added sugar as possible. I can, after all, add more if I think the pudding needs it. Above all, avoid the cheap blocks of 'chocolate flavour' cake covering.

Melting chocolate is simple enough, but you must pay attention to it. If you overheat most brands of chocolate, they will change swiftly from a glossy unctuous dark pool, to a lumpen grainy matt mass. The same thing happens if you inadvertently splatter the hot melted chocolate with cold water. To be on the safe side, I usually heat the chocolate together with any liquid flavourings, or add them well after the melted chocolate has been incorporated with other ingredients. Cheap white chocolate is a false economy; quite apart from the taste, when heated it separates into a hard grainy mass in a pool of oily liquid.

To melt the chocolate, break into squares and place in a bowl with any liquid flavourings such as brandy or coffee. Set the bowl over a pan of *gently* simmering water, making sure that the base of the bowl never comes into contact with the water. Stir occasionally, and take the bowl off the pan as soon as the chocolate has melted.

I now use my microwave to melt chocolate – no fears of overheating it if I get caught up in some other activity. Break up the chocolate and place in a bowl with the other flavourings. Microwave in short bursts of 30 seconds on the lowest setting, stirring between each one, until melted.

COCONUT MILK

Tinned coconut milk can often be purchased in small Asian shops, and if you like the taste as much as I do, it makes sense to keep a couple of tins stashed away at the back of the cupboard. Use instead of water when cooking rice. White cabbage stewed gently in coconut milk with a chilli or two is unusually good. Or use instead of milk to make baked or unbaked sweet custards.

You can make your own coconut milk from a block of coconut cream, or from desiccated coconut. If you use coconut cream, cut 60 g (2 oz) off the block, and chop roughly. Pour over a generous 150 ml (¼ pt) of boiling water, and stir until dissolved. Strain to remove the strands of coconut. You can also add the coconut cream, grated first, straight to a stew or soup.

Alternatively, put 90 g (3 oz) desiccated coconut into a bowl, and pour over 250 ml (⅜ pt) of boiling water. Leave it to steep for 15 minutes, then strain into a bowl. Squeeze the coconut to extract as much milk as possible.

CORNMEAL AND POLENTA

Cornmeal and polenta are both ground maize. Italian polenta (from Italian delicatessens) is coarser ground than the West Indian or American cornmeal (from many West Indian food shops and some supermarkets). They can be used interchangeably, although the finished texture of the dish will vary accordingly. Cornmeal is thrillingly cheap, deliciously sweet and nutty, and remarkably filling.

It can be used in all sorts of way – simply simmered with hot water, milk or stock to make a thick porridge to replace mashed potatoes (finish with a generous knob of butter and grated parmesan), in dumplings, bread, biscuits, cakes, noodles, fritters and more.

Blue cornmeal is beginning to make its way to this country. It has been very fashionable in smart restaurants in America for some time. It is actually a dramatic dark grey-purple when cooked, with a less sweet taste than ordinary cornmeal.

CRAB MEAT

Steer well clear of frozen crab meat. Utterly tasteless. Even my cats find it dull as ditchwater and will barely sniff at it. For preference buy newly-cooked crab from a reputable fishmonger. Second best is the fresh crab meat that comes in neat little vacuum packs sold in many supermarkets.

CROÛTONS AND CROSTINI

I usually bake croûtons rather than fry them. They absorb less oil this way, and cook more evenly. Whenever I fry them I always end up with several that are verging on burnt, while others are only half-done.

Use day-old bread, crusts removed and cubed as large or small as you like. Toss briefly in a little oil and spread out on an oiled baking sheet. Bake in a hot oven for 5–10 minutes, shaking the tray occasionally to redistribute, until evenly browned.

Crostini are thick slices of bread, with or without crusts, baked until crisp. Generously oil or butter a baking tray. If you use butter, spread one side of the bread with butter and lay the bread butter-side up on the baking tray. If you use oil (preferably olive oil), press the bread on the oiled baking tray so that the underneath absorbs some of the oil, then turn it over. Bake in a moderate-hot oven (200C/400F/Gas 6–220C/425F/Gas 7) until crisp and golden, turning over once.

FRENCH DRESSING

A decent French dressing or vinaigrette is easy enough to make. Its purpose is to enhance and complement the flavours of the salad, not to drown them or overwhelm with the acidity of vinegar. Always taste the dressing before using, since both vinegar and mustard can vary in strength. If it catches on the back of the throat or puckers your mouth with its sharpness, gradually add more oil until you reach a pleasing balance.

When adding the dressing to the salad, use as little as you can get away with – enough to coat each leaf or element, but not enough to set them swimming.

Basic French dressing can be varied *ad infinitum*. Try using tarragon vinegar, or balsamic or sherry vinegar, or a tablespoon of walnut or hazelnut oil. Crushed garlic can be thrown in, fresh herbs, finely chopped shallots, chilli, or ginger, and so on.

Basic French Dressing

>1 tablespoon wine vinegar
>salt and pepper
>½ teaspoon dijon mustard
>4 tablespoons good olive oil, or light oil, or half and half

Either place all the ingredients in a screw top jar, seal and shake well, taste and adjust the balance; or beat the vinegar with salt and pepper and the mustard, beat in the oil 1 tablespoon at a time, taste and adjust the seasoning.

HERBS

Whenever possible use fresh herbs, not dried. Fresh parsley is available throughout the year and there is no good substitute. Dried parsley is a dead loss, imparting a musty taste.

When it comes to other herbs, if the one you want is unavailable then by and large it is better to change the flavourings by substituting an alternative fresh herb, than to resort to dried ones. You may even discover a wonderful new combination and never go back to the original.

The only dried herbs I use are thyme, bay leaves, rosemary, mint, oregano and, if pushed, sage, but even so I'd rather have them fresh if I can.

MUSSELS

Sweet, plump, delicious and cheap, mussels take just a few minutes to cook once they've been well cleaned. The rub is that the cleaning does require time and patience – allow a generous half an hour to prepare 1½ kg (3 lb) of them.

Tip them all into the sink and cover with cold water. Scrub each one under the cold tap, scraping off barnacles and wisps of 'beard'. Tap open mussels against a hard surface. If they don't close up throw them out. Throw out, too, any mussels that feel abnormally heavy – they are probably full of sand and mud. Once you've cleaned all the mussels, rinse them twice in cold water to flush out as much sand as possible.

Cook them according to the recipe, discarding any that refuse to open in the heat. When a recipe calls for cooked mussels, either steam them open or place in a wide large pan, with a glass of water or white wine, cover and shake over a high heat until they open.

Save the cooking juices, strain through a muslin-lined sieve and, if not used in the recipe, freeze to add to fish soups and stock.

NUTS

Nuts contain a high percentage of oil, which can quickly turn rancid if exposed to air. Buy shelled nuts in small quantities, from a shop with a rapid turnover. Store them in airtight bags or jars (but not metal) in the fridge.

Toasting until golden brown transforms the taste of most nuts, and is the easiest way to skin hazelnuts and peanuts. Spread the nuts out on a baking tray and whizz into a hot oven (230C/450F/Gas 8) for 4–8 minutes until browned, shaking the tray every couple of minutes to distribute evenly. To remove the papery skins of hazelnuts and peanuts, tip the toasted nuts into a wire sieve and roll them around in it over a sheet of newspaper or the bin to catch the flakes of skin.

Unskinned almonds are much cheaper than the skinned ones, but they may need to be blanched before using. Pour boiling water over them and leave for 30 seconds. Drain and pop them out of their tight skins. If necessary dry them, spread out on a baking sheet in a low oven 10–20 minutes, before using.

OIL

Olive oil is my basic every day cooking oil. It tastes great, and is positively good for you. What more can you ask for? Pure olive oil has a mild flavour, ideal for frying or brushing over meat and fish to be grilled or roast when you don't want too powerful a lick of oliviness. Mind you, since I do usually long for a clear hit of flavour, I may well use stronger cold-pressed extra virgin olive oil for cooking.

The only time I find olive oil too powerful is in mayonnaise. Then I prefer to dilute it with an equal quantity of groundnut or some other light, bland oil. In the end, it all comes down to personal preference. When olive oil is used in the recipes in this book, use whichever kind suits you best. If you find the taste of olive oil too much, substitute part or all groundnut, sunflower, or grapeseed oil, all virtually tasteless.

Like wine, extra virgin olive oils vary wildly in taste, from delicate and grassy, to full, heavy and fruity. There are brand name extra virgin olive oils, carefully blended so that each bottle tastes exactly the same. Then there are the more expensive 'estate' oils, unblended, varying from year to year, individual, usually the stars of the olive oil market. These should be saved to be used in salad dressings, or as a condiment, added at the end of cooking to give a final lift to a dish.

Store olive oil in a dark, cool cupboard, but not in the fridge. Use within a year at most.

Wherever I have not stipulated any particular sort of oil, use a light, virtually tasteless oil. Sunflower oil is perfectly acceptable in most instances, although I find it a little too heavy and greasy for use in salads. For these, I prefer groundnut, grapeseed or safflower oil.

PASTRY

Puff Pastry

I'm no paragon of virtue when it comes to puff pastry. On average, I make my own puff-pastry once every 18 months. It's great fun, tastes sensational, and takes ages. The rest of the time I resort to frozen puff pastry.

Shortcrust Pastry

Shortcrust is another matter, and unless I'm really rushed for time, I do make it myself, usually in double quantities, freezing the excess for another time. For most purposes I use a basic rich shortcrust which has a short crumbly texture, or even better Anne Willan's marvellous rich oil and butter shortcrust. When I want a stronger casing (for instance for pies or pasties to be taken on a picnic), I stick with the ordinary eggless shortcrust.

Whichever recipe you use, handle the dough as little as possible. Overhandling develops gluten which hardens the pastry. If you have one, use a processor for best results: whizz the flour with the fat, then add the egg, if using, and slightly less water than you would normally use. Process again briefly and gather up the crumbs with your hands to form a ball.

Whatever method you use, pastry needs plenty of time to 'relax'. Once made, wrap in cling film and rest in the fridge for at least 30 minutes before using. Let it come back to somewhere near room temperature before rolling out.

Rich Shortcrust

175 g (6 oz) plain flour
pinch of salt
90 g (3 oz) butter
1 egg yolk, beaten
1½ tablespoons iced water

Sift the flour with the salt. Rub the butter into the flour until it resembles fine breadcrumbs. Make a well in the centre and add the egg and iced water. Mix quickly to a soft dough, adding extra iced water if needed.

Anne Willan's Rich Shortcrust

250 g (8 oz) plain flour
125 g (4 oz) butter
1 egg
1 tablespoon oil
pinch of salt

Make as for rich shortcrust, beating the oil with the egg before adding. If necessary, add a little iced water to bind.

Plain Shortcrust

175 g (6 oz) plain flour
pinch of salt
90 g (3 oz) butter
iced water

Make up as rich shortcrust.

Baking Blind

Soggy pastry is the ruination of many an open-topped quiche or tart. To avoid it, use a metal tart tin, not china, and always bake the pastry blind before adding the filling. Roll the pastry out thinly on a lightly floured board and line the tin. Cover loosely and rest in the fridge for 30 minutes.

Meanwhile, place a baking sheet in the oven, and heat to 200C/400F/Gas 6. Prick the base of the tart with a fork, line with foil or greaseproof paper and weigh down with dried beans or ceramic baking beans. Bake on the hot baking sheet for 10 minutes. Take out of the oven and remove the beans and paper. Return to the oven for 5–10 minutes to dry the pastry, without browning.

For a fully baked pastry case, return the case to the oven for 10–15 minutes or until golden brown.

Filo Pastry

Paper-thin sheets of filo pastry are a useful and potentially glamourous standby to keep in the freezer. They can be used to make crisp delicate pastries, savoury or sweet, small or large: Austrian strudels, Greek *baclava* or Middle Eastern *boreks*. Or make little money pouches oozing a hot melting filling, to be served as a quick first course, or tiny puddings: cut 13 x 13 cm (5 x 5 in) squares, brush with melted butter, take 2 together and fill with a teaspoon of mashed goats cheese and a square of apple, or a paste of ground almonds, sugar and cream, gather the edges together and twist to make a money bag shape. Bake in a hot oven for 7–10 minutes until brown and crisp – and that's all there is to it. Turn to page xx for more detail, and a pair of sweet fillings.

When using filo pastry, the important thing to remember is never to let it dry out. Take the number of sheets you need from the roll and keep them covered with a sheet of greaseproof paper, and over that a damp tea-towel (damp, not wet – wring the tea-towel out well before using). Divide the remainder into smaller rolls of 4–6 sheets each, wrap well in cling film and plastic bags, label and return to the freezer to be used whenever you need them.

You can buy packets of filo pastry from Greek and Middle Eastern bakeries and food shops, good delicatessens and some supermarkets. If local shops cannot provide, then you can even buy it by post! Contact Pittos Pastries, 25 Old Farm Avenue, London N14 5QS for details. They also mail out *kadaifi* or *konafa* pastry – the thread-like 'shredded wheat' pastry.

PEAS

Fresh or frozen? In theory, of course, the answer is fresh when they are in season. Unfortunately, in practice fresh peas in their pod are not always as good as they should be. These days much of the best of the crop, small and juicy, gets swept off to the processing plants to be frozen within hours of picking. It's often the rejects that find their way into the shops, fresh and unpodded.

Still, if you shop carefully, choosing fresh peas with pods that are sprightly looking, small and relatively undamaged, or pick your own from the farm or garden, then you can look forward to a real treat. Don't let them get lost in the morass of meat and two veg, but serve them separately, maybe stewed gently with butter, a few shreds of Parma ham, onion and herbs, accompanied by triangles of fried bread or crisp crostini*.

For most dishes, where peas are one of several or many ingredients, I resort to frozen petits pois, the smaller peas, thawing them before using. Since they have already been blanched during processing, they need virtually no extra cooking – just a few minutes to heat them through thoroughly.

Fresh mangetouts have become extremely popular over the past few years, and rightly so. A newer arrival, the sugar-snap pea, is nicer still. They look like a plumper version of the mangetout, or maybe a very young and perfect ordinary pea. Like mangetouts, they are cooked and eaten whole (topped and tailed first), but they contain discernible peas within the edible pod. Both mangetout and sugar-snaps need very little cooking (boil, steam, stir-fry or microwave), only enough to soften slightly. Both can be eaten raw in salads, or as part of a collection of *crudités*.

PEPPERS

Sweet peppers, capsicums or bell peppers, come in a whole rainbow of colours these days, from the familiar green and red, to yellow, orange, purple-black and ivory-green. Reject any that are wrinkled, damaged or have squidgy patches on them. The skin should be uniformly glossy and taut.

Although the crisp, juicy sweetness of raw peppers is refreshing and enjoyable in a salad, the true delight of these fruit-vegetables really only comes out when they are cooked, and it is best of all when they are grilled or roast until the skin blackens and blisters. The flesh acquires a smokey sweetness and a unique voluptuous texture.

The peppers can be grilled in several ways (see below). Once they are charred, drop them into a plastic bag and knot the end. The trapped steam loosens the burnt skin. When they are cool enough to handle, strip off the skin. If absolutely necessary, rinse briefly under the cold tap, but keep this to a minimum as you lose some of the natural juices this way. Then, if the peppers are whole, slit open and discard the stem, seeds and white inner membrane. Cut up as directed for the recipe. Grilled peppers can be prepared 24 hours in advance – to store, place in a dish, drizzle over a trickle of olive oil and coat the peppers in it, then cover and keep in the fridge. Bring back to room temperature before using.

Grilling Methods

1. This is a good method for grilling a single pepper, but too time-consuming for any quantity. Spear the pepper on the tines of a fork and turn in the hot flame of a gas burner until blackened and blistering all over.

2. This only works well if your grill is terrifically hot and you can arrange the grill pan close to the heat. If it is not searingly hot, the flesh dries out before the skin is burnt enough to remove.

Quarter the peppers, discarding the stem, seeds and white membrane. Pre-heat the grill thoroughly and grill the peppers, skin to heat, until blackened and burnt.

3. Grill whole peppers on a very hot barbecue, turning occasionally, until blackened and blistered.

4. Heat your oven to its highest setting and bake the peppers in it, turning occasionally, until blackened and blistered. This should take 20–30 minutes – any longer and they will start drying out before they are ready. Since ovens vary considerably from one type to another, I'd suggest that you try this out with a single pepper first, before throwing in a whole basketful.

POTATOES FOR SALADS

Common or garden floury potatoes do not make the best salads. Even assuming that you stand over them as they cook and whip them out of the water at the exact moment when they are just tender but not yet inclined towards collapse, they will still absorb frightening quantities of dressing and end up fuzzy at the edges. The result tends to be a greasy mushy salad with scant visual charm.

The answer is to use either new potatoes, or waxy-textured 'salad potatoes', which hold their shape well and absorb just enough dressing. Until recently, the latter were virtually unheard of in this country, but the big supermarket chains have gradually been introducing several varieties into their larger stores, and they are filtering through to many greengrocers' shops as well.

Look out for varieties such as La Ratte, Pink Fir Apple, Cornichon, Belle de Fontenay, Charlotte, among others. Don't limit their use to salads – they're good hot, steamed, or boiled, or tossed in olive oil and roast in the oven.

RICE

There's more to rice than long-grain, pudding and brown. If a recipe stipulates a particular type of rice, you would be ill-advised to replace it with whatever happens to be sitting at the back of the cupboard, unless you are sure that both have similar characteristics. You cannot, for instance, make a proper risotto with anything but 'risotto rice'. There are several different sorts, available from Italian delicatessens and other good food shops. I usually plump for *arborio*, but *carnaroli* and *vialone* also work well. All three absorb liquids well without softening to a mush, producing the perfect risotto – creamy, tender, but still with a bite to the grains of rice. Never wash risotto rice before using.

Basmati rice has a distinctive fragrance, long grains and holds its

shape well. This is the best rice to use for biriani and pilau. For
many Chinese and Japanese dishes, opt for glutinous rice with a
high starch content.

Pudding rice is a short grain rice that absorbs vast quantities of
liquid but, unlike risotto rice, cooks to a soft sticky consistency.

Brown rice is the whole rice grain complete with its outer layer of
bran. It has a delicious nutty taste, is good as a side-dish and doesn't
deserve its dull and worthy reputation. Look out, too, for the packs
of mixed rices – brown, wild, black and Wehani – available in some
healthfood shops.

SQUID

Squid has a reputation for being tough and rubbery. It isn't or at
least fresh squid isn't. It only gets chewy when it has been frozen or
overcooked. Fresh squid is tender, full of flavour, and needs only
the briefest cooking. Always check that you are buying squid that
has not been frozen before you hand over your money.

When I first gave instructions for cleaning squid in my column in
the London *Evening Standard*, it produced a flurry of correspon-
dence in the letters page, one writer describing it as *cuisine horreur*.
This surprised me. I enjoy cleaning squid. It is a satisfyingly easy
and neat process, far less gungey than gutting fish, for instance. I
can only suppose that to the uninitiated it sounds much worse than
it is. Don't be put off. You can buy ready-prepared squid, but it has
usually been frozen and the tentacles have been discarded along
with the rest of the debris. Far better to tackle the job youself.

To prepare whole squid, pull the heads gently away from the
body, bringing with it the innards. Try not to break the tiny black
ink sacs lodged in the middle – there's an extraordinary amount of
dye hidden in there and, although it is easily rinsed away, it does
have a tendency to spread all over the place.There are some very
good recipes which use the ink in the sauce. Cut off the tentacles
and reserve. Throw the rest of the head and innards away. Using
your fingers, pull any remaining bits out of the body sac and
discard. Pull the thin purplish skin off the body. Now the squid is
ready to be cooked.

STEAMING

I bought my big metal steamer just after I left university. It seemed an extraordinary extravagance at the time, and it took up a huge amount of room in the pokey cupboards of my bedsit. I never once regretted it. It is still going strong, in regular use, mostly for cooking vegetables and fish. With its 3 layers, stacked one on top of the other, I can cook enough vegetables to satisfy a tableful of guests using just one gas ring. The flavour of steamed vegetables is superb, since little is washed away during the cooking. The only vegetable I don't steam is broccoli, because it always turns out a drab sludge green.

You don't have to have a proper steamer to steam food, although it does make life easier. Instead you can rig up an impromptu arrangement – a sieve or colander sitting over a pan of simmering water, lid clamped on top, will do. Or use one of the cheap 'flower' steamers that can be adjusted to fit in any pan. Use these carefully – they do have a tendency to collapse into the pan at just the wrong moment. Chinese bamboo steamer baskets are very cheap if you buy them from a Chinese supermarket, and are pretty enough to serve food in.

Before you begin to steam, make sure that the water in the base of the steamer or pan is bubbling happily, producing plenty of steam. Once the vegetables or whatever are in place and the lid is on, adjust the heat so that the water doesn't bubble right up and engulf them. Don't turn it down too low, either. If you use the steamer for a lengthy period of time (more than 15 minutes, say) check regularly that there is enough water – at least 2 cm (¾ in) in depth. If the level has fallen lower, top up with *boiling* water.

Either place the foods to be steamed straight on to the steamer basket or, where you want to save the natural juices, arrange the food on a heat-proof plate at least 2½ cm (1 in) smaller in diameter than the steamer, or line the basket with silver foil, crumpling the edges to form a shallow 'dish', again leaving a good gap all the way round so that the steam can circulate.

Don't pile food up high but spread it out in a flat layer, using 2 or 3 baskets if necessary. To prevent drips of condensed steam dropping on to the food, line the lid with a clean towel, folded in half.

STOCKS

I'm sorry, but stock cubes just won't do. There are no instant substitutes for real stock. A good stock gives soups, stews and sauces depth and body. Basic stocks are pretty easy to make but, with the exception of fish and vegetable stock, they do need several hours simmering, and it is all too easy to forget that they are there, ending up with irretrievably burnt pans. I've lost several this way.

Actually, chicken and other poultry stocks can now be made quickly, if you have a microwave. Unless I'm making them in a vast quantity, I always use the microwave (see below for method). Fish stock can also be made in the microwave, but I've found that it is very easy to overcook, developing an unpleasant bitterness. Since it only takes 30 minutes on the hob, it hardly seems worth the risk.

The simplest vegetable stocks are no more than the cooking water left over from boiling vegetables. Before you cast it down the drain, have a quick taste. If the flavour is good, save it. If it is good, but weak, it can be boiled down to concentrate.

All stocks can be frozen for later use. To save space in the freezer, pour the stock into a wide frying pan and boil hard until reduced to a small quantity. Freeze, making a note of the original quantity on the label. When needed, thaw and make up to the full quantity with water.

If you've got a few tubs of chicken, fish and vegetable stock stashed away in the freezer, you can tackle most recipes that call for stock. Chicken stock is the all-rounder (unless you are vegetarian, of course), and if it is lightly flavoured (but not watery) can often be used in fish recipes. Where a recipe calls for a lamb or beef stock, a more concentrated chicken stock (boil it down a little if need be) can usually be substituted without too much damage.

There are no hard and fast rules about the ingredients for a stock. Treat all recipes as guidelines. The aim is to end up with a well-balanced, fully-flavoured cooking liquid. If you don't have, say, any celery, add a leek instead, or spring onions, or leave it out altogether. When you are making a stock specially for a particular dish, throw in a few sprigs of the herb that will be used to flavour the final number. Use your imagination, your own taste, but think before you throw in a bit of everything from the vegetable drawer. Don't add anything that will dominate to disadvantage – Brussels sprouts, for instance. Never add salt to a stock. You may want to boil it down later to concentrate the flavour. If it is already salted it will be disgusting.

Vegetable Stock

This is a basic recipe, but you can add all kinds of other vegetables and herbs to vary and improve the flavour. Save the trimmings from asparagus, broccoli, celeriac, spinach stalks, lettuce, fennel and so on, and add those too.

Rather than spend all that time chopping the vegetables, I usually just prepare and chop them roughly, then whizz them all up together briefly in the processor. The aim is, after all, to extract all their flavour, so there is no need to worry about the perfection of your chopping technique.

MAKES ¾–1 litre (1½–2 pt)

2 tablespoons olive oil
2 onions, chopped
2 leeks, chopped
2 carrots, chopped
4 stalks of celery, chopped
1 medium sized potato, chopped
2 cloves of garlic, chopped
2 bay leaves
6 stalks of parsley
2 sprigs of thyme
1 small sprig of rosemary

Heat the olive oil in a large pan. Add the vegetables and herbs, and stir to coat well. Cover and sweat over a low heat for 15 minutes, stirring occasionally to prevent burning. Add 1½ litres (2½ pt) water. Bring to the boil and simmer for 30 minutes. Strain, squeezing as much liquid as possible out of the vegetables.

Chicken Stock

MAKES around ¾ litre (1½ pt)

The carcass and, if available, giblets (not liver) and scraps of skin
    from 1 chicken
1 onion, quartered
1 carrot, sliced
2 sticks of celery, sliced
1 bay leaf
3 stalks of parsley
1 sprig of thyme
6 black peppercorns

Place all the ingredients in a large pan and cover generously with water. Bring to the boil and simmer for 2–3 hours, occasionally skimming off any scum that rises to the top. Add extra boiling water if the level drops severely. Strain and cool. If you have time, chill in the fridge and lift off any fat that rises and sets on the surface.

Microwave Chicken Stock

The ingredients are exactly the same as for an ordinary chicken stock. Put them all in a large microwave bowl, breaking up the carcass so that it all fits snugly. Cover with boiling water. Cover tightly with cling film (no need for a vent), and microwave on full power for 25 minutes (650–700W oven). Stand for 30 minutes before straining.

Fish Stock

Use the trimmings and bones from any white fish, or even a few cheap whole fish, cleaned thoroughly and roughly chopped. Avoid oily fish such as mackerel or herring. Don't overcook fish stock – it develops a nasty bitterness.

MAKES about 1 litre (2 pt)

¾–1 kg (1½–2 lb) bones and trimmings of white fish, or shells
    and heads from prawns or other crustaceans.
1 onion, quartered
1 carrot, sliced
1 stick of celery, sliced or 1 leek
3 stalks of parsley
1 bayleaf
2 sprigs of thyme
6 peppercorns
1 glass of white wine or 1 tablespoon white wine vinegar

Put all the ingredients into a pan with enough water to cover generously. Bring to the boil and simmer for 20 minutes. Strain.

TOMATOES

It is one of those sad facts of life that most of the tomatoes we can buy in this country have little flavour. Marble-sized cherry tomatoes are an exception, but are too expensive and fiddly for making sauces and soups. In the summer, tomatoes grown out of doors, not under glass, can occasionally come up trumps, but in the winter I always use tinned tomatoes, usually the ready-chopped kind, for cooking.

To skin tomatoes

Pour boiling water over the tomatoes and leave for 30 seconds. Drain and run under the cold tap. Skin. If the skin still clings tenaciously, repeat.

Raw Tomato Sauce

This is a favourite summer sauce, marvellous when made with fully flavoured sun-ripened tomatoes. It can be served with hot and cold foods – lovely with grilled meats, or tossed into hot pasta. Double the quantity of lemon juice or vinegar, and oil, and it can also be used as a dressing for pasta or lentil salads.

SERVES 4–6

½ kg (1 lb) tomatoes, skinned, seeded and finely chopped
1 small, sweet red or white onion, or 2 shallots, skinned and finely chopped
2 tablespoons olive oil
1 tablespoon lemon juice, or balsamic or sherry vinegar
1 large clove of garlic, very finely chopped
6 basil leaves, torn up, or 1 tablespoon fresh marjoram, chopped
salt and pepper

Mix all the ingredients, cover and chill for 20 minutes. Taste and add more oil or lemon juice if needed, and adjust the seasoning. If necessary, add a pinch of sugar to bring out the flavour.

VANILLA PODS AND VANILLA SUGAR

Vanilla essence (but never fake 'vanilla flavour' essence or 'vanilla flavouring') may seem like the simplest way to get the taste of vanilla into cakes, puddings, sweet sauces and pastries, but real vanilla pods and vanilla sugar are easier to use and give a truer, more even flavour. What's more, vanilla pods last for ages and can be used time and again.

Store vanilla pods in a large airtight jar of sugar. Within a week the sugar will have taken on the scent of the pods, to become vanilla sugar. Three or four pods will be more than enough to perfume 1 kg (2 lb) of sugar. Top up the jar every now and again, mixing the new sugar with the old.

After you have used a vanilla pod, perhaps for flavouring a custard, simply rinse and dry it well and bury it safely back in the jar of sugar.

YEAST

The relatively new 'easy-blend' or 'easy-bake' dried yeasts shorten the time it takes to make up a yeast-raised dough. These fine-grain yeasts are added dry to the flour, no need to 'sponge' them first in warm water. If you are in a real rush, you can even get away with letting the dough rise only once, although the texture and flavour are better if you stick with the traditional double risings.

All the yeast recipes in this book are geared for using this type of yeast. If you use ordinary dried yeast or fresh yeast (in which case you need double the weight of dried yeast), the method will have to be adjusted. Begin by stirring either kind (crumble fresh yeast first) into half the liquid, warmed to blood temperature. It will be about the right heat when you can hold your finger in the liquid for a slow count of 10 before it becomes unbearable. Stir in, too, a teaspoonful of sugar or honey to encourage the yeast to liven up.

Leave it in a warm place for 10 minutes. If you have used fresh yeast it should be frothing up on the surface by then. Dried yeast looks less dramatic, but it should be gently fizzing. If it isn't then the yeast was old and past it. Chuck it out, buy some more and start again. Add the yeast mixture to the dry ingredients, and from there on follow the recipe as it reads.

Index